Challenge

CHALLENGE

an encounter with Lubavitch-Chabad

PUBLISHED BY THE LUBAVITCH FOUNDATION OF GREAT BRITAIN

© 1970 by the Lubavitch Foundation, 109/115 Stamford Hill, London N.16
and distributed by Vallentine, Mitchell & Co. Limited, 18 Cursitor Street, London E.C.4

SBN 901927 03 1

Original artwork by Charles Front and Zalman Kleinman
Designed and printed in Great Britain by Jarrold & Sons Ltd, Norwich

Rabbi Menachem M. Schneerson
THE LUBAVITCHER REBBE שליט״א

RABBI MENACHEM M. SCHNEERSON
Lubavitch
770 Eastern Parkway
Brooklyn 13, N. Y.

HYacinth 3-9250

מנחם מענדל שניאורסאהן
ליובאוויטש

770 איסטערן פּאַרקוויי
ברוקלין, נ. י.

By the Grace of G-d

Greeting and Blessing:

... You asked me to explain the following problem:

Having been brought up to believe that G-d is
Master of the world, Whose omnipotent power is not
limited in time and place, and Who, moreover, is the
Source of goodness and desires His human creatures to
live a life based on justice and morality, and insofar as
Jews are concerned - a life fully in accord with the
Torah and Mitzvos --

I find it difficult to understand why such a life
is often burdened with difficulties, sometimes even
seemingly insurmountable obstacles ?

I wish to add that I raise this question not as a
sceptic, but because I believe in Divine Providence.
Indeed, the more deeply I feel about G-d's benevolent,
and at the same time unlimited, Providence, the more
difficult I find it to reconcile this seeming anomaly.

This problem is, of course, not new. It is as old as humanity itself. The
question has been asked and discussed in many a religious-philosophical work
throughout the ages. But the question is still being asked, because the average
contemporary thinking individual no longer has direct access to Jewish
religious philosophy, either by reason of a language barrier, or for lack of time
or knowledge to find the sources. So an attempt will be made here to give at
least one explanation, and this, too, necessarily in a limited way, within the
limitations of a letter. Obviously, the subject matter could fully be dealt with
only in a book or lengthy treatise. Nevertheless, I believe that the salient
points raised below hold the key to the problem.

Starting from the same basic premises that G-d is the Essence of Goodness,
and that "It is in the nature of the Good to do good," it follows that G-d not
only desires the true good, but also that this good be enjoyed in the fullest
measure. If such good were given to man by Divine grace, in other words, if
it were to be achieved without effort, it would have an intrinsic flaw, for it would
be, what our Sages call -נַהֲמָא דְּכִיסּוּפָא- "bread of shame."

To be sure, G-d could have established a world order, wherein morality and
ethics would reign supreme, with little or no effort on the part of man. However,
obviously there is no comparison between something received as a gift and the

same thing attained through hard personal efforts, after overcoming difficult obstacles both within and without, both material and spiritual, and sometimes even obstacles which appear insurmountable. Yet, knowing that there is a Divine command to follow a certain path in life, the person is resolved to fulfil his Divine mission, no matter what the difficulties may be. Indeed, the very difficulties and obstacles which he encounters are regarded by him as a challenge to be faced unflinchingly and to be surmounted; and far from being stymied by such obstacles, they evoke in him untapped powers which reinforce his determination and stimulate his effort to the maximum degree.

Coupled with this is the feeling of satisfaction which is commensurate only with the amount of effort exerted in the struggle which makes the fruits of victory so much more delicious.

And from the above to a still further point and deeper insight:

The true and perfect way of fulfilling G-d's Will, which is embodied in the Torah and Mitzvos, is not when it is prompted by a desire to discharge an obligation towards G-d and fellowman; nor is it the gratifying feeling of having contributed something towards the world at large, that matters, a world that is apart from and outside himself. For so long as the Jew's compliance with the Will of G-d is externally motivated - however commendable such motivation is in itself - it is not yet quite complete. The perfect fulfillment of the Torah and Mitzvos is achieved when such fulfillment is an integral part of one's life, to the extent of being completely identified with the individual, that is to say when the Torah and Mitzvos permeate his very essence and being and become inseparable from him in his daily living. This is the deeper meaning of the words which we declare daily in our prayer, "For they (the Torah and Mitzvos) are our life" - meaning that just as a person and his life are one, making him a living person - so are the Torah and Mitzvos and the Jew one and inseparable. Such real identification with a thing cannot be achieved and experienced if the thing is come by without effort, or with little effort. Only that thing becomes an integral part of one's life which entails extraordinary effort in striving for it, even to the extent of staking one's life in obtaining and holding it. Conversely, only a matter which is regarded as an indispensable and integral part of one's life can evoke one's innermost powers, even self-sacrifice.

*　　*　　*

The above provides an insight also into the meaning of the Golus (the exile and dispersion among the nations of the world) which is at the root of most, if not all, the difficulties and obstacles confronting the Jew in his desire to live his G-d given Torah-way of life.

To be sure, we recognise the Golus as a punishment and rectification for failure to live up to our obligations in the past as, indeed, we acknowledge in our prayers: "For our sins we were banished from our land." But punishment, according to our Torah, called Toras Chesed (a Torah of loving kindness), must also essentially be Chesed. Since G-d has ordained a certain group, or people, namely the Jewish people, to carry the difficult and challenging task of spreading - in all parts and remotest corners of the world - the Unity of G-d (true Monotheism) through living and spreading the light of Torah and Mitzvos, a task which no other group was willing or capable of carrying out -- the greatest reward is the fulfillment of this destiny, or, as our Sages put it, "The reward of a Mitzvah is the Mitzvah itself." Thus the ultimate purpose of the Golus is linked with our destiny to help bring humanity to a state of universal recognition of G-d.

Our Divine Prophets and Sages explained at length the state of the ideal world which will eventually be attained, when all evil will be eradicated and "the wolf shall dwell with the lamb," etc., "they shall not hurt nor destroy," etc. Here again, at first glance, one may ask: "Why was it necessary to create vicious beasts in the first place, if they were ultimately - when the world will be filled with the knowledge of G-d - destined to be turned into docile and peace-loving creatures, so that "a small child shall lead them"? But the answer is the same as above.

*   *   *

Paving the road to the gradual achievement of the said destiny has always been the persevering and indomitable work of determined individuals and groups conscious of their responsibility. They dedicated themselves to the vital need of strengthening and spreading the Torah and Mitzvos among the widest sections of our people.

In recent generations, more than ever before, the main emphasis has been on the need to bring the knowledge and practice of the Torah and Mitzvos to the widest possible segments of our people, in the greatest number of locations, without waiting for them to seek it - in the hope that they will sooner or later realise the need of it themselves. The most effective way to accomplish this is, of course, through organised Torah-true education of the young, the young in years and "young" in knowledge. The pattern has been set by the founders of Chassidus and of Chassidus Chabad, who exemplified this approach with dedication and selflessness. The Baal Shem Tov, before revealing himself and his way of life, was a Melamed - a teacher of small Jewish children. Similarly, the Alter Rebbe, founder of Chabad, a disciple of the Baal Shem Tov's disciple and successor, began his work by founding his well known three "Chadorim". This road has been followed also by his successors, the heads of Chabad, each in his generation. They personified an indomitable spirit and a disdain for any and all difficulties and obstacles in their work for the dissemination of the Torah and Mitzvos. They also made it plain for all to see that whatever the difficulties, these are nothing but a challenge, to be expected and overcome. And by facing up to, and eventually overcoming, all obstacles, they had verified the truth of the basic tenets of our faith, namely that G-d's Providence extends to each and everyone individually, and that "He who is determined to purify himself and others, receives aid from On High." It is a matter of common experience that when there is a firm will and unshakeable determination, it soon becomes apparent that the difficulties are often largely imaginary, and even when real - not insurmountable. The forces of good are cumulative and self-generating, as our Sages indicated in their well known dictum, "One Mitzvah brings another in its train." If evil can be contagious, good is certainly much more so, and many who stand at the sidelines are inspired and willing to join in constructive and positive action, provided the lead is given and the way is shown.

The challenge of our time is to spread the knowledge of the Torah and Mitzvos, particularly through the education of our young, until each and every Jew will attain the level of "Know the G-d of your father and serve Him with a perfect heart," and the fulfillment of the prophecy "They all shall know Me, small and great, and the earth will be filled with the knowledge of G-d, as the waters cover the sea."

With blessing, M. Schneerson

contents

the founders of general Chassidism
and the heads of Chabad

the Founder of Chassidism

Rabbi Israel Baal Shem Tov
Elul 18, 5458–Sivan 6, 5520 (1698–1760)

Successor

Rabbi Dovber of Meseritch
(Date of birth unknown)–*Kislev 19, 5533 (?–1772)*

Founder of Chabad

Rabbi Shneur Zalman of Ladi
Elul 18, 5505–Teves 24, 5573 (1745–1813)

Second Generation

Rabbi Dovber
(the son of Rabbi Shneur Zalman)
Kislev 9, 5534–Kislev 9, 5588 (1773–1827)

Third Generation

Rabbi Menachem Mendel
(grandson of Rabbi Shneur Zalman; son-in-law of Rabbi Dovber)
Elul 29, 5549–Nissan 13, 5626 (1789–1866)

Fourth Generation

Rabbi Shmuel
(son of Rabbi Menachem Mendel)
Iyar 2, 5594–Tishrei 13, 5643 (1834–1882)

Fifth Generation

Rabbi Sholom Dovber
(son of Rabbi Shmuel)
Cheshvan 20, 5621–Nissan 2, 5680 (1860–1920)

Sixth Generation

Rabbi Joseph Isaac Schneersohn
(son of Rabbi Sholom Dovber)
Tammuz 12, 5640–Shevat 10, 5710 (1880–1950)

Seventh Generation

Rabbi Menachem Mendel Schneerson שליט״א
(sixth in direct paternal line from Rabbi Menachem Mendel,
son-in-law of Rabbi Joseph Isaac)
Born *Nissan 11, 5662 (1902)*

A significant part of the genius of the Jewish people is a compulsion to preserve its identity at whatever cost. Much of that identity is vested in the practices of the Jewish religion. But these practices, prescribed by laws first given long ago, are often incomprehensible to modern Jews.

These moderns are frequently unable to see how the ancient ideas which are their inheritance can help them to tackle the contemporary problems which confront them. Modern Jews with modern problems require modern answers, they reason.

Yet in every age there have been "modern" Jews with these same doubts, convinced that their religious problems were different from those of their ancestors. So that the same questions have been asked again and again.

Lubavitch-Chabad, with its intellectual yet uncompromisingly Orthodox approach to Judaism, is familiar with these questions, and continues to present its own answers to them in a manner which it believes makes them soluble for every Jew.

For Chabad Chassidism this is essential, because its philosophy is based on unconditional love for all Jews.

This dynamic approach, permeated with warmth and devotion and associated with intellectual awareness of the problems of the Jews in the world as it is, have won for Chabad respect and admiration throughout the world—even among those who do not agree with its principles.

CHALLENGE offers both to the friends of Lubavitch-Chabad and to those who have not yet encountered it, an introduction to its history, philosophy and activities.

We of Chabad believe that we have the capacity and the philosophy to meet the challenge of our and all times. We offer that strength to all who are aware of that challenge. To those who have the honesty to ask profound questions, we submit fundamental answers.

I

the beginning of Chassidism

the Baal Shem Tov
5458–5520 (1698–1760)

On *Elul* 18 in the year 5458 (1698) the founder of *Chassidism*, Rabbi Israel Baal Shem Tov, known by the abbreviation "*BeShT*", was born in the small town of Akop in the Carpathian Mountains of Poland.

His birth came exactly fifty years after the Chmielnicki pogroms which had decimated the Jewish communities in the Ukraine, Podolia, Volhynia and Poland.

Whole communities had been wiped out and the remaining Jews plunged into despair. The effects of this great disaster were still apparent when the *BeShT* was born, and a large part of his life was dedicated to alleviating this sense of despair.

However, it would be wrong to suppose that *Chassidism* was designed solely as a kind of spiritual medicine, necessary when one was ill, but of no value for the healthy. It was an important teaching of the *Baal Shem Tov* that *Chassidism* was vital for the spiritual well-being of every Jew.

This is important for understanding the life and teachings of the *Baal Shem Tov*, because it is often said that *Chassidism* was meant primarily for the downtrodden, ignorant masses. Although the *BeShT* and his followers aimed much of their energies at helping poor, illiterate Jews, it would be incorrect to regard this as the main characteristic of *Chassidism*, for the movement also brought new vision and depth to the world of *Torah* and *mitzvos* as practised by scholars.

The teachings on which *Chassidism* is based were known previously to a select few, but the time had come for them to be transmitted to the Jews as a whole. The *Baal Shem Tov*'s mission was to begin this work and to establish the roots of *Chassidism* from which it would grow and develop to become an intrinsic part of Jewish life.

It was not conceived as a mere luxurious addition to this life, but as a necessary support without which the essential character and essence of Jewish existence could not long survive.

At the age of five the *Baal Shem Tov* became an orphan. His father, a pious and saintly man, left him this legacy: "My son, be not afraid of anyone but G–d. Love every Jew with all your heart and soul."

The young orphan became the ward of the community and received the customary education for Jewish boys in those days. He enjoyed spending his free time in the beautiful natural surroundings of his native town, where his sensitive soul could appreciate the majesty of the Creation.

At the age of fourteen the *BeShT* joined a group of *Nistarim*, the followers of Rabbi Adam Baal Shem of Ropshitz. Their mission was to wander from town to town, speaking with Rabbis, scholars, poor workers and wealthy businessmen, encouraging and giving hope where before there was only pessimism.

Four years later, at the *BeShT*'s suggestion, the *Nistarim* assumed responsibility for the religious education of these communities. They organised suitable schools and provided pious, qualified teachers for them, paying special attention to the needs of the poor.

After the death of Rabbi Adam Baal Shem, the *Baal Shem Tov* was elected to serve as the leader of the *Nistarim*. Upon his election, the *BeShT* directed the establishment of *chadorim* for the young and *yeshivos* for the older boys in hundreds of Jewish communities.

With the religious educational apparatus thus firmly established, the way was clear for serving G–d and fulfilling the commandment of *ahavas Yisroel*. As a second objective, the *Nistarim* focused their attention on raising the masses from the morass of ignorance to the heights of *Torah*.

During this period in his life the *BeShT* came into possession of a number of manuscripts which had belonged to Rabbi Adam Baal Shem. These manuscripts revealed many *Kabbalistic* secrets and instructions which he studied avidly.

For a time, the *BeShT* settled in Brody, where he married the sister of a renowned scholar, Rabbi Abraham Gershon Kutover. A son, Rabbi Zvi, and a daughter, Adel, were born to the *BeShT* and his wife.

For the ten years from 5484 (1724) the *BeShT* led a secluded life dedicating himself to intensive study of the *Torah*. It is recorded that during this period the *Baal Shem Tov* received instruction from Ahiya of

Shilo, the ancient prophet of King David's time, who appeared regularly to the *BeShT* and taught him the secrets of the *Torah*. Then in 5494 (1734), at the age of thirty-six, the *BeShT* moved to the city of Mezibush. Here he settled and began to teach the doctrines of *Chassidus* publicly.

It must be remembered that, at that time, *Torah* scholarship alone was the path of Judaism—the illiterate and unlearned were regarded as "second rate" Jews.

The *Baal Shem Tov* taught that Judaism and *Torah* are the property of all Jews; that every Jew, regardless of station or background or endowments, is perfectly capable of serving G–d; and that *ahavas Yisroel* must embrace the willingness to sacrifice oneself for the good of another Jew.

He urged that worship is vital in the full life of every Jew; that the religious potential of prayer is incalculable. Prayer, however, is not petitioning G–d to grant a request, though that is one end of prayer, but cleaving—the feeling of oneness with G–d; the state of the soul when man gives up the consciousness of his separate existence and joins himself to the eternal being of G–d. Such a state produces a type of indescribable joy —*simcha*—which is a necessary ingredient in the true worship of G–d. *Simcha shel mitzvah*—joy in the performance of a commandment—and warmth and affection in dealing with others, these attributes became the hallmark of *Chassidism*.

Many people flocked to Mezibush and became ardent followers of the *BeShT*. Numbered among the thousands of his disciples were some of the most highly esteemed and erudite Rabbis and *Talmudic* scholars of the time. One of the greatest, Rabbi Dovber of Meseritch, became the *BeShT*'s successor and the teacher of the celebrated Rabbi Shneur Zalman of Ladi.

These outstanding scholars and Rabbis helped to spread the teachings of the *BeShT* in their communities, so that before long the new *Chassidic* movement spread throughout Poland and the neighbouring provinces.

Some Rabbis who were not acquainted with the teachings of the *Baal Shem Tov* became suspicious lest here was yet another false "messianic" movement,[1] and began to oppose it. These suspicions were without foundation. The *Baal Shem Tov* and his followers were, in fact, among the most active antagonists of such movements.

The first open opposition to the *BeShT* and his movement came in the year 5515 (1755), some twenty years after the *Baal Shem Tov* began his public work. But the opposition could not stem the tide of the *Chassidic*

[1] Between 1660 and 1676, a certain Sabbatai Zvi claimed to be the Messiah, and gathered round him a band of supporters. Sabbatai Zvi converted to Islam in 1666, but even this and his death in 1676 failed to shake the devotion of his followers. As late as the second half of the eighteenth century, Jacob Frank found in Eastern Europe enough smouldering belief in the pseudo-Messiah of a century before to be able to put forward his claims as his reincarnation, and to found a sect which he led over to hybrid Christianity after the disputation of Kameniec (June 20, 1757).

movement, which was gaining more and more adherents, both among the masses and among scholars and Rabbis.

Thus, in the final years of his life, the *Baal Shem Tov* witnessed the beginning of the struggle which later, for a time, divided the Jewish people into two camps, the *Chassidim* and the *Misnagdim*.

But he could also visualise the eventual victory of his teachings and their ultimate acceptance by the Jewish people everywhere. When this came to pass, the *BeShT* taught, the ground would have been fully prepared for the coming of the *Moshiach*.

Rabbi Israel Baal Shem Tov passed away on the first day of *Shovuos* (*Sivan* 6) in the year 5520 (1760), at the age of sixty-two. He left no written works, but his teachings and doctrines were recorded by his disciples and published in their works and in special collections.

As a system of thought and as a philosophy of Jewish life, the teachings of the *Baal Shem Tov* are contained in the extensive *Chabad* literature, particularly in the writings of Rabbi Shneur Zalman, the founder of the Lubavitch-*Chabad* movement.

The far-reaching influence of Rabbi Israel Baal Shem Tov continued with growing momentum even after his death.

Soon, the breach between the *Chassidim* and *Misnagdim* began to heal, and the *Chassidim* were no longer suspected of heretical ideas. Instead, they were recognised as the pious representatives of traditional Judaism. Within fifty years, half the Jewish population of Eastern Europe belonged to the *Chassidic* movement.

Today, over 200 years after the death of the *Baal Shem Tov*, the *Chassidic* movement, in all its colourful ramifications, constitutes one of the most, if not the most, vigorous, dynamic and creative forces of Orthodox Jewry.

Rabbi Dovber—*the Maggid of Meseritch*
?–5533 (?–1772)

Little is known about the immediate background and early life of Rabbi Dovber, later known as the Maggid of Meseritch.

Even the exact year of his birth is unknown, but it would appear that he was born at the end of the seventeenth century at about the same time as the *Baal Shem Tov*. His parents (Abraham and Chavah) traced their ancestry back to the royal house of King David. It is told that when Rabbi Dovber was five years old his home was destroyed by fire. His mother stood by the charred remains and wept bitterly. "It is not for the house that I weep," she explained to the child, "but for the records of our family tree which have been burnt."

"Then start a new line from me," returned the child.

How aptly those words described the rôle he was later to play; for the boy was destined to become the successor to the *Baal Shem Tov*.

All his time was devoted to the study of the *Torah* and he was recognised as a great *Talmudical* scholar. As was not uncommon among *Torah* scholars in those days, Rabbi Dovber delved into the significant ethical treatises of the mediaevals and the tracts of the Lurianic *Kabbalah*. From these he adopted their prescriptions of strict fasts and mortifications. He lived an austere life of great poverty by choice rather than of necessity, for it is recorded that he refused to accept numerous calls to become Rabbi and spiritual leader of great communities.

A popular story about him relates to this fact. After the *Maggid* had already become his disciple, the *Baal Shem Tov* asked a follower, who was due to pass through Meseritch, to convey his regards. With great difficulty the messenger found the *Maggid*'s small and derelict home. Entering the poor abode, the visitor found Rabbi Dovber seated on a rough block of wood. Before him were his pupils seated on planks of wood supported by similar blocks of wood. The only other furniture in the room was a wooden table.

As the *Maggid* was in the midst of teaching, the visitor agreed to return later. When he did so, he found the scene changed. The pupils had gone; the "table" had been converted into a "bed"; the *Maggid* was still seated on the block of wood, studying alone. The visitor could not hide his astonishment at the conditions in which the great Rabbi lived. "I am far from wealthy," he said, "but in my home you will find a chair, a bench, a bed and other home furnishings."

"At home," replied his host, "one indeed needs a chair, a bed, a table and a lamp. But on a journey things are different."

To the *Maggid* his earthly dwelling was not his "home". Here on earth he was but a sojourner and, as such, only those values which bring the traveller to his ultimate destination were of real and lasting importance.

The *Maggid* suffered from lameness in his left foot and was generally of a weak constitution. His life of self-denial aggravated his condition. His ill health, however, was one of the causes for his first meeting with the *Baal Shem Tov*. It is related that his teacher, the famed author of the *Pnei Yehoshua*, endeavoured to persuade him to visit the *Baal Shem Tov* to seek a cure for his ailments.

Strange are the ways of Providence leading to the first meetings between the *Baal Shem Tov* and some of his principal disciples. Many of them were far removed from *Chassidism* in thought and practice and yet, after initial opposition, they became the very pillars of the movement. The first meeting between the *Baal Shem Tov* and the *Maggid* is of particular interest. It took place late in 5513 or early in 5514 (1753); less than eight years before the *Baal Shem Tov's* passing.

The two sages had corresponded during 5513 (1752). The *Maggid* had grave doubts whether to undertake the journey; the slanderous rumours spread by the opponents of *Chassidism* deterred him from taking that step. The *Baal Shem Tov*, in his replies, assuaged the *Maggid's* suspicions and hesitations and urged him to come, foreseeing the meeting to be of great significance to *Chassidism*. The *Maggid* eventually decided to see for himself whether the *Baal Shem Tov* was as great as his followers reputed him to be.

The journey to Mezibush was long and arduous and the *Maggid* was unable to study. This caused him much anguish and he began to regret his decision. He consoled himself by assuming that when he reached his destination he would surely hear profound words of *Torah* from the *Baal Shem Tov*. When his coach finally arrived in Mezibush, he lost no time in seeking out the *Baal Shem Tov*.

Rabbi Israel Baal Shem Tov received his visitor cordially and told him a short, seemingly insignificant story. The interview ended. They met again on the second day and again the *Baal Shem Tov* told him only a short story.

Rabbi Dovber, the assiduous type, to whom every moment was precious, regretted having come and having wasted so much time. He made plans to return home; he would leave the same night, as soon as the moonlight would make travelling possible. But before he could leave, a messenger came from the *Baal Shem Tov* asking Rabbi Dovber to come to the master's house. When he arrived, the *Baal Shem Tov* asked him: " Are you well versed in *Torah*?" Upon receiving an affirmative reply, the *Baal Shem Tov* asked: "Are you familiar with the teachings of the *Kabbalah*?" Again, an affirmative reply. The *Baal Shem Tov* then asked the *Maggid* to interpret a passage in *Etz Chaim*, the basic work of the Lurianic *Kabbalah*. Rabbi Dovber carefully examined the passage and offered his interpretation. The *Baal Shem Tov* rejected his words. Rabbi Dovber deliberated again and reiterated his previous statement, adding: "The meaning of this passage is as I stated. Should you have a different interpretation, tell me and we will see who is right."

At this stage the *Baal Shem Tov* read the passage to him. As the *Baal Shem Tov* read and spoke, it seemed to the *Maggid* as though the whole house had become full of light and that a Divine fire surrounded them. It appeared to the *Maggid* as though he actually saw the angels whose names were mentioned in the discourse. Afterwards, the *Baal Shem Tov* said: "Your interpretation was correct, but there is no soul in your learning."

Rabbi Dovber remained with the *Baal Shem Tov* for some time, to learn from him.

Reports show that the *Maggid* visited the *Baal Shem Tov* only twice. The second time he remained for six months. Rabbi Dovber related that the *Baal Shem Tov* taught him everything to the most intricate details of the various works of the *Kabbalah* and the "language of the birds and trees".

When he wished to return home, the *Baal Shem Tov* did not agree and delayed him several times. When asked for the reason, the *Baal Shem Tov* explained that as long as the *Maggid* was with him, his own mind was "as a gushing well, and the more one draws from a well the more it pours forth."

Though Rabbi Dovber may not have seen the *Baal Shem Tov* again, they remained in touch through messengers and correspondence. Occasionally, Rabbi Dovber served as interim leader of the *Chassidim* in the absence of, and at the request of, the *Baal Shem Tov*.

Even though *Chassidism* is generally opposed to self-mortification, the *Maggid* appears to have continued for some time in his erstwhile habits. The *Baal Shem Tov* warned him to cease these practices and to guard his health.

During the period between his first meeting with the *Baal Shem Tov* and his becoming leader of the *Chassidim*, Rabbi Dovber was appointed *Maggid* of the communities of Meseritch and Koritz.

The year 5520 (1760) saw the passing of Rabbi Israel Baal Shem Tov. His son Rabbi Zvi assumed leadership of the *Chassidim* and remained in that position for one year. On the day following the *yahrzeit*, Rabbi Zvi addressed the assembled *Chassidim*, and upon concluding his discourse said: "Today, my father came to me and told me that the Heavenly Court had decided that I must relinquish the leadership to Rabbi Dovber." All those present rose in respect and remained standing to hear Rabbi Dovber's first discourse.

The *Chassidic* centre now moved from Mezibush to Meseritch. Rabbi Dovber was to remain leader of the *Chassidim* for the next twelve years and under his leadership *Chassidism* struck its roots deeply and widely. The seeds which had been planted in Mezibush grew in Meseritch. Attended by a unique group of followers, compounding the greatest minds and spirits of the time, Rabbi Dovber externalised the creative, seminal thoughts and teachings of the *Baal Shem Tov* and formed them into a comprehensive system.

Within three months of the beginning of the *Maggid*'s reign a new spirit had been breathed into the *Chassidic* camp. Throughout Poland and Lithuania, the ranks of the *Chassidim* swelled. The already established centres in Volhynia and Podolia made their influence felt even more strongly than before, and Meseritch itself was a scene of constant activity.

The *Maggid* was a stabilising force to his followers, directing their energies towards achieving the ideal combination of emotional excitement and intellectual restraint in serving G–d.

Like the *Baal Shem Tov* before him, the *Maggid* preached that *ahavas Yisroel* is the key to true love of G–d. "The meaning of *ahavas Yisroel*", the *Maggid* declared, "is to love the worst sinner in the same way as the most righteous."

He impressed this principle of love upon his followers, and moulded it into a main factor in the *Chassidic* outlook. One of his closest disciples, Rabbi Levi Yitzchak of Berditchev, addressed everyone as "my heart".

In the autumn of 5533 (1772) Rabbi Dovber took to his bed. On *Kislev* 18, he summoned the members of the "Holy Society", and said to them: "My children, always stay together and you will overcome everything. You will go ever forward and not back."

On Tuesday, *Kislev* 19, 5533 (1772) Rabbi Dovber, the great Maggid of Meseritch, returned his holy soul to heaven. Thus ended an era. His task was accomplished.

A new line had not only been started, but set firmly on a solid foundation. It was now the work of others to carry it on.

what is Chabad?—a synopsis

Chabad Chassidism is a system of Jewish religious philosophy which teaches understanding and recognition of the Creator through the application of the three intellectual qualities of "Chochmoh", "Binoh" *and* "Daas". *The initials of these three Hebrew words form the word* "Chabad".

While faith and belief in G–d form the foundation of our religion, Chabad *insists on intellectual study and understanding of religious truth by everyone according to his intellectual level, in order to come closer to the service of G–d in both mind and heart.*

Though Chabad Chassidism *is a system that reaches into the deepest mysteries of the Creation, it makes ample use of illustrations and examples from experience, so that it becomes understandable even to those who are little gifted with the power of theoretical and abstract thinking.*

The virtue of this Chassidic *philosophy is that it does not stop at theoretical teachings. It motivates and induces those who study it to translate their intellectual knowledge into actual deeds and put them on a higher level of religious feeling and practice, inspired by the knowledge and intellectual appreciation of the basic truths which* Chabad *expounds.*

Chabad Chassidism *is thus a practical guide to all Jews in all walks of life, showing them how to enrich their religious experience by developing the attributes of both mind and heart through a concerted effort that comes from their perfect harmony.*

But the leaders of Chabad Chassidism *have not concerned themselves only with the spiritual standard of our people. Together with their tremendous influence in the spiritual field, they have devoted attention to the general conditions of the Jewish community, being motivated by their boundless* ahavas Yisroel, *which is one of the mainsprings of their* Chassidic *system. To love a fellow-Jew means to love him completely and unconditionally. Thus, their work has a dual purpose—to improve the material conditions of their people, as well as their spiritual standards.*

Chabad Chassidism

יאר פני לק ארדמור הרב הנאון האלקי ההסיד אור עולם נר ישראל קדוש ה מנונה מוהר שניאור זלמן בהרב מלה ברוך נבגם זלע בעל המחבר ספר התניא והשלע ותלאונלקת

The history of the portrait of Rabbi Shneur Zalman of Ladi which is reproduced above is given on page 24

Rabbi Shneur Zalman of Ladi

5505–5573 (1745–1812)

founder of Lubavitch-Chabad Movement

The rise and growth of the *Chassidic* movement was rapid. Under the slogan of *"Rachmonoh liboh boey"*, the leaders of this genuine renaissance recaptured the happiness and bliss of the Jewish faith for the common man.

In and through it even Jewish peasants, traders, labourers and craftsmen found themselves in the warm haven of the *Torah* universe from which they had been excluded because of their limited scholarship. No longer forced to consider their religion a "Paradise Lost", they eagerly absorbed the inspired message of the *Torah* on the emotional level upon which *Chassidism* projected it for them.

Like other movements, *Chassidism* might have dissipated after the initial emotional momentum had been spent. Divine Providence however, sent great and inspiring leaders who, by virtue of their exalted personal qualities and intellectual creativeness, provided the spark that induced *Chassidism* to grow into a dynamic body reconciling divergent schools of thought. It has attracted staunch adherents for generation after generation, right up to the present day.

One of the greatest of these outstanding personalities was Rabbi Shneur Zalman of Ladi, later famous as the *Rav*. This saintly man became the founder of *Chabad Chassidism*, a movement which developed into one of the strongest and most dynamic branches of *Chassidism*.

This movement, founded in Lithuania in 5533 (1773), grew far beyond the boundaries of this once mighty centre of Jewish life, and gained enthusiastic adherents throughout the world.

Rabbi Shneur Zalman was a direct descendant of the *MaHaRaL* of

Prague. His great-grandfather later lived in a village in Posen. The family moved eastward, wandering through Galicia and Poland and finally settled in Vitebsk, then a flourishing centre of *Torah* and *Talmudic* scholarship.

It was there that Rabbi Shneur Zalman's father, Rabbi Baruch, was born and reared in the spirit and tradition of learning. Later he moved to Liozna, near the town of Lubavitch which was to become famous as the seat of the dynasty of the *Rav's* descendants.

Here Shneur Zalman was born. Here, too, he received his first instruction, and from his earliest youth he showed unusual brilliance, diligence and devotion to his studies.

In order to develop further his son's scholarship, Rabbi Baruch took him to a renowned teacher of the time, Rabbi Issachar Ber of Kobilnik, who lived in Lubavitch. Under Rabbi Issachar Ber's tutelage the young scholar traversed the "sea of the *Talmud*" in all directions and familiarised himself with *Kabbalah*, the esoteric side of traditional *Torah* wisdom.

In his spare time the eager boy further increased his knowledge through the study of science and mathematics. Before long, Rabbi Issachar Ber sent for Rabbi Baruch and told the overjoyed father of his student: "There is nothing more that I can teach your son; he has grown beyond me."

Rabbi Baruch now took Shneur Zalman to Vitebsk. The twelve-year-old boy won immediate recognition and fame as a genius, and he was accepted as an equal by the great scholars of the city.

In later years a wealthy man selected him as a son-in-law and supported him, so that he could devote his undivided attention to the exclusive study of *Torah*.

Numerous tales of those years attest to the unquenchable thirst for knowledge of Rabbi Shneur Zalman. His sagacity and proficiency as a scholar won the admiration of everyone who came into contact with him.

At the age of twenty, this brilliant young man, with his wife's consent, left his home and family to search for the fulfilment of a yearning in his soul. Despite all his knowledge, he felt that he was missing an element of Jewish religious experience which could not be captured in the solitude of the four walls of his own study.

Two centres of Jewish learning and leadership competed for his attention: Vilna, the main seat of *Talmudic* scholarship and the fortress of the opposition to the young yet rapidly growing *Chassidic* movement; and Meseritch, the seat of Rabbi Dovber, the famed Maggid of Meseritch, heir to the ideology of Rabbi Israel Baal Shem Tov and to the leadership of the *Chassidic* movement.

From the very outset, Rabbi Shneur Zalman realised that the sober, rationalistic atmosphere of Vilna and its scholars, headed by the *Gaon* Rabbi Elijah, could not offer him that for which he was searching. Already an acclaimed *Torah* scholar, Rabbi Shneur Zalman felt that his need was not for *Talmudic* instruction but for guidance in *avodah*. Therefore he decided to try Meseritch where a new world called. A world, it was said, that taught its people how to pray.

Full of hope and expectation, but with few material resources, he set out on the long journey. To pay his way the eminent scholar did any chores which came along, chopping wood and working in the fields. Yet he still had to make most of the long trek to Meseritch on foot.

The first impression of the inner circle of disciples gathered about Rabbi Dovber of Meseritch was not very encouraging to Rabbi Shneur Zalman. He had expected a large academy brimming with sparkling personalities, scholars and wise men. Instead, he found a group of unobtrusive people who, at first sight, seemed to possess little that made seeking worth-while. Nor was he particularly inspired by the pious admonitions that the Maggid of Meseritch addressed to the crowd that gathered in his *shul*.

He was about to leave, when his eyes were opened to the true nature of the master and his inner circle. Rabbi Shneur Zalman had decided to pay his respects to the *Maggid* before returning to Liozna. He entered the master's house and stood among the crowd, when the eyes of Rabbi Dovber singled him out. They bored deeply into the very abyss of Shneur Zalman's soul, exploring and evaluating its every quality.

After a few minutes of pregnant silence, the master not only told him what had been in his mind, but without having been asked, gave Shneur Zalman astoundingly simple, yet convincing answers to some test questions the young scholar had prepared in order to assure himself of a worthy master. Deeply impressed, Rabbi Shneur Zalman begged to be admitted into the inner circle of Rabbi Dovber's disciples.

A new world now unfolded itself before the eager eyes of the scholar from Liozna as he absorbed the *Maggid*'s daily lectures on the teachings of the *Baal Shem Tov*. In the company of Rabbis of great renown, he delved into the realm of the holy relations that unite G–d, Israel, the *Torah* and the world into one insoluble system of universal scope.

Rabbi Dovber's young son, Rabbi Abraham, who by his saintly conduct earned the title of "*Malach*", was his guide to this higher sphere of wisdom and knowledge. In return, Rabbi Shneur Zalman instructed him in the realm of *Halachah*—the major part of the *Talmudic* and Rabbinic literature dealing with Jewish law.

Thus, the young *Rav* absorbed the fundamentals of *Chassidus* and satisfied the yearning in his soul which had driven him from his home and family. He never regretted having chosen Meseritch in preference to Vilna.

Rabbi Shneur Zalman enjoyed little prestige at first among the established followers of the *Maggid*, until one day Rabbi Dovber disclosed the *Rav*'s extraordinary qualities and revealed him as a "light in Israel". He commanded Rabbi Shneur Zalman, then at most twenty-five years old, to rewrite the Code of Jewish Law so as to include the latest decisions.

Roughly two hundred years had passed since Rabbi Joseph Caro had published his master-work, the *Shulchan Aruch*, and throughout this period generations of *Acharonim* had added to and elucidated what was to have been the final word in the discussion of Jewish law.

Rabbi Shneur Zalman gave full consideration to this further two hundred years of commentary on the *Shulchan Aruch*, and by careful editing, he presented the Code of Jewish Law in a precise and handy form.

This was obviously a most difficult task. Yet the young scholar carried it out in such a masterly fashion, that he was at once acclaimed as one of the truly great of his time, not only by the *Chassidic* world, but by scholars of all ranks.

After the death of Rabbi Dovber on *Kislev* 19, 5533 (1772) his disciples separated. Each one shouldered the task of propagating *Chassidism* in the country assigned to him.

Rabbi Shneur Zalman inherited the most difficult of all missions. He was to capture the stronghold of the *Misnagdim* in Lithuania for the *Chassidic* ideology and way of life. This he was to accomplish, first, together with Rabbi Menachem Mendel of Vitebsk, and after the latter's departure for *Eretz Yisroel*, by himself.

A man of lesser stature as a *Talmudist* could not have undertaken such a mission, for the opposition included some of the most illustrious scholars of the time. But Rabbi Shneur Zalman was well equipped to meet them on their own ground.

His attempts to meet with the *Gaon* Rabbi Elijah were harshly rejected. Nevertheless, he carried on his work with undiminished zeal. To the surprise of his contemporaries, friends and opponents alike, he succeeded to a degree hardly thought possible.

Facsimile of a letter in Rabbi Shneur Zalman's handwriting

The history of the letter reproduced above is as follows:

During the height of the persecution of the *Chassidic* community by the opponents of the movement, the followers of the *Rav* in Vilna held a conference at which many of the younger *Chassidim* urged the adoption of strong countermeasures. This was contrary to the policy of the moderate *Chassidim* of Vilna, led by Meir ben Rafael, who had for five or six years (5551–56) unsuccessfully endeavoured to bring about peace. Rabbi Moshe Meisels, a leading *Chassid*, supported the demands of the younger *Chassidim*, and under stress of a suffering and bitterly disappointed heart, voiced strong disapproval of the policy of Meir ben Rafael.

A special delegate of the *Rav* attended that conference and brought a message from the *Rav*, to the effect that while their mood was quite justified, *Chassidism* taught that the mind should govern the heart. To have control over one's heart and feelings, and to reserve them for true love and fear of G–d, leading to practical deeds of kindness and charity to fellow man—this is the primary objective of every *Chassid*, the *Rav* said, promising the ultimate triumph of the cause.

In the month of *Elul* of that year, the *Rav* sent the letter to Rabbi Moshe Meisels, in which he urges him to make a public apology to Meir ben Rafael.

Rabbi Shneur Zalman was not a dreamer who lived in the clouds, but a true leader who was fully alive to the material needs of his co-religionists no less than to their spiritual shortcomings. His extensive work for the economic welfare of his brethren is a chapter in itself. Space permits only a brief mention here of some of his notable efforts in this field.

The *Rav*'s interest in his brethren spurred him to action immediately after his wedding. He began a campaign to induce more Jews to settle on the land and engage in farming. Rabbi Shneur Zalman devoted to this cause not only a great deal of effort, but his entire dowry.

From about the year 5532 (1772), Rabbi Shneur Zalman was engaged on an extensive plan to induce large numbers of Jews living on the Russo-Polish border to move eastwards, into the interior of Russia, where the opportunities for economic existence were more promising.

Rabbi Shneur Zalman also devoted himself to fund-raising activities in order to support the newly established *Chassidic* settlements in *Eretz Yisroel*. However, his efforts were subsequently distorted by his opponents, who slandered him and denounced him to the Russian Government, accusing him of sending funds to the Turkish Government. Relations were strained between the two countries at that time.

When a decree was issued in 5568 (1808) for the expulsion of Jews living in rural areas and on farms, depriving thousands of Jewish families of their means of livelihood, Rabbi Shneur Zalman undertook an extensive fund-raising journey throughout Russia, with a view to meeting the emergency and creating the means for the rehabilitation of these unfortunates.

This work was carried on in addition to advising and guiding his thousands of followers, who turned to him individually in all their complicated problems.

During the years of struggle for the betterment of the spiritual life and economic conditions of his co-religionists, the *Rav* developed his magnificent philosophy of *Chabad Chassidism*.

Of the people who flocked to him after his return to Liozna, he demanded much more than the unquestioning adherence required by the other schools of *Chassidic* thought. Whereas their ideology centred on the *Tzaddik* as a person of supernatural powers, he posed the idea of the *Tzaddik* as a spiritual guide, a teacher rather than a miracle worker.

The *Chassid* was to train himself for a life of faith and *avodah*, which would carry him to the highest level of *Chabad*: *Chochmoh*, *Binoh* and *Daas*, forming a bond between heaven and earth.

Upon this basic thought Rabbi Shneur Zalman built the structure of *Chabad* ideology. Total man serves G–d with mind, heart and deed in unison, each complementing the other. The mind understands, the heart feels and the hand performs.

The substance of Rabbi Shneur Zalman's teachings can be found in his major contribution to Rabbinic literature, the *Likutei Amarim*, better known as the *Tanya*,[1] after the first word of this treatise. It contains a concise outline of his philosophical system as a way of life, and attests to his vast knowledge and the depth of his understanding and mastery of both the exoteric and esoteric teachings of our Sages.

The *Tanya* has been and still is a sacred text for the thousands of followers of *Chabad*. It is religiously studied and memorised by the youngest as well as the oldest members of the Lubavitch movement, and seems inexhaustible at every level of approach and interpretation. Rabbi Shneur Zalman, the *Baal haTanya*, known to *Chabad* adherents as the *Alter Rebbe*, was also the author of many other works which are classics of Chabad literature.

With the rapid expansion of the *Chassidic* movement under Rabbi Shneur Zalman's leadership, its opponents resorted to the most extreme measures to undermine his work. He was denounced to the Russian Government as a traitor and heretic, an accusation levelled also against certain other *Chassidic* Rabbis.

In the year 5558 (1798), Rabbi Shneur Zalman was arrested and taken to the capital, St Petersburg, where he was thrown into prison to face trial for high treason and subversive political activities.

Numerous tales of his sagacity, presence of mind and majestic poise attest to the impression he made on the Czarist commission selected to try his case. Czar Paul I incognito and other men of the highest social and military standing visited him to test his sincerity and to fathom his wisdom. On *Kislev* 19 in the year 5559 (1798), he was freed on the express orders of the Czar. This date has since been a festival amongst *Chassidim*.

Hardly two years after the first attempt, the extreme opposition again denounced Rabbi Shneur Zalman on false charges. Again he was brought to the Russian capital and imprisoned, but as before, he was cleared of all guilt and released with the approval of Czar Alexander I, who shared the admiration of his predecessor for the venerable leader of the Lithuanian *Chassidic* movement.

During the war between France and Russia, Rabbi Shneur Zalman espoused the Russian cause, and through the co-operation of his followers proved of great service to the Russian High Command.

Other *Chassidic* leaders, such as the famous Maggid of Kosnice, were loud in their acclaim of Napoleon who promised freedom and equality to all the oppressed, including the Jews. But Rabbi Shneur Zalman realised that the spread of French influence might bring greater moral harm than all the hostility of the Czarist regime.

[1] The *Tanya* was designed by its author to appeal to the widest possible audience, from those with analytical and searching minds to the less scholarly. The former find in it an inexhaustible profundity; the latter, each according to his intellectual capacity, find it edifying and profoundly stimulating. These qualities and its authoritativeness account for the widespread recognition which the *Tanya* has commanded from the time of its appearance to the present day.

Accompanied by his family and a number of close disciples he took to the road, barely keeping ahead of the onrushing French armies. Though he escaped capture several times, Rabbi Shneur Zalman's weakened body was not equal to the harrowing strains of the flight. He became seriously ill and died in Piena, a small village near Kursk, on *Teves* 24, 5573 (1813). He was laid to rest in the Jewish cemetery at Haditz, a small place near Poltava.

It used to be said: "In Vilna they knew how to study; in Meseritch they knew how to pray." Rabbi Shneur Zalman, the saintly Sage of Ladi, knew how to do both. He bridged the gap between the mind and heart by his masterly synthesis of intellect and emotion within the framework of *Chabad* ideology.

History of the Portrait of Rabbi Shneur Zalman of Ladi:

The portrait of the *Alter Rebbe*, Rabbi Shneur Zalman of Ladi, which has been reproduced on page 16, was executed by using text from the *Tanya* in the body of the picture.

It is itself based on a portrait which has been certified as a good likeness of the *Alter Rebbe* by various Lubavitcher Rabbis of their generation and its history is of interest.

This original portrait was discovered only through a chance meeting of the *Maharash* with some Russian Government officials.

In 5615 (1855) the *Tzemach Tzedek* received a command from the local authorities to attend a conference on matters appertaining to Jewish education. Because of ill health he was unable to go, but one of his two emissaries was his son, the *Maharash*.

During one of the many breaks in the talks, a senior official who had been showing every courtesy to the *Maharash* requested an appointment to meet him. It transpired that the official was a gifted artist and wanted an opportunity to paint the Rebbe. His father was also an artist of repute and had handed down a large art collection. During the conversation, the official told the *Maharash* that among his collection was a painting of a great Rabbi who had been imprisoned on treason charges. His father, who was one of the prosecution officials at the time, instructed an artist to make the portrait of the imprisoned Rabbi. The *Maharash* requested that he be allowed to view the portrait and to his amazement saw that it was none other than that of his great-grandfather, Rabbi Shneur Zalman. The portrait was clearly titled with Rabbi Shneur Zalman's name and that of his father, and dated 1798, the year of his imprisonment.

Rabbi Dovber
5534–5588 (1773–1827)

the second generation

Rabbi Dovber, the son of the founder of *Chabad*, known popularly as the *Mittler Rebbe* (intermediate Rabbi, i.e. the middle one of the first three generations of the fathers of *Chabad*), expounded the philosophy of his father and interpreted the meaning and implications of all its intricate phases in a most lucid manner.

His commentaries on his father's original texts are filled with detailed discussions of the ideology and philosophical concepts of Rabbi Shneur Zalman, and by their volume, preciseness and clarity testify to the great mental stature of their author.

It is interesting that when news of the death of Rabbi Shneur Zalman reached St Petersburg, the War Minister called a special session of the Cabinet to send a message of condolence to the bereaved family.

The official address was brought to Rabbi Dovber at Krementchug by representatives of the Governors of Poltava, Tchernigow and Odessa, with an enquiry as to the best way in which Russia could repay the Lubavitcher Rebbe for the support and encouragement Rabbi Shneur Zalman had given the Czar during the Napoleonic war.

The son and successor of the first *Chabad* leader asked nothing for himself, but requested a benevolent attitude by the Russian Government towards the Jews, and the improvement of their economic position.

Asked for specific suggestions, he requested the co-operation of the Government in settling numerous Jews on the land, a project which his father had taken up just before the Franco-Russian war broke out. In this way, the famous Jewish settlements of Kherson came into being.

Rabbi Dovber continued the work started by his illustrious father, following the path he had pioneered. In addition to further expounding the doctrines and philosophy of *Chabad*, he devoted himself to the communal and social activities initiated by his father. Intellectually he was exceptionally gifted and he was also a fluent and sparkling speaker.

Inevitably, the Napoleonic war had disastrously disrupted Jewish life. However, during the days of Rabbi Dovber, there was a revival of *Chassidus*, and there was a marked increase in the knowledge of it among young students.

The Rebbe had instructed that young men should study *Chassidus* for at least three hours daily, and in time every *Chassidic* community produced a growing number of youthful scholars. Later, many of these learned young men became teachers in different communities. This had a marked effect on the local *Chassidim*, since the study and knowledge of *Chassidus* promptly increased.

The *Mittler Rebbe* endeavoured to persuade the Jewish masses to leave the precarious occupations in which they were then engaged. He urged them to go and live in villages and settlements where they could learn to till the soil, or acquire skills and learn crafts which would provide them with an honest, steady income. This would eliminate the constant worry and insecurity that accompanied their existing occupations.

Of great importance was the fact that this way of life would not interfere with their living and practising their religion completely and sincerely. In this connection, a letter from the *Mittler Rebbe* to the community is of interest. It is quoted below in full:

> I have the following proposal to make concerning the decrease of income and the sharp increase in the number of those without a source of income who suffer extreme poverty in the cities, and the resulting evils of unemployment and the misdirected energies of the youth who really want to work.
>
> Only a small minority are employed in shops and open businesses, and even fewer practise manual trades. Those who have some capital are gradually losing it, and we find the Jewish masses in an increasingly dangerous state of impoverishment.
>
> My own suggestion, for the attention of the wise who understand the problem, is that strict regulations be introduced in the Jewish communities, whereby the women and children, boys and girls, learn some basic trades, such as the various types of weaving and spinning and allied crafts which are employed in factories.
>
> The training of artisans should likewise be organised and aided in an orderly manner, and should be properly regulated for the children of the poor and middle class as well. They should have teachers and

instructors paid for by the communities and under communal supervision.

They should not despise agriculture. They should acquire good fertile land, large plots or small, and work on the soil; G–d will surely send His blessing on the soil, so that they will at least be able to feed their children properly. No doubt they will have to hire experienced non-Jewish farm hands for two or three years, until they are sufficiently trained to do all the work themselves.

They should not be ashamed of tilling the soil. Were not the fields and vineyards the source of our subsistence in the Holy Land, the richer farmer using Jewish servants and good workers? Why, then, should we be different from our forefathers, even though we may live in exile among non-Jewish people, provided there are opportunities to follow our ancient occupation as tillers of the soil?

Perhaps we may be permitted to buy land outright, or at any rate to rent it for a long time. When I visited the Southern Steppes, I saw with my own eyes Jewish farmers with their wives and children working the soil every week-day with zeal and enjoyment.

Up to thirteen years of age every boy there learns in the *cheder*. If he shows promise of becoming a scholar he continues studying the *Torah*; if not, he leaves the *cheder* and works in the fields. The Jews there are happy and satisfied —free from worry—and they remain G–d-fearing, righteous people, supporting themselves honestly and decently.

Although the work may not bring them any riches and luxuries, fancy clothes and jewellery, they have all they require. They sell their crops, the produce of their dairy farming, or their sheep and cattle to the neighbouring provinces. I saw their way of living and liked it very much; the soil is fertile in those parts.

We may, if we try hard, acquire good fields here which would greatly aid the poor. I have already corresponded with responsible people, and I believe that G–d will bless the land, and our people will earn as much as they need. As it is written, "If thou wilt eat by the toil of thy hands, happy art thou." Thus, those who slander us will have no food for talk, and the nobles and officials will look favourably on the farmers. It cannot be otherwise, for there is no other hope; only the prospect of even greater poverty for the Jewish masses.

And who knows what lies ahead? Perhaps, G–d forbid, they will be driven away to distant lands. Enough of this, and those with intelligence will understand. These words come from one who wishes well for the Jewish people and desires their prosperity.

Dovber, son of the great Gaon Rabbi Shneur Zalman of blessed memory.

From this letter and other sources we know how deeply Rabbi Dovber was concerned at the economic plight of the Jewish masses, and how much effort he put into various attempts to better their lot.

Rabbi Dovber was at all times interested in aiding the *yishuv* in the Holy Land. In 5583 (1823) he was the first to establish a colony in Hebron,

Handwriting facsimile of Rabbi Dovber of Lubavitch—the Mittler Rebbe of sainted memory. The English text of this letter appears on page 26

and he continued to support it financially. He personally acquired a synagogue there, which bears his name.

At the time of his father's death Rabbi Dovber was in Krementchug in Little Russia, and from there he went to settle in Lubavitch in White Russia.

En route, *Chassidim* provided him with means to establish himself in his new home. Upon his arrival, however, he decided to distribute these funds to the needy and wrote to a relative about forming a committee of three to supervise the allocation. In this letter he referred to a "considerable" sum.

Years later this letter came into the hands of the recipient's heir, an unscrupulous and vengeful enemy of Rabbi Dovber. He harboured an implacable hatred of the Rebbe for some personal family "slight". With judicious doctoring the figures in the letter, "three or four thousand rubles" became "one hundred and three or four thousand". Indeed a "considerable" sum. What could be its purpose? And how did he gather such a sum on so short a journey? Obviously he was planning a revolution!

The money was destined for the Turks who then ruled the Holy Land. The regular remittances to needy scholars there lent an air of credibility to the charges.

Other weird accusations were made concerning the dimensions of the Rebbe's synagogue being similar to those of the Jerusalem Temple, and that meant that he intended to be king of Israel!

The similarity to the charges levelled against Rabbi Shneur Zalman in 5558 (1798) is striking.

In the autumn of 5587 (1826) Rabbi Dovber was instructed to appear in Vitebsk, the provincial capital. This was done in a most respectful manner through high-ranking officers and the arrangements were made to suit the Rebbe.

Hundreds accompanied him from Lubavitch, and at every village the elders met him with the traditional bread and salt. The honour accorded him by Jew and gentile deeply impressed the officials.

Governor-General Chavanski, a harsh man who had little affection for Rabbi Dovber, conducted the investigation. Important dignitaries interceded on his behalf. He was treated courteously and later he was permitted to worship publicly and to lecture on *Chassidus*.

He was officially informed that he was completely exonerated of all suspicion and released on *Kislev* 10, a date which has since been a festival amongst *Chassidim*.

His death, a year later, on *Kislev* 9, 5588 (1827), exactly fifty-four years after his birth, marked the end of an important chapter in the history of *Chabad*.

Rabbi Dovber had plumbed the depths of his father's teachings, explored their implications, developed the doctrines in detail and depth. His father was the creative, original thinker, the founder of a movement. Rabbi Dovber achieved its consolidation and advanced *Chabad*'s manifold activities.

Rabbi Menachem Mendel
5549–5626 (1789–1866)

the third generation

Third in the line of leaders of the *Chabad* movement was Rabbi Menachem Mendel, popularly known as the *Tzemach Tzedek*, after the title of his voluminous *Talmudic* responsa.

Rabbi Menachem Mendel was born on *erev Rosh Hashonoh* 5549 (1789). His mother, Devorah Leah (daughter of Rabbi Shneur Zalman of Ladi), passed away three days after his third birthday, and from that day the young orphan was reared and educated by his famous grandfather.

The young lad's prodigious abilities soon became evident. By the time he was twelve he had written many treatises on matters of *Halachic* importance and had begun recording the *Talmudic* and *Chassidic* teachings of his grandfather, supplementing them with his own comments and explanations.

While still in his teens, he was appointed by Rabbi Shneur Zalman to engage in the necessary research and reply to the numerous *Halachic* enquiries pouring in from scholars in Russia and Europe.

When Rabbi Menachèm Mendel was only eighteen years old, the manuscript of his famous *Chassidic* discourse, *Basis of the Precept of Prayer*, which he had tried to conceal, was discovered by his grandfather. Rabbi Shneur Zalman was so delighted with his find that he thereafter allotted more time for their study together.

Rabbi Menachem Mendel was only twenty when he was appointed to take charge of most of Rabbi Shneur Zalman's communal affairs.

After the death of Rabbi Shneur Zalman in 5573 (1813), Rabbi Dovber (the father-in-law of the *Tzemach Tzedek*) was appointed his successor. At this time Rabbi Menachem Mendel commenced a period of fourteen years' seclusion, during which he devoted himself to study and prayer. He emerged to play his part in public life in 5587 (1826), at the time when Rabbi Dovber was accused of subversive activities. His first undertaking was the organisation of a committee to defend Rabbi Dovber.

When Rabbi Dovber died in 5588 (1827), the *Chassidim*, in recognition of Rabbi Menachem Mendel's outstanding abilities, called on him to accept the leadership of the Lubavitch-*Chabad* movement. For many months he rejected the tremendous responsibility of this position, but finally, he reluctantly answered the call.

Rabbi Menachem Mendel was a prolific writer. His works contain a unique synthesis of the hidden and the manifest in which *Talmudic*, *Midrashic*, *Kabbalistic* and *Chassidic* thought are harmoniously and lucidly blended.

He would certainly have liked nothing better than to continue his writings, edit the works of his grandfather and father-in-law, and lead the countless *Chassidim* who had swelled the ranks of Lubavitch. But this era had its own share of problems with which Jews were confronted.

Jews in Russia were barred from most occupations and business opportunities, and poverty was rampant among them. Deeply interested in the economic position of the Jewish people, the *Tzemach Tzedek* advised the *Chassidim* to engage in agriculture wherever possible, and he gave financial aid to those who followed his advice.

At that time it was the policy of the Russian Government to make it difficult for Jews to settle in the villages, so the *Tzemach Tzedek* bought a large tract of land near the city of Minsk on which to settle many Jewish families. In 5604 (1844) he bought another large area of land with some adjoining forests in Minsk Province from Prince Shzedrinov, and established the settlement of Shzedrin. A council was organised to direct its affairs.

The founding of Shzedrin made a deep impression on Jews and non-Jews alike. In a Government report from the officials of the Province of Minsk to the Minister of the Interior, they spoke of Rabbi Schneersohn of the city of Lubavitch with respect and praise.

The report mentioned that he had acquired a large tract of land and established there a settlement for Jews, thereby raising their living conditions and improving their position. It also spoke of the great influence of the Rabbi of Lubavitch on all the Jews living within the pale of the Russian Empire and of the manner in which he constantly tried to improve their material living conditions.

In the year 5587 (1827) Czar Nicholas I instituted the "Cantonist" edict, which introduced the conscription of children for military training and service. Originally it applied to children of the age of twelve years and older. The Jewish communities had to supply a quota of ten children per thousand (non-Jews had a smaller quota and more liberal exemptions).

Since the communities were unable to supply the full quota of older children, youngsters of eight or even seven were often caught and delivered as cantonists. Confusion and despair reigned among the people.

The children were sent away by Government officials and distributed among the peasantry, or sent to special schools until the age of eighteen. They were then removed to barracks for military service for twenty-five years.

This meant that the children were torn from home and from *cheder* for the greater part of their lives, and were subjected to treatment calculated to estrange them from their own people.

No parent would willingly yield a child for such a callous scheme, but the community was obliged to provide its quota, so the children had to be taken by force. This led to the appearance of a despicable character, the "catcher", whose job was to "catch" or kidnap the children and hand them over to Government officials. Heart-breaking scenes, with children being torn from their mothers' arms, became common occurrences. The brunt of the tragedy fell upon the poorer Jews, who were unable to buy their children's freedom from the "catchers".

The *Tzemach Tzedek* attacked the problem without regard to the dangers involved. It was necessary to save as many as possible of the children who were actually conscripted. With this in view the *Tzemach Tzedek* organised a special council for the following three purposes:

First, to study the position of the individual Jewish communities, with a view to helping them decrease the number of children they would have to supply.

Secondly, to engage in freeing those who had been captured. It was arranged to achieve this through the organisation of a special clandestine society known as "*Techias Hameisim*".

The method employed was to pay a ransom for each child to the officials concerned. They would return the child, at the same time reporting to the authorities that the child in question had died during the journey. They would also officially inform the community concerned of the "death" of the child. These "death certificates" brought great happiness to the parents.

Obviously, the children had to be hidden for a long time. Those who were saved were called "members of the *Techias Hameisim* society". They were then sent to *chadorim* or *Talmud Torahs* far from their home towns.

Thirdly, to send special trustworthy people to the places where the cantonist children were stationed, to encourage and urge them to remain faithful to their religion and to their people.

Apart from the huge expense it involved, this responsible work was highly dangerous, for it amounted to an act of treason. Yet this underground programme was successfully carried out and was never betrayed.

At the same time, the *Tzemach Tzedek* concentrated his efforts on supporting the agricultural centres in the districts of Vitebsk and Minsk. He dispatched Rabbi Hillel of Paritch, one of the leading *Chassidim*, to the settlements in the district of Kherson, where he spent several months each summer.

Besides instructing the Jews there in the study of the *Torah* and the fear of G–d in accordance with *Chassidic* teachings, he inspired them to rise to a high level of brotherly love, mutual help and generally high moral conduct.

During the twelve years from 5587 to 5599 (1827–1839), Rabbi Menachem Mendel concentrated his efforts on communal activities in the field of material aid; the protection of Jewish children from kidnappers and their maintenance in safety; and spiritual help for the cantonists.

The *Tzemach Tzedek* devoted particular attention to the requirements of the Jewish conscripts in the Russian army. He ensured that there should be special representatives at every place where Jewish troops were stationed, with the specific aim of concerning themselves with the troops' moral conduct. These representatives were to encourage the soldiers and strengthen them in the observance of the Divine commandments, and prevent them from falling into the traps of conversion laid for them by eager missionaries.

Rabbi Menachem Mendel also worked for the support of needy *Torah* scholars studying at the *yeshivos* and advanced institutes of learning.

During all these years he carried on his work without any interference from the opponents of *Chassidism* in either the religious or the so-called "enlightened" groups in Russia. During this time also, there was no conflict between *Chassidim* and *Misnagdim*. On the *Tzemach Tzedek*'s frequent visits to *Chassidic* communities in Minsk and Vilna, the *Misnagdim* always accorded him great honour and attended his *Chassidic* and *Talmudic* discourses.

In 5603 (1843) the Russian Government announced that a conference was to be held at St Petersburg for the purpose of deciding important religious problems. It was the intention of the government, at the instigation of the *Maskilim*, to use the conference as a means to introduce into the school system innovations which would interfere with traditional procedures in Jewish education and prayer.

A Rabbinical Commission composed of leaders of *Chassidim* and *Misnagdim* was convened to plan how best to combat the threat the conference posed. Rabbi Menachem Mendel was appointed to the Commission.

The first meeting between the *Tzemach Tzedek* and Rabbi Yitzchok of Volozhin, the leader of the *Misnagdim*, made a favourable impression on both of them. Observers remarked that the meeting proved to the *Misnagdim* that the *Chassidim* were scholars, and convinced the *Chassidim* that the *Misnagdim* were pious.

This rapprochement and communal co-operation had salutary effects on the general relationship between *Chassidim* and *Misnagdim*. The antagonists were re-united and began to work together for the common cause of traditional Judaism.

At the first meeting of the conference in 5603 (1843), Rabbi Menachem Mendel expressed his opinion that the purpose of the conference could only be to encourage religious observance among the Jews and he reiterated the indefensibility of tampering even with Jewish custom, since customs are also considered *Torah*. Despite threats by the chairman of the conference, a Minister of the Government, and being placed under house arrest on numerous occasions during the four-month period of the conference, Rabbi Menachem Mendel showed unswerving determination to oppose any proposed change of any Jewish custom whatsoever.

"We were not summoned to legislate", he said. "We are here to clarify statutes previously decided in the laws of the Mosaic faith. We are here to clarify, too, the customs of Israel, to protect both the commandments of G–d and Jewish usage from tampering."

The conference ended without the adoption of any of the changes proposed by the *Maskilim*. Rabbi Menachem Mendel's resoluteness and selflessness impressed all the participants and enhanced his already considerable reputation.

The granting of honorary citizenship papers signed by Czar Nicholas was one of the honours bestowed on Rabbi Menachem Mendel in 5604 (1844), in recognition of his valuable work at the St Petersburg conference the previous year.

This great honour bestowed on the *Tzemach Tzedek* by the Government made a deep impression on the Jewish population throughout the Russian Empire. Whenever an important problem arose concerning the Jewish community in White Russia, the *Tzemach Tzedek* was consulted and asked to negotiate with the Government. The communal activities undertaken by Rabbi Menachem Mendel thus spread into even wider fields.

He made every effort to improve the economic conditions of the Jews in the "Pale of Settlement". Of all the inhabitants of Russia, only the Jews were discriminated against in the matter of where they could live. They were allowed to settle only in certain districts forming a belt or "pale"; hence the Pale of Settlement. Even there, they were restricted to the urban areas and kept out of the rural areas.

At the conclusion of the Rabbinical conference, the *Tzemach Tzedek* submitted a report to the Minister of the Interior on the economic situation of the Jews in the Pale of Settlement, and petitioned the Government to extend it.

The reaction of the Minister of the Interior was favourable, and at the suggestion of one of his assistants, he invited Rabbi Menachem Mendel, together with two interpreters—Mr Feitelson and Mr Chaikin—to come and see him in the capital in order to elaborate on his proposals. The Minister received the *Tzemach Tzedek* courteously, and assured him that his proposals would be submitted to the next session of the Cabinet.

Several days later, one of the assistants of the Minister of the Interior announced that, although Rabbi Schneersohn's proposals concerning the economic plight of the Jews in the Provinces of Vitebsk, Mohilev and Minsk had not been accepted in full, a decree had been promulgated forbidding the expulsion of Jews from villages and estates if they were already settled there. The precarious position of many Jews was thus legalised, and the Pale was in fact extended.

News of the new regulation gained by the *Tzemach Tzedek* spread among the Jews, and hundreds of Jewish families took advantage of the new development to infiltrate into the "new zone", finding ways to antedate their move so that it would meet the requirements of the law.

During the summer of 5604 (1844), several hundred families settled on the land and earned a good livelihood. Furthermore, as a result of the exodus from the cities, the problems of overcrowding and competition was eased.

Rabbi Menachem Mendel's personal magnetism drew tens of thousands of *Chassidim* from all parts of Europe and Russia, and his thirty-eight years as leader of the movement were a colourful and flourishing period for *Chabad*. His efforts, like those of his predecessors, served as an inspiration to his successors.

Rabbi Shmuel

5594–5643 (1834–1882)

the fourth generation

Fourth in succession to the leadership of *Chabad* was Rabbi Shmuel, son of the *Tzemach Tzedek*. Rabbi Shmuel continued to spread the teachings of *Chabad* among the Jewish people, and at the same time to engage in communal activities to improve the spiritual and material conditions of the Jewish masses within and beyond the ranks of the *Chassidic* movement.

In 5615 (1855), at the age of twenty-one, Rabbi Shmuel's father requested him to participate actively in communal work. Together with a colleague, Rabbi Shmuel travelled to the Russian capital in order to take part in a conference called by the Russian Government to discuss the problems connected with the publication of textbooks with a German translation for use in the instruction of Jewish children.

This conference was under the chairmanship of one of the assistants of the Minister of the Interior. Despite his youth, Rabbi Shmuel voiced his opinion clearly and vigorously to the officials of the Czarist Government.

Between the years 5616 and 5626 (1856–1866) he travelled extensively throughout the country and abroad, in order to meet and influence important Jewish leaders. The friends that he made and the confidence he inspired at these meetings were to be of great assistance to Judaism in later years.

After the death of the saintly *Tzemach Tzedek* in the spring of 5626 (1866), Rabbi Shmuel was elected to succeed him as head of the *Chabad Chassidim*. His leadership, which lasted from 5626 to 5643 (1866–1882), coincided with one of the stormiest periods of antisemitism in Russian history, originating in the highest circles of the Czarist court in

Handwriting facsimile of Rabbi Shmuel Schneersohn—the Maharash of Lubavitch, of sainted memory

St Petersburg. Many princes were among the violent Jew-baiters who constantly schemed to cause trouble to the Jewish communities and to instigate pogroms.

Rabbi Shmuel, keenly aware of his great responsibility, was among the foremost fighters in the battle for the survival and defence of the Jews. He was the moving spirit in all actions taken to save the Jewish masses or defend them against the vicious attacks from Government circles.

In 5629 (1869) Rabbi Shmuel organised a permanent council of leaders of the St Petersburg Jewish community. The council's task was to be well-informed in all matters concerning the Jewish people and to be on constant guard to defend their interests and rights. From 5630 to 5640 (1870–1880), Rabbi Shmuel again made many trips to various parts of the Russian Empire and abroad, with complete disregard for personal safety.

During 5639 and 5640 (1879–1880) there was a considerable rise in anti-semitism throughout Russia. In many cities and towns the enemies of the Jewish people incited the local populations to carry out pogroms against the Jewish communities. Rabbi Shmuel again travelled to St Petersburg to try to stop this new wave of persecution.

He had many personal friends and acquaintances among Government officials, princes and nobles. They assured him that the antisemitic campaign would be stopped, but pogroms broke out again in 5640 (1880) in Kiev and Nieshin.

Rabbi Shmuel had just returned from a visit abroad in connection with the problems of the Jewish communities, when the sad news reached him. He at once set out for the Russian capital, and with the aid of Professor Bertenson, court physician to the Czar, he was able to obtain an immediate audience with the Minister of the Interior.

Filled with sorrow because of the desperate situation, the Lubavitcher Rebbe went so far as to reproach the Minister for not having kept his word to suppress the antisemitic outbreaks. He made it clear that continued failure to do so would create a very bad image of the Russian Government among the highest circles in foreign countries.

In the course of his meeting with the Minister, Rabbi Shmuel mentioned that he had received letters from many personalities and bankers in other countries who had international influence. They all wanted to know what attitude they were to take, in view of the sad news concerning the plight of the Jews in Russia, and what they could do to protect the lives and property of the Jewish population in Russia.

The Minister asked: "What was your reply?"

"I have delayed my reply till I receive positive assurances in this matter from the Russian Government", answered Rabbi Shmuel.

"Rabbi of Lubavitch," said the Minister, "do you dare to intimidate the Russian Government with threats of the power of foreign capitalists? Are you threatening a revolution in this country?"

"Your Excellency does not have to interpret my words as an attempt at intimidation", replied the Lubavitcher Rebbe. "Regard them, rather, as a serious fact to be reckoned with, for this concern is shared by capitalists and great men even of the non-Jewish world, who are shocked by such barbaric and inhuman outbreaks as have occurred here. As to the second question, it appears to me that it is the negligent and weak conduct of the Imperial Government in the past that could now bring about a revolution in this country."

That very evening, on returning to his hotel, Rabbi Shmuel was informed by the Government that he was under arrest. Two policemen stood guard at the entrance to his room for two days. On the third day, however, he was called before the Minister of the Interior and given a positive reply to his request.

This is but one example of the numerous occasions when Rabbi Shmuel turned to the Ministers and princes of Russia on behalf of the Jewish people, displaying complete disregard for any threats of punishment to himself.

Such was his conduct in all his communal work. He was not deterred by the rich capitalists or the sophisticated *Maskilim*, nor was he intimidated even by the highest Government officials. He voiced his views clearly, forcefully and with dignity on every occasion that it was necessary to do so in the interests of the Jewish people and his outstanding leadership was reflected by the respect shown for his pronouncements and interventions. During this time the adherents to *Chabad* increased in number and like the leaders of *Chabad* since the inception of the movement he ministered to their individual needs and enquiries, strengthening their devotion to *Torah* in the especially difficult times in which they lived. He was the author of many volumes of *Chassidic* literature.

Rabbi Shmuel's short but vital and purposeful period as leader of *Chabad* also heralded the next phase of its work, which is characterised by the campaign to spread the knowledge and study of *Torah* and the spirit of tradition and G–dliness among the Jews of the world.

This world-wide activity was spurred by the growing mass emigration of Russian Jews. While concentrating on Russia, including its outlying provinces of Grusia, Bokhara and Caucasia, *Chabad* activities spread to *Eretz Yisroel*, Poland and the Baltic countries and, more recently, to the United States, Canada, Western Europe, Australia, North Africa, South America and elsewhere.

It is noteworthy that these activities have been carried out with equal zeal and determination whether the Jews concerned have been of Oriental, *Sephardi* or *Ashkenazi* origin, once again emphasising the all-embracing character of the *Chabad* movement as one belonging to the whole People of Israel.

Rabbi Sholom Dovber

5621–5680 (1860–1920)

the fifth generation

The fundamental approach of the leaders of *Chabad* was the path followed by Rabbi Sholom Dovber, the fifth Lubavitcher Rebbe, son of Rabbi Shmuel. Like his predecessors, he devoted a great deal of his time to the furthering of Jewish education, and sent his representatives and delegates to all parts of the country for this purpose.

Rabbi Sholom Dovber took a personal interest in the "*Berg Yidden*", living in the Caucasian mountains and other remote parts of the country. He investigated their position and learned that they had neither teachers nor spiritual leaders, and that their youth was growing up without any knowledge of the *Torah*.

Already, because of lack of learning, many had become largely estranged from the faith of their forefathers. The situation was deteriorating rapidly, and the prospect was that within a short time, a generation or two at most, the last vestige of Jewishness would be gone from these isolated elements of the nation.

Rabbi Sholom Dovber planned a determined campaign to save these groups of straying Jews before they became completely alienated from the Jewish faith. To head this campaign, he selected the distinguished scholar and *Chassid*, Rabbi Shmuel Halevi Levitin, who had been Rabbi of the Jewish community of Rakshik up till then, and appointed him his personal representative with full authority to organise *Talmud Torahs* and *yeshivos* throughout the provinces of the Caucasian Mountains. Rabbi Shmuel Levitin travelled to this far corner of the country and devoted all his time and efforts to this sacred mission entrusted into his care by his revered Rebbe.

Handwriting facsimile of Rabbi Sholom Dovber Schneersohn of Lubavitch, of sainted memory

The Jews in these areas numbered over 100,000. The majority were *Sephardim*, and at first Rabbi Shmuel Levitin found that the immense amount of work to be done was impeded because these *Sephardi* Jews found it difficult to accept the authority and teaching of *Ashkenazi* Rabbis. However, the sincerity of the *Chabad* representatives so impressed the *Sephardim* that they soon overcame their initial prejudices.

Chabad's aims in this region were twofold. First, immediate action to save the children and bring them back to *Torah* and the fear of G–d.

Secondly, the establishment of institutes for the training of Rabbis, teachers, *shochetim* and cantors, so that the *Sephardim* would in due course produce their own spiritual leaders to carry on this work.

The *Sephardim* sent their children to these schools, and the name of *Chabad* won fame and favour among these thousands of Jews living in the Caucasian provinces.

The basic principle of the leaders of the *Chabad* movement in their work for education was that the *chinuch* for *Torah* and *mitzvos* should be conducted in the pure spirit of tradition, in the manner handed down to us through the centuries, originating in the Divine revelation on Mount Sinai.

In 5669 (1909) Rabbi Sholom Dovber became increasingly perturbed by the innovations being introduced in certain so-called *Torah* institutions in *Eretz Yisroel*. The following are extracts from a letter which he wrote to *Eretz Yisroel* at that time:

> There is an increasing number of distinctive reformers, whose only goal is to destroy the Jewish faith and deprive it of its sacred character. Shrewdly enough, they persuade fathers, and even more so mothers, who are soft-hearted, easily convinced and ready to fall for the lures of the new ideas, to deliver their children to certain destruction. . .
>
> Experience has shown that unless we are able to implant the light of the *Torah's* sanctity into the hearts of the children while they are still young and pliable, there is little hope that they will follow the path of righteousness. He who wants to make sure that his son will grow up in the true spirit of the *Torah* and *Yiddishkeit* must make certain that the child will not be exposed to the temptation of these new ideas that were foreign to our forefathers.
>
> It is hard for anyone to remain calm in the face of such serious inroads into the very heart of Judaism. They have broken and cut into small fragments the grandiose structure of the *Torah*, the very *Torah* which is the life and soul of our nation, and for the preservation of which our ancestors were prepared to die, by the thousands, as martyrs.

It was in this spirit that Rabbi Sholom Dovber fought the forces of reform and assimilation, which had made progress within certain circles of our people.

Residents of the new Lubavitch village in Israel—Nachalat Har Chabad—joyously carry two Sifrei Torah *sent to them by the Lubavitcher Rebbe, Rabbi Menachem Mendel Schneerson, from New York. Nachalat Har Chabad is located in the Negev, near Kiryat Malachi, and was established in 1969 by the Rebbe for settlement of 400 immigrant families. These families, all* Sephardi Jews, *are direct descendants of the* Berg Yidden *referred to in this article*

When the Bolshevik Revolution toppled the Czarist regime in Russia, the country was proclaimed a Republic, with the slogan: "Liberty and freedom for all." Rabbi Sholom Dovber feared that the desire to break free from all bonds and traditional ties might also invade the Jewish world and induce the Jewish masses to throw off the traditions of our faith and do as they please in the matter of religion.

He suggested that a strong non-political Jewish corps should be organised by all the faithful Jews in every city and village in Russia, and that they should work as a unified force, putting aside "selfish individual interests" to strengthen the cause of *Torah* and religion everywhere.

Particular attention was to be paid to encouraging the observance of the Sabbath, kosher slaughtering, family purity and other vital facets of Jewish life. He further suggested that these groups should consult each other about the problems they encountered, and plan their activities.

Rabbi Sholom Dovber was at all times conscious that the future of Judaism depended entirely upon the young, the future generation. He therefore stressed the importance of strengthening the work of *limud Torah* particularly for younger children.

The leadership of Rabbi Sholom Dovber, spanning as it did a period of great political upheaval in Russia and the world at large, illustrated clearly how the leaders of *Chabad*, each in his generation, carried on the golden chain of sacred work for *Torah* education and the spreading of *Torah* knowledge among young people wherever Jews lived.

They worked incessantly to strengthen every weakness in the fortress of the Jewish religion. They faced without fear the forces who stood in the way of their sacred work or threatened to undermine our faith.

Rabbi Joseph Isaac Schneersohn
5640–5710 (1880–1950)

the sixth generation

Rabbi Sholom Dovber, the fifth leader of the growing *Chabad* movement, was constantly kept busy by the growing number of public meetings, conferences and important Rabbinical convocations which he had to attend.

The endless stream of *Chassidic* delegations, people seeking his advice and guidance, the need to supervise and instruct his followers in addition to his personal need for Biblical and *Chassidic* study, made increasing inroads into working days which already stretched from early morning until late at night.

He decided to appoint a personal secretary to relieve him of part of this enormous burden. His choice was his fifteen-year-old son, Rabbi Joseph Isaac Schneersohn. Born on *Tammuz* 12, 5640 (1880) in Lubavitch, Russia, the young man had proved his ability in the field of study and was already acknowledged as a brilliant scholar. He was soon to prove himself to be no less a brilliant administrator with an outstanding talent for communal and civic activities.

In 5655 (1895) the young Rabbi participated in the great conference of religious and lay leaders in Kovno, and again in the following year in Vilna.

On *Elul* 13, 5657 (1897), at the age of seventeen, Rabbi Joseph I. Schneersohn married Nehamah Dinah, the daughter of Rabbi Abraham Schneersohn, a prominent man of great scholarship and piety (and the grand-daughter of the *Tzemach Tzedek*).

During the week's celebrations that followed the wedding ceremony,

Rabbi Sholom Dovber announced the founding of the famous Lubavitch *Yeshivah*, Tomchei Tmimim, and the following year appointed his son to be its executive director. Under the able direction of Rabbi Joseph I. Schneersohn and guided by his ever-watchful father, the Lubavitch *Yeshivah* flourished and developed and many branch *yeshivos* were formed throughout Russia.

The first two decades of the twentieth century were to test the young Rabbi's unbounded energy, zeal and ability to the full. Only the briefest mention can be made here of even the most important of the events contained in those twenty years.

As part of the strenuous efforts being made to improve the economic status of the Jews in Russia, Rabbi Joseph I. Schneersohn was delegated by his father to conduct an intensive campaign for the establishment of a textile factory in Dubrovna.

This campaign, in the year 5661 (1901), took Rabbi Schneersohn to Vilna, Lodz and Koenigsberg. He obtained the co-operation of leading Rabbis and of the famous philanthropists, the brothers Jacob and Eliezer Poliakoff, and the textile factory was duly established with some 2,000 Jewish employees.

We already know of the difficult position of the Jews under the Czarist regime and how the Lubavitcher Rebbes continually interceded on behalf of their brethren, both with the Government and with the Court. Rabbi Joseph I. Schneersohn undertook many such missions and often travelled to the capital of St Petersburg and to Moscow.

When the Russo-Japanese war flared up in the Far East in 5664 (1904), Rabbi Joseph I. Schneersohn became active in the campaign inaugurated by his father to provide the Jewish soldiers on the Far East front with *matzos* for *Pesach*.

In the widespread unrest that followed in the wake of that war, a new wave of pogroms swept the Pale of Settlement. Rabbi Joseph I. Schneersohn was sent by his father to Germany and Holland, and was successful in obtaining the intercession of prominent statesmen on behalf of Russian Jewry.

In the year 5668 (1908), he again participated in the Rabbinical convocation in Vilna. In the following year, he went to Germany to confer with Jewish leaders there. Upon his return, he took part in the preparation for the next Rabbinical convocation in the year 5670 (1910).

His energetic and far-reaching public activities, his watchful defence of the rights of Russian Jewry and his constant fight against the local and central authorities aroused the displeasure of the Czarist regime at that time.

Between 5662 and 5671 (1902–1911), Rabbi Schneersohn was arrested in Moscow and St Petersburg on four occasions. Since Government enquiries elicited nothing incriminating in his activities, he was released each time with a stern warning.

These incidents did not deter Rabbi Schneersohn from continuing his work, but spurred him to even greater efforts. In the years 5677 (1917) and 5678 (1918) he again took a leading part in the convocations of Rabbis and laymen in Moscow and Kharkov.

Upon his father's death on *Nissan* 2, 5680 (1920), Rabbi Joseph I. Schneersohn was requested by the entire *Chabad* world to accept the leadership of the movement and become the next Lubavitcher Rebbe.

By that time conditions had greatly changed. As a result of the war and the October Revolution, Russia was in a state of constant internal strife. As usual, the Jews suffered most.

In those days Rabbi Schneersohn found himself practically alone, facing a task that required superhuman effort—the rehabilitation of Jewish communal and religious life in Russia.

He fought his struggle on two fronts, the material and the religious. Russian Jews had been reduced to the most abject poverty and suffering, and the future of traditional Judaism was gravely threatened by the policy of the G–dless *Yevsektzia*. (The Jewish branch of the Soviet Communist Party, responsible for anti-Jewish activities. It was subsequently dissolved by the Soviet Government.)

During his single-handed fight for the preservation of traditional Judaism in Russia against overwhelming odds, Rabbi Joseph I. Schneersohn realised that a new country would have to supersede Russia as a great *Torah* centre. He therefore founded a Lubavitch *yeshivah* in Warsaw, in the year 5681 (1921), and helped many students and staff of his Russian *yeshivah* to make their way to Poland and continue their work there. The Lubavitch *Yeshivah* in Poland, like its counterpart in Russia, rapidly developed into a whole system of *yeshivos*, and hundreds of students were enrolled in its many branches.

In the meantime, Rabbi Joseph I. Schneersohn fearlessly conducted his work in Russia, establishing and maintaining *yeshivos*, *Torah* schools and other religious institutions.

At that time Rabbi Schneersohn had his headquarters in Rostov (on the River Don), but because of libellous accusations it was necessary to move from there. He took up residence in Leningrad (St Petersburg) from where he relentlessly continued to direct his activities. He organised a special committee to help Jewish artisans and workers who wished to observe the Sabbath, and he sent teachers, preachers and other representatives to the most remote Jewish communities in Russia to strengthen their religious life.

Realising the necessity of organising *Chabad* communities outside Russia, the Lubavitcher Rebbe formed the Agudas Chassidei Chabad of the United States of America and Canada, and maintained regular contact with his followers in the New World.

In 5687 (1927) the Rebbe founded the Lubavitch Yeshivah in Bokhara, a remote province of Russia.

His stand against those who wanted to undermine the Jewish religion became even more perilous. The *Yevsektzia* was determined to stop him, and even resorted to intimidation and mental torture.

One morning, when the Lubavitcher Rebbe was observing *yahrzeit* for his father, three members of the *Yevsektzia* rushed into his synagogue, guns in hand, to arrest him. Calmly, the Lubavitcher Rebbe finished his prayers and followed them.

Facing a council of armed and determined men, the Lubavitcher Rebbe again reaffirmed that he would not give up his religious activities, whatever threats might be made. When one of the agents pointed a gun at him, saying: "This little toy has made many a man change his mind", the Lubavitcher Rebbe calmly replied: "That little toy can intimidate only the kind of man who has many gods—passions, and but one world—this world. Because I have only one G–d and two worlds, I am not impressed by your little toy."

His struggle came to a head in the summer of 5687 (1927), when the Rebbe was arrested and placed in solitary confinement in the notorious Spalerno prison in Leningrad. He was sentenced to death, but the timely intervention of leading foreign statesmen saved his life. Instead of being executed, he was banished to Kostroma, in the Urals, for three years.

Giving way to further pressure by these statesmen, the authorities decided to release the Lubavitcher Rebbe. He was informed of this decision on his birthday, *Tammuz* 12. The next day he was permitted to leave and settle in the village of Malachovka, in the vicinity of Moscow. Further intervention resulted in permission for the Rebbe to leave Russia for Riga, in Latvia. The day after *Succos*, together with his family and the bulk of his valuable and historic library, the Rebbe left for Riga.

Without pausing to rest, he renewed his activities, beginning by establishing a *yeshivah* in Riga. In the years 5688 and 5689 (1928 and 1929) he ensured the provision of *matzos* for the Jews of Russia.

In the year 5689 (1929) the Lubavitcher Rebbe visited *Eretz Yisroel*, afterwards proceeding to the United States. In New York he received a civic welcome and was granted the freedom of the city. Hundreds of Rabbis and lay leaders welcomed the Rebbe and sought personal interviews with him. During this visit, he was received by President Hoover at the White House.

Returning to Europe, he continued his various activities, but in order to have better facilities for his work he took up residence in Warsaw in 5694 (1934). The activities of the Lubavitch *yeshivos* in Poland had by now gained considerable momentum. The central *yeshivos* in Warsaw and nearby Otvock attracted many hundreds of scholars from all parts of Poland and other countries, including the United States. Two years later the Rebbe took up residence in Otvock and directed all his activities from there.

At the outbreak of the Second World War in September, 1939 (5699), the Rebbe refused every opportunity to leave the inferno of Warsaw until he had taken care of his *yeshivos* and done everything possible for his suffering brethren in the Polish capital. He remained there throughout the terrible siege and bombardment of Warsaw and its final capitulation to the Nazi invaders.

Even during this time he managed to evacuate a great many of his students to safer zones, and all the American boys who had been studying at the Lubavitch Yeshivah at Otvock were safely transported back to their homes in the United States.

His courage and fearlessness (he had a *succah* built and observed the *mitzvah* of "dwelling in the *succah*" at the height of the bombardment) were a source of inspiration to the suffering Jewish community of Warsaw.

Only when he realised that nothing more could be done for them did the Lubavitcher Rebbe finally agree to heed the urgent requests of his many followers in Warsaw and abroad, to attempt to leave the shattered and charred ruins of the Polish capital and make his way to the United States.

With the co-operation of the Department of State in Washington, the Rebbe's friends and followers worked incessantly to arrange his journey from Warsaw to New York. Finally, the Lubavitcher Rebbe and his family were offered safe conduct to Berlin and thence to Riga—Latvia was still neutral at that time. Once there, the Lubavitcher Rebbe continued to help the numerous refugees who had succeeded in escaping from Poland to Lithuania and Latvia.

On *Adar Sheni* 9, 5700 (March 19, 1940) the Lubavitcher Rebbe arrived in New York on the s.s. *Drottningholm*. He was enthusiastically welcomed by thousands of followers and many representatives of various organisations, as well as civic authorities.

Immediately upon his arrival, the Rebbe made it known that it was not for his own safety that he had made the trip to the United States, but because he had an important mission to fulfil during his sojourn there. This was to make America a *Torah* centre, which would take the place of the ruined Jewish communities of Europe.

The decade that had elapsed between the Rebbe's first and second visits to the U.S.A. had left its scars on his constitution. But, although his health had become greatly undermined by suffering and martyrdom, Rabbi Schneersohn devoted himself at once to his new mission.

The Tomchei Tmimim Lubavitch Central Yeshivah was soon established, and it became the forerunner of many *yeshivos* and day schools throughout the United States. The Rebbe continued his efforts on behalf of his war-afflicted brethren overseas, and at the same time concentrated on his avowed intention to bring about a religious revival in the United States.

After a short stay in New York City, the Rebbe moved his headquarters to Brooklyn. The first issue of the monthly, *Hakriah Vehakdusha*, made its appearance as the official organ of the World Agudas Chassidei Chabad and continued throughout the war.

During the ten years of his life in America, the influence and accomplishments of Rabbi Joseph Isaac Schneersohn in strengthening Judaism, furthering Jewish education, and establishing institutions of Jewish learning were so great, that Judaism and *Torah* learning in America, and subsequently in other countries, took on an entirely different complexion.

In addition to the establishment of the Lubavitch Yeshivos Tomchei Tmimim in the U.S.A. and Canada, the Rebbe founded Machne Israel, Merkos L'Inyonei Chinuch, Beth Rivkah and Beth Sarah schools for Jewish girls, and the Kehot Publication Society, dedicated to the issue of books in the true spirit of *Torah* and tradition.

Mesibos Shabbos groups for boys and girls were also established, to make Jewish children and teenagers conscious of their great spiritual heritage. Meeting every *Shabbos* in a congenial atmosphere, and led by a young person of their own age and from their own neighbourhood, these children are imbued with the fundamentals of the Jewish religion, of the sanctity of the Sabbath and other precepts.

At the end of the war in 5705 (1945) Rabbi Joseph I. Schneersohn established his Refugee, Relief and Rehabilitation Organisation, Ezras Pleitim Vesidurom with a regional office in Paris. Many refugees were helped by this office to emigrate to *Eretz Yisroel*. In 5708 (1948) the Lubavitcher Rebbe established the *Chabad* village (Kfar Chabad) near Tel Aviv.

A short while before his death, Rabbi Joseph I. Schneersohn turned his attention to the needs of North African Jewry. The foundation was laid for a network of educational institutions, including *yeshivos*, *Talmud Torahs*, and schools for girls, all of which have continued to flourish under the name "Oholei Yosef Yitzchak Lubavitz".

A similar network of educational institutions was established in Israel, and day schools in Melbourne, Australia.

Many Jewish communal workers and leaders have taken heart from the successful work of Rabbi Joseph I. Schneersohn and have redoubled their own efforts. New organisations and institutions have sprung up in the field of Jewish education and Sabbath observance, and their influence is making itself increasingly felt. It can be truly said that this great man was one of the pillars of world Jewry in our generation.

Rabbi Joseph Isaac Schneersohn passed away on *Shabbos, Shevat* 10, 5710 (1950), after thirty years of indefatigable endeavour as head of *Chabad* and a leader of world Jewry.

News of his death saddened Jews all over the world, and they mourned with a sense of personal loss the passing of so eminent, devoted and inspiring a leader. However, they find comfort in the knowledge that his spirit lives on in the unbroken chain of *Chabad* leadership; and that the institutions which he founded continue to thrive and expand under the leadership of his successor, the present Lubavitcher Rebbe and head of *Chabad*, Rabbi Menachem Mendel Schneerson. שליט״א

Rabbi Menachem Mendel Schneerson
the Lubavitcher Rebbe שליט״א
the seventh generation

The Lubavitcher Rebbe, Rabbi Menachem M. Schneerson שליט״א, is the seventh leader in the Lubavitch-*Chabad* dynasty.

Born in the Russian town of Nikolaev in 1902, he was named after his great-grandfather, the third *Chabad* leader who was the grandson of Rabbi Shneur Zalman of Ladi, the founder of the Lubavitch-*Chabad* movement.

In 1907, the Rebbe's father became the spiritual leader of the community of Yekatrinslav and here the Rebbe spent most of his youth until 1927. Until the age of twenty-seven, when he married the second daughter of the late Lubavitcher Rebbe, he studied diligently under the guidance of his father. Before arriving in the United States in 1941, he spent some time in various countries which included Russia, Poland, Germany and France. It was during this period that he also took courses at the Universities of Leningrad and Berlin and at the Sorbonne in Paris.

Soon after his arrival in New York he was appointed as chairman of the executive committee of the Merkos L'Inyonei Chinuch—the educational arm of the Lubavitch movement. The publications division rapidly expanded under his guidance and many of its works contained his own notations.

At the age of forty-eight, in 1950, Rabbi Menachem M. Schneerson was called upon to assume the leadership of the Lubavitch movement which has continued to flourish ever since. The vitality and strength of the movement, and the esteem in which it is held by people from every walk of life, is a tribute to his leadership.

Lubavitch spans the globe

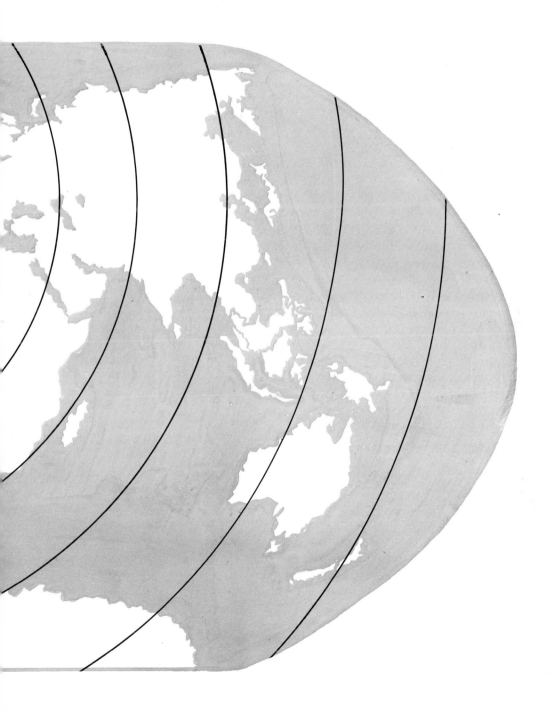

No word could be more descriptive of the activities of Lubavitch in the last two decades than the first word of its motto "Ooforatzto"—"And you shall spread out. . . ."

Represented as it is in each of the five continents, Lubavitch can now truly be termed world-wide. The representation may be open or underground. It may take the form of a *cheder*, a school or a *yeshivah*. It may be by a *Rav* of a community or a Merkos office; by an established Lubavitch organisation spanning a country, or by a single *Chassid* in some faraway foreign town. Whatever form it takes, its purpose is the same. It is a mission to Jews by Jews.

Chabad has a unique outlook on religion. It is both severely practical and inspired. *Chabad* recognises the good in each man, the Divine spark which is sometimes dimmed by varying circumstances. It considers that it has the sacred duty to rekindle the flame, and it does so by patient application and dedicated self-service.

Its success is due in large measure to its dynamic and realistic approach to Judaism. But it has been helped by a revived interest in Judaism, even amongst the most estranged.

In today's world, panaceas have lost their attractiveness. Disillusion has replaced the dreams of economic, political, cultural cures for man's and society's ills. The Second World War gave the coup de grâce to secular idealism. A generation or two ago, any number of ideologies attracted some of the finest minds and spirits among Jewry's young people and led them away from *Torah* and Judaism. Today our young people are searching for something different. Many of them, quick to sense *Chabad*'s sincerity and honest intellectual approach to authentic Judaism, have turned to *Chassidus* in enquiry and hope.

Why to *Chassidus*? Here is one possible reason. In today's three largest Jewish communities, *Chassidus* has demonstrated its ability to fire the imagination and command the allegiance of our young people, where other approaches have not had this success.

In the Soviet Union, despite vicious and relentless attempts to destroy Judaism, the adherents of *Chabad* have succeeded in raising generations of loyal *Torah* Jews. In Israel, *Chabad* has demonstrated that it can successfully address the most hostile and indifferent. In the United States, *Chabad* has sunk deep and fruitful roots. A movement, a school of thought, that flourishes under such different circumstances, deserves the thoughtful attention of anyone interested in the perpetuation of Jewry and Judaism.

The *Chabad* approach is largely through education, and its schools and

1. *Lubavitch Representatives with Senator Javitz at White House Conference on Youth*

2. *The Mayor of Kfar Chabad received by the Mayor of Montreal*

3. *Display of Merkos Publications at World Fair N.Y.*

4. *Professor Block with University Students*

5. *At "Encounter with Chabad" in New York*

1. *Rabbi I. H. Sufrin of London visits servicemen in Iceland especially to read the* Megillah *for them—*Purim *1969*
2. *Rabbi S. Lew visits servicemen in Greenland to conduct services for* Yom Kippur, *1964*
3. *A morning service at the Lubavitch* Yeshivah *in Tunisia*

yeshivos throughout the world are renowned as seats of learning. It is, however, the personal contact, the concern for the spiritual and material welfare of all Jews, that has become the hallmark of Lubavitch *Chassidism*.

Visits to universities, colleges and military camps; a summer camp where children can learn *berochos*; a once-a-month kindergarten for a small number of Jewish children miles away from the nearest synagogue; sending representatives with *siddurim* and *Tefillin* to the jungles of Panama, a Rabbi to conduct *Yom Tov* services for a few servicemen in Alaska, a *mohel* to circumcise Jewish children on a remote Caribbean island, *shelichim* to small groups of Jews in Tokyo, Afghanistan, India, Burma, Hong Kong, Singapore and the Philippines. For, in the service of *Yiddish-keit*, no task is too large for *Chabad*—or too small.

It will be readily seen that CHALLENGE, with its limited space, cannot do justice to the manifold and varied work of *Chabad* throughout the world. It is hoped that the following section on the Lubavitch Foundation in England and the articles on the European Bureau of Lubavitch in Paris, *Chabad* in Israel, Australia and Italy will, however, give some indication of its scope in different environments and under different conditions. Similarly, there has been included as an example, an article on one of the many Lubavitch institutions in the United States—the Merkos L'Inyonei Chinuch in Minneapolis. In addition there is a short description of the work of Zeirei Agudas Chabad.

CHALLENGE would have liked to include a contribution on *Chabad* in Soviet Russia. Unfortunately, the time has not yet come for this tale of heroism to be committed to print.

A complete volume could be devoted to the organisations which *Chabad* maintains in Belgium, Canada, Holland and Scandinavia and to its many activities in the Latin American countries.

Perhaps one day, too, someone will write a book on "770"—770, Eastern Parkway, a not too salubrious building in Brooklyn, New York, which houses the office of the Lubavitcher Rebbe—the power-house of *Chabad* and the hub of the Lubavitch "empire". It is from here that *Torah*-true Judaism continues to spread out until it will encompass every Jew, every-where. May that time come soon.

Artist's impression of stage two of Lubavitch schools building programme including existing new community centre

LUBAVITCH SCHOOLS

Architects: David Stern & Partners

OFFICE OF THE CHIEF RABBI

ADLER HOUSE,

TAVISTOCK SQUARE,

LONDON, w.c.1

TELEPHONE:
EUSTON 7867

Chanukah 5729

MESSAGE FROM THE CHIEF RABBI TO "CHALLENGE" - 1969/5729

The impetus to Anglo-Jewry's religious life, and in particular to Jewish education, of the Lubavitch Movement has presented the community with a hopeful ray of brightness in a scene otherwise still beset by much sordid darkness.

Together with all lovers of Torah, I am thrilled at the success which has rewarded the enthusiasm and selfless efforts of what were once but a handful of dedicated pioneers and what has now grown into a massive Torah-force, already encompassing many hundreds of adults and especially children.

I am particularly heartened by the achievements of the Movement in establishing several vibrant educational and communal centres to enrich the religious life of Anglo-Jewry.

As one of the many admirers of the creative enterprise of Lubavitch in so many parts of the World, especially in the field of Jewish education, I send you my most heartfelt felicitations on these significant additions to the spiritual fortifications of our people.

May the light of Torah shining forth from the institutions of Lubavitch illumine ever more homes and communities to brighten their path towards the sanctification of Jewish life everywhere.

Dr. Immanuel Jakobovits
Chief Rabbi

Lubavitch Foundation of Great Britain

the Rebbe sends a sheliach

The year 1968 saw the official opening of the new Lubavitch Community Centre in London, almost exactly twenty years after the first Lubavitch *cheder* was started in the same area in the home of a Lubavitcher *Chassid*.

The story of Lubavitch in England during the first half of those twenty years is the story of that Lubavitch *Chassid*, Rabbi Benzion Szemtov.

Before the end of the Second World War there was no organised Lubavitch movement in England. In Manchester there were two synagogues, founded by Russian and Lithuanian immigrants, which had a strong association with Lubavitch. There, too, two Rabbis at the *yeshivah* taught *Chassidus* as an extra-curricular subject, whenever possible, to interested pupils, thereby spreading *Chabad* philosophy within a limited circle.

In London the picture was similar. Before the outbreak of war in 1939, there had been a synagogue in Old Castle Street, in East London, which had an association with Lubavitch. In Stamford Hill a small group regularly met together for prayer at the *Beis Hamedrash* of the late Rabbi Benyaminson, a Lubavitcher *Chassid*.

It was this group, led by the late Mr Solomon Perrin, which welcomed Rabbi Szemtov to London in 1948. He had been sent there by the previous Lubavitcher Rebbe, charged with the task of bringing the message of *Chabad* to Britain.

It was no new task for this little man. Born in Warsaw, he had been one of a number of *shelichim* of the Rebbe, who had worked in Russia organising *chadorim*, *Talmud Torahs*, *mikvaos* and, under the most dangerous conditions, bringing *Yiddishkeit* to our oppressed brethren on the other side of the Iron Curtain.

He had been rewarded for his pains by being sent to a prison camp in Siberia. Released after six years, he had managed, after sojourns in other countries, to reach Paris, where Lubavitch had established a centre.

Now London. A new scene—but the same task.

Those who did not already know will have gathered from the pages of this book that whatever the country, whatever the era, the challenge, the task, has always been the same—and it has always been the lot of a few dedicated idealists.

If the task has not altered, neither has the method of tackling it. Modern facilities have speeded communication and transport; science has found new and quicker methods of curing ailments of the body. But those who are concerned for the spiritual welfare of others have found no short cut to tackling the problem.

The answer has always been the same. A *cheder* for a few children; a *Talmud Torah*; a day school; adult education; interesting and influencing individuals; slow painstaking progress if one is successful. And if one is not successful? But that possibility can never be countenanced.

The year 1948 in England was not greatly different from any other year anywhere else. True, there was freedom to carry out the work, but a generation had grown up in the war with little or no Jewish education. War service and evacuation had played havoc with Jewish home life. Families had drifted away from practice and observance.

Rabbi Szemtov was aware of the magnitude of the task and the difficulties it involved, but he also realised the immense possibilities. This was the challenge. The Siberian snow had not cooled his ardour or his own personal warmth—a warmth that was to make itself felt in the years that followed.

A start had to be made, and Rabbi Szemtov made it in the traditional manner—by starting a *cheder* in his own home. He then visited local secular schools to make contact with Jewish pupils who were not receiving any Jewish education, and these children formed the nucleus of his first classes.

Hampered by his lack of English, he realised that it was necessary to find and to train English-speaking young men in the *Chabad* tradition and philosophy, so that they, in turn, could train and impart their knowledge to others. Where to find these young men was another matter. Many of the established *yeshivos* did not encourage the teaching of *Chassidus*.

The ten years between 1948 and 1958 were spent by Rabbi Szemtov in an organised "assault" on the problems which faced him.

First the problem of Jewish education. The *cheder* in his own home grew. Helped by his late wife, members of his family and a few interested friends, he started other *chadorim* in Stamford Hill and the East End of London. The pupils were often literally pulled in off the streets, and there was no shortage of parents who came to remonstrate with Rabbi Szemtov for his "interference". He was not repentant. Patiently but forcefully, he explained the need for Jewish education and observance. His dedication and sincerity were apparent to all, and he soon mollified the irate parents.

Of these not infrequent confrontations, one of his then small band of teachers, now the Director of Education of the Lubavitch Foundation, recalls: "They came in like lions and went out like lambs", adding, "and it was not unusual for these parents themselves to become interested in the work of the *chadorim*."

This was just what Rabbi Szemtov wanted and envisaged. For it is the experience of Lubavitch that their fellow-Jews really want a Jewish education for their children and themselves, but that they need to be made aware of their true feelings.

The interest of the Jewish community was the second problem. Rabbi Szemtov travelled regularly throughout Britain, to all the Jewish centres. Whenever he met people they saw in him the embodiment of a different type of *Chassidism*, Lubavitch *Chassidism*, which concerned itself with all Jews, not only its adherents. From them he won the interest and support that was so necessary for the growth of *Chabad* in the British Isles.

Last, and possibly most important in the long term, was the task of carefully choosing, influencing and teaching the young men he needed

The sheliach *returns.*
Rabbi B. Szemtov affixing a Mezuzah *at the opening of the new Lubavitch Community Centre*

One of the first Cheder *classes in London*

to work with and for Lubavitch. They were young men from varying backgrounds. *Yeshivah* students in Manchester and Gateshead; others with little or no religious background or learning. But they all had one thing in common—in them he could ignite the spark of *Chassidus*. They were encouraged to go to the Lubavitch *yeshivos* in New York and Montreal, so that when they graduated they would be the new *shelichim* of the Lubavitcher Rebbe, in Britain and in other countries of the world.

In 1959, when Lubavitch acquired a house in Stamford Hill in which to concentrate their activities, there was not, on the surface, a great deal to show for over a decade of hard and devoted work by Rabbi Szemtov and his helpers. But the foundations had been well and truly laid for the period of expansion and achievement that followed and is still continuing.

Rabbi Szemtov now lives in New York working, as always, on some project for the Rebbe. It is not easy to measure success, but as the section of CHALLENGE devoted to Lubavitch in England shows, Rabbi Szemtov has visible proof of a job well done.

He knows, too, that the majority of the *Chassidim* who today form the executive and staff of the Lubavitch movement in England, are the young men who were influenced by him and his family in those early days, and that some of the first pupils in his small *chadorim* are now graduates of Lubavitch *yeshivos*, working for *Chabad* in Britain and as far away as Australia.

He would be the first to insist that this story is not unique, and that it is only an example of what has happened, and is happening, in many parts of the globe. That he is one of many *shelichim* who are proud to work wherever they are sent, wherever their particular talents are deemed to be needed, by the Lubavitcher Rebbe, in his direction of the world-wide activities of *Chabad* in the service of Jews and Judaism.

the dream — stage 1   *by David Stern* FRIBA, AA Dipl.

The new Lubavitch School and Community Centre is not just a building made of concrete and brick and steel. It has a soul. Long before the builders moved out, it pulsated with animation, activity and a sense of urgency.

Do not allow yourself to be deluded by the apparent simplicity and inevitability of the design; this building did not "just happen". It was created room by room from an urgent need to solve a thousand problems, but with the resources to deal with only a fraction of them. Only a few of these pressing needs were recognised or clearly appreciated at the outset, and the solution had to change as frequently as new requirements came to light.

Priorities were, as always, impossible to establish. Should the first stage be a boys' primary school, or perhaps a girls' secondary school, or a kindergarten and mixed primary? Or perhaps a *yeshivah?* Important though the children were, what about the adults who need a meeting room, a library, a synagogue?

These were some of the major issues which formed the subjects of my early meetings with the indefatigable Rabbi Sudak, Rev. Sufrin and Rabbi Vogel, and some, even now, remain to be settled.

It was in 1961 that I was first asked to advise upon a new dining room and other facilities to be added to Nos. 109–111 Stamford Hill. However, it was apparent that although every square inch was being used to the fullest, these houses were too old to justify major extensions, quite apart from the considerable upheaval they would cause to the working of the school.

The Old . . .

. . . and the first stage of the New

I therefore advised the purchase of Nos. 113–115 on which to build the first stage of the Rebbe's dream, and like so many events during later stages, the idea materialised somehow and the sites were acquired.

Then began the second miracle; not making oil for one day last for eight, but fitting ten pints into a quart pot. The planning problem was almost insuperable: seven girls' classrooms; kitchens and dining halls for boys, girls and infants; an assembly hall, gymnasium, synagogue; a library and community centre for adults; a banqueting suite, administrative and school offices; a bookshop and publications store; club rooms and junior synagogue; club bar. . . . All, with conflicting requirements, claimed priority.

Eventually and incredibly a coherent scheme gradually emerged which solved most problems—as far as we then knew them! The rest would have to await Stage II.

Lengthy negotiations with the local authorities on planning, building lines, drainage, means of escape and many other technical matters were finally concluded, and tenders for construction were invited.

With the help of our quantity surveyors we had worked out a fairly accurate assessment of the probable cost, and we were very relieved when the lowest tenders fell within our budgeted figure and contractors were appointed.

Demolition of Nos. 113–115 was the first essential. No. 113 was full of children, books and furniture, but thanks to Lubavitch forethought, all were accommodated elsewhere and the contractors moved in.

It would be satisfying to write that from that point on everything went smoothly—but life is not like that, and unusual problems continued to present themselves at all levels, requiring ingenious solutions.

The large windows in the hall also had to withstand use in a gymnasium, and had to be of armourplate glass; sliding trolleys on tracks under the stage were designed to store the seats out of sight. The stage, with the curtain closed, also serves as a changing room for the gymnasium, and, with a net curtain lowered, as a ladies' gallery for services. Serving as a screen to the hall, the Ark also contains a sliding *omud*, a book store and a school trophy case; the dining rooms "double" as club rooms, and classrooms 6 and 7 become the Library and Lounge until Stage II is completed.

A major problem arose over the serving of lunches for up to 600 children in not more than two sittings. The critical factor was the time taken to wash and dry hands before the meal—if this took too long, service

Main Hall . . . In use as gymnasium

. . . converted to use as synagogue

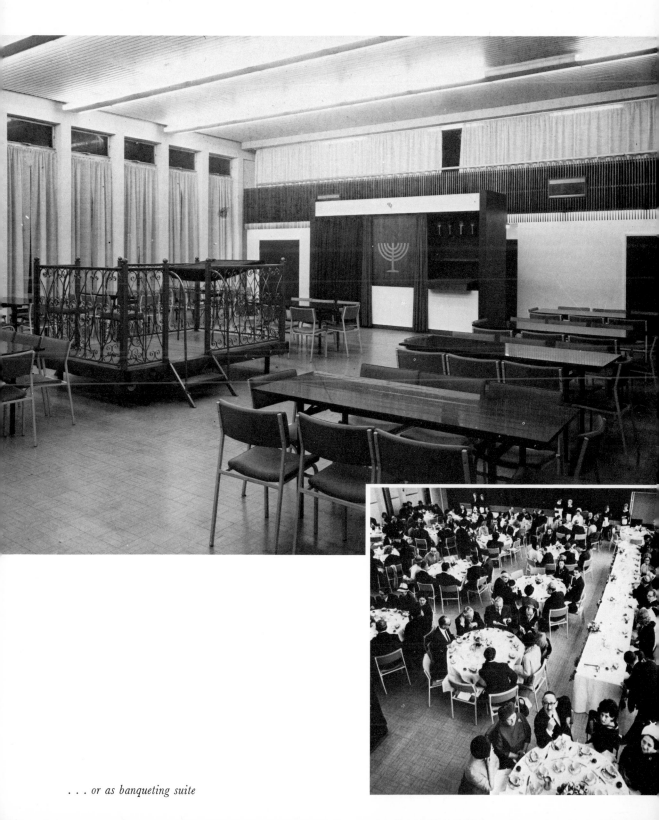

. . . or as banqueting suite

1. *The Lounge*
2. *The Library*
3. *Folding Ark in Youth Synagogue*
4. *School corridor with pupils' art display*

would be delayed and the whole school timetable would be disrupted. A wash corridor with long troughs solved this problem.

The general contractors strove to maintain their programme and progress, and were always co-operative and cordial—although sometimes distraught.

Throughout the organised chaos which characterises every building project, the three Rabbis, next door, never more than ten yards from the site, supervised, scrutinised, criticised and eulogised, adding new requirements with a reassuring smile which changed a problem into a challenge which had to be tackled.

Gradually, however, a bond of confidence and a working relationship were forged as each came to know and respect the other's difficulties and capabilities.

Furnishing and decorations are always a severe test of faith in the architect, and were in this instance particularly trying. A building to serve so many different and sometimes conflicting needs requires very careful thought in the choice of finishes, colours and materials. At this stage, I am pleased to say that these matters were left to us—with the instructions that they were to be practical, good-looking, but not luxurious.

Maintenance and running costs are particularly important in a building of this kind used seven days a week by large numbers of children and adults. Floor and wall finishes were carefully selected to stand up to hard wear with the minimum of maintenance. Floor heating was chosen—operating in off-peak hours—for trouble-free uniform heat, and the building is thoroughly insulated and double-glazed throughout for economy and comfort.

At all times everyone was aware of the need to use ingenuity in place of money wherever possible to ensure that donations diligently sought and generously given were not wasted on non-essentials.

Long before Stage I was complete, the next stage was being discussed, and now plans are under way for a new main block including a girls' secondary school with laboratories, domestic science rooms and studies, a small indoor pool, club rooms and a kindergarten.

The three Rabbis are as irrepressible as ever, and the first stage is throbbing with life and echoing with children's voices in new surroundings, which they all seem to enjoy. No, the Lubavitch centre is not merely a building—it is the realisation of a dream and the justification of faith.

opening of the new community centre

Rabbi Szemtov brings a message from the Lubavitcher Rebbe to the participants in the opening of the new Lubavitch Community Centre

RABBI MENACHEM M. SCHNEERSON
Lubavitch
770 Eastern Parkway
Brooklyn 13, N. Y.

HYacinth 3-9250

מנחם מענדל שניאורסאהן
ליובאוויטש

770 איסטערן פארקוויי
ברוקלין, נ. י.

FREE RENDITION

By the Grace of G-d
7th of Adar, 5728
Brooklyn, N.Y.

To All Participants in the Opening
of the New Lubavitch Community Centre
in London,

G-d bless you all-

Greeting and Blessing:

The Opening of the New Lubavitch Centre and attending
events taking place in the week of Purim, will surely be imbued with the sublime spirit of those auspicious days.

The essential aspect of Purim is the miraculous escape
of the Jewish people from the decree which, as the Megillah
tells us, threatened the annihilation of the entire Jewish
people, "young and old, infants and women in one day." According to our Sages of blessed memory, the decree was nullified
when Mordechai gathered 22,000 Jewish children, and so inspired
them, by word and education, that they were prepared to give up
their very lives rather than depart from Yiddishkeit.

The relevance of the Purim events to our day is pointedly
emphasized by the Baal Shem Tov, whose disciple and successor
was the teacher of the Alter Rebbe, author of the Tanya and
(Rav's) Shulchan Aruch, and the father of the Chabad-Lubavitch
system. Referring to the Mishna (Megillah 17a), the Baal Shem
Tov declared that the words, "He who reads the Megillah 'back-
ward,' does not fulfil his duty" allude also to "one who thinks
that the miracle of Purim was valid 'back in those days', but
not now".

Thus we are reminded emphatically that all the events that
took place on Purim are equally applicable today. And although
no such decree, G-d forbid, now hangs over our people, and, on
the contrary, Jews can, thank G-d, live in peace and even prosperity - the secret of Jewish survival remains the same: it is
to be found in the kosher education of Jewish boys and girls to
the degree of Mesiras Nefesh (self-sacrifice) for Yiddishkeit.

This precisely is the basic function of the Lubavitch
Centre: To gather Jewish children - children in the plain sense
of the word, as well as "children" in terms of knowledge of G-d,
His Torah and Mitzvoth - in order to reveal their inner soul and
true essence, that they should recognize that "You are children
of G-d your G-d," and should continue to forge the golden chain
of their ancestral tradition to the point of veritable self-
sacrifice for the preservation of the Jewish way of life,
the way of the Torah and Mitzvoth.

Such Mesiras Nefesh includes, of course, also complete
dedication to helping others, both spiritually and materially.

We have seen these features personified in my father-in-
law of saintly memory, the leader of Chabad-Lubavitch of our
generation, as they came to light in his eventful life, from
his earliest youth. (Thus, for example, at the age of eleven
he was arrested and imprisoned for coming to the aid of a Jew
harrassed by a Russian official).

May G-d grant that the new edifice should be filled to
capacity with "our young and our old, with our sons and with
our daughters," who will follow in this path and in this spirit.

It is impossible to overstate the extraordinary Zechus of
all those who have lent a hand in the erection and equipment of
the new centre, and who have been and will continue to be its
ardent supporters, and participants in its activities. For every
good deed by any of the youngsters who are educated within its
walls and atmosphere will be attributable to the everlasting
credit and Zechus also of the builders and helpers of this great
institution.

With esteem and blessing for much
Hatzlocho and good tidings in all
above, and for a joyous Purim -

Signed: /Menachem Schneerson/

Opening of the new Lubavitch Community Centre in London

Speech delivered by Sir Isaac Wolfson, Bart., F.R.S., on the occasion of the opening of the Lubavitch Community Centre on March 10, 1968.

In recent years the Lubavitch movement has become ever more widely acclaimed, and has won ever greater support. This recognition has come from greatly different people from all walks of life: from the President of the State of Israel to quite ordinary citizens; from Rabbis to men who had already wandered far from their Jewish origins. Many of them appeared to have little in common, perhaps no other link at all, except their response to the attraction, the pull, which the Lubavitch movement has for them.

One might ask, why is this, particularly just now? I believe the answer is to be found in the very spirit of the Lubavitch movement itself, in *Chabad*, the three pillars—Wisdom, Understanding, Knowledge—on which it is built. These represent the loftiest goals to which man can reach. And just because in this age we are constantly told that we have reached the nadir of materialism and the depths of cynicism, people have revolted and looked for ways by which to lift themselves.

For us Jews the means by which we can do this are clear, and the Lubavitch movement illuminates them, as the Chief Rabbi, from the moment of his taking on his high office—and even before—has thrown added light on them. For in a phrase, what we need is to provide more intensive Jewish education.

The Lubavitch movement took the initiative in presenting itself as a movement for the regeneration of our people, and has gone out—having adopted modern commercial methods and fashioned them for its own purpose—to sell Judaism. In that field it has proved a successful supermarket—even a mail order business!

I was happy to see that for the promotion of the *Tefillin* Campaign, the Lubavitch movement acted together with the Chief Rabbi and the United Synagogue.

It was a perfectly harmonious partnership, in which neither side attempted a take-over bid of the other, though I can assure you that a ready welcome awaits any "chabadniks" who want to join the United Synagogue. However that may be, you showed that action taken for a common aim—in this case to teach and promote the observance of one of the most important commandments laid on the Jewish people—can be rewarding to all engaged in it.

I believe that if we can get more such co-operative campaigns going among those concerned with reawakening loyalty to our Jewish faith, then we can expect great achievements. In the very recent past we have seen that considerable anxiety has been aroused in many congregations about the state of Jewish education—as was witnessed by the questions raised about the London Board for Jewish Education. I was pleased, as I am sure was also the Chief Rabbi, to know that there are a growing number of people in the community intent on doing something to see that Jewish education is improved.

What is important now is to drive home the point that the weekly classes which provide at most a few hours of tuition a week, though they may have a part to play in our present society, have been allowed to obscure the real needs instead of fulfilling them. To rely on them as the principal method for providing Jewish education, as has been done for so long, inevitably had the effect of lowering their standards, till they have become a problem instead of a solution.

Had the community sensed the need for Day Schools, in which Jewish children could get their proper Jewish education fitted into their ordinary school life, instead of having it as an inconvenient adjunct, then the schools would have influenced the weekly classes and given them also greater scope. I can tell you of my own experience that only a few short hours a week given over to Jewish education is absolutely inadequate.

Now that we have reached a crisis in these affairs, and have been shown where the fault lies, I hope that an example will be taken of your Community Centre, for it is clear that such an institution can be a guide for others.

For here you have taken a kind of double slogan: "It's never too early to begin—It's never too late to make up for lost time." You take children when they are still tiny tots, through nursery, kindergarten, primary and secondary schooling, provide evening classes for those who did not have the opportunity for such an education earlier, give facilities for adult education, study groups and the like.

In this way you train the children, inculcate into them Jewish and *Chabad* values, which will surely remain with them all their lives, and equip them to make the most of their own lives, and to contribute their best to the community to which they belong, and what more can be done for anyone?

That is why I count it a privilege to be associated with you here today for this Official Opening. And I take this occasion to tender my congratulations to the committee responsible for the Centre and my felicitations to the teachers who work in it, and my best wishes to the children and adults who will benefit from the facilities offered here—for all are engaged in the holy task of ensuring the survival of our people in accord with the teachings of our *Torah*.

At the opening of the new Lubavitch Community Centre

Telephone: 01 - 387 3952   Telegrams: DEPUTIES, LONDON, W.C.1

THE LONDON COMMITTEE OF DEPUTIES OF THE BRITISH JEWS

generally known as

THE BOARD OF DEPUTIES OF BRITISH JEWS

WOBURN HOUSE,
UPPER WOBURN PLACE,
LONDON, W.C.1.

23rd November 1968.

All communications to be addressed to **The Secretary.**

<u>Message from the President.</u>

I am delighted to have this opportunity of sending a message, through the columns of CHALLENGE, to the many thousands whose privilege it is to count themselves supporters of the Lubavitch Foundation.

It was a thrilling experience to have been present at the Official Opening of the New Lubavitch Centre in Stamford Hill, and to have seen the splendid equipment made available, and the arrangements made for hundreds of our Jewish Youth, from all sections of the Community.

It is on our Youth that our future depends. Our hopes of strengthening the Jewish consciousness of British Jewry depend on our ability to fire the interest and enthusiasm of our young people, at their most impressionable age. The flame of "Yiddishkeit" in its widest sense, which was transplanted to these islands of Freedom, can only be kept alight, and made to burn more fiercely if we take steps to make our Jewishness attractive and meaningful to the younger generation. This great task is being nobly discharged by the dedicated band of workers in the Lubavitch Movement. May it go from Strength to Strength in its great and noble work.

Alderman Michael M. Fidler, J.P.
President
Board of Deputies of British Jews.

Some of the many personalities at the opening of the new Lubavitch Community Centre

Lubavitch schools

The Lubavitch Day Schools in London were founded for English-speaking pupils whose parents were interested in ensuring that their children received a well-balanced education, encompassing both religious and secular aspects of their upbringing.

The first classes were formed in August, 1959 and consisted of a small group of children of nursery age and a small group of five-year-old girls. In ten years this small nucleus has developed into a large school system, consisting of boys' and girls' schools with parallel classes in junior and senior departments. Included in the system is a nursery, which acts as a natural source of pupils for the schools, although entry is not limited to pupils of the nursery.

The nursery, boys' and girls' schools had by early 1969 grown to about 450 pupils who are accommodated in separate premises at Stamford Hill.

The junior girls' school is now accommodated in the new Community Centre, and the plans for the second stage of building contain provisions for the accommodation of the nursery and senior girls' school.

In 1963 the Lubavitch Grammar School for Boys was opened at Kingsley Way, Hampstead Garden Suburb, in fine premises previously built and equipped as a private school.

The opening of the Grammar School was the idea of Mr N. Vogel who wanted his son to have a grammar school education coupled with a comprehensive Jewish education. Its fruition and success are in great measure due to him. Obtaining financial support for the project, although not easy, was a much smaller problem than convincing parents of the need for such a school and persuading them to entrust their sons' more advanced secular education to it.

The school opened with only two pupils but now has over fifty, some of whom sat for the University of London General Certificate of Education 'O' levels in 1968 and 1969 and achieved excellent results.

The curricula for all the schools have been formulated so that pupils are taught both religious and secular studies in equal proportion. They are designed also to develop and train future teachers and leaders, who will be able to continue and practise the teachings they have received during their school life. It is a source of great pride that the first group of girls has recently left school to join seminaries. Half of them have gone to Lubavitch seminaries to train as teachers in Jewish schools.

All the latest educational theories and practices are examined and,

The Lubavitch Grammar School in London

A Gemorrah class

Part of the Chemistry Laboratory

The presentation of a Sefer Torah *to the Grammar School*

Hebrew prep.   *A French class*

where appropriate, implemented. Constant research is undertaken by the Schools' management to ensure that the pupils will, without impairing their secular education, have a much greater advantage and chance for their future lives as good Jews than their counterparts who attend normal secular schools.

To achieve this result, classes are kept to small numbers so that the highly qualified staff are able to give pupils almost individual attention. This ensures that, in the time available, pupils can attain the necessary secular standard—General Certificate of Education level—while also receiving a comprehensive religious education. On leaving, pupils are ready not only for advanced secular education, but also for entry to colleges of further Hebrew education.

The teachers of religious studies utilise every possible opportunity to train pupils to practise the concepts and teachings of our religion in their day-to-day life, so as to make this part of their education a living ideal. All the members of the staff are trained not only to impart knowledge, but also to interest themselves in the difficulties and problems of the individual student and to help him to surmount them.

The success of the Lubavitch Day Schools policy, unique in Great Britain, is evidenced by the increasing number of pupils being enrolled from the widest possible range of Jewish groupings in all areas of the Metropolis.

All work and no play. . . .

90

Some of the children at the Lubavitch School

A knotty problem?

The world at their fingertips

A chemistry demonstration in progress

Needlework, Art and Music are important parts of the wide curriculum in the Lubavitch Girls' Schools

Ritual washing before meals

"When you have eaten and are satisfied . . .

. . . You shall bless The L–rd your G–d"

An example of the Art projects undertaken by the pupils

Evening classes

evening classes

The original Lubavitch *chadorim* have been extended to provide a special programme of religious instruction for children attending secular schools.

These evening classes are staffed by a group of teachers who, in addition to providing a basic knowledge of religious subjects, have been specially chosen for their ability to help and encourage the pupils to practise the Jewish religion, in spite of the many difficulties which a large number of them have to face.

The love and devotion shown by these teachers to their pupils is unparalleled.

The pupils of these evening classes, like those at the day schools, are encouraged to attend the youth activities, summer camps and seminars, where they are shown how to "live" religion while, at the same time, being a twentieth-century child.

The success of this programme is unequalled. Many boys have taken courses in higher religious studies, several have been ordained as Rabbis, and others are training as teachers. All are imbued with the feeling of wishing to help others; to pass on the knowledge they have gained, and to show to others the love shown to them.

The effects of this training have also reached into their homes, bringing whole families closer to Judaism, and influencing many to become fully observant.

Lubavitch youth organisation

Chinuch in the *Chabad* sense is not restricted to a classroom or a *shiur*. It pervades every aspect of *Chabad*'s endeavours, each and every one of its activities. Education in the *Chabad* sense is not only instruction; it also includes the equally important aspects of example and practice.

This attitude to education is exemplified by the Lubavitch Youth Organisation. Its programmes include recreational and social activities supplemented by religious instruction and observance, all in an authentic Jewish environment.

Football, netball, table tennis, gym activities and weight lifting, handicrafts, first aid classes—all normal youth club activities are included and enthusiastically and actively pursued—but so are a youth *minyan*, *melavei malka* and *farbrengens*.

The girls' and boys' clubs meet separately, and the groups making up

*Some of the activities
at the boys' Youth Club*

Girls' Youth Club

the Lubavitch Youth Organisation cater for young people between the ages of six and seventeen. Within its spectrum, which ranges from those engaged in full-time Jewish education to those whose only contact with *Yiddishkeit* is through the Lubavitch movement, all the needs of Jewish youth are met.

The groups meet up to three times a week during the school year and more frequently during the school holidays. The Boys' Grammar School at Hampstead has its own club, which meets at the school premises. These regular meetings supplemented by outings, seminars, and week-end and summer camps, all supervised by experienced youth leaders, help to fuse the various groups into self-contained units.

A youth *minyan* meets each *Shabbos* and on all *Yomim Tovim*. All the services are conducted by the young people themselves who, in this way, become active participants in the practice of their religion, rather than onlookers at adult services.

The older boys' activities each *Shabbos* reach a climax at *shalosh seudos*— the third *Shabbos* meal. This lively and popular weekly event has an atmosphere all of its own, and provides a warm social and religious occasion for the young participants.

Similarly, the religious content of the programmes for the girls' groups is on both instructive and practical lines. The girls also enjoy participating in their own *melavei malka*, *shalosh seudos* and *shiurim*, and they receive instruction in traditional Jewish cookery.

The annual summer camps for boys and girls have become such popular events that it is necessary each year to find new venues capable of accommodating the increased numbers applying to attend. Winter reunions are also held in London or Manchester.

All the activities are designed to provide an ideal background for today's Jewish youth. The social interchange they promote among young people of varied backgrounds enriches their experience.

The popularity of the activities of all the groups is evidenced by the steady increase in membership, and underlines the need for clubs which are Jewish in content as well as in name. It is worth mention that a significant number of boys and girls whose first contact with authentic Judaism was through the Lubavitch Youth Movement, have been drawn much closer to Jewish thought and practice. The new Lubavitch Community Centre, with its greater facilities and space, has already permitted a much-needed expansion of this important section of the Lubavitch Foundation.

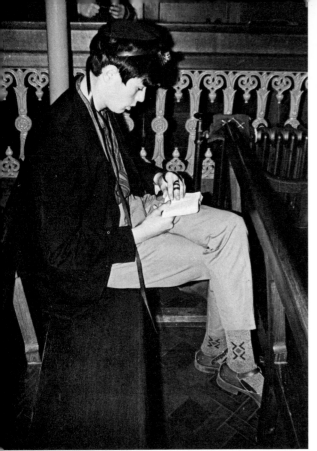 

Above: Boys' Summer Camp.   *Below: The late Mr S. Perrin presenting prizes at camp reunion*

Girls' Summer Camp

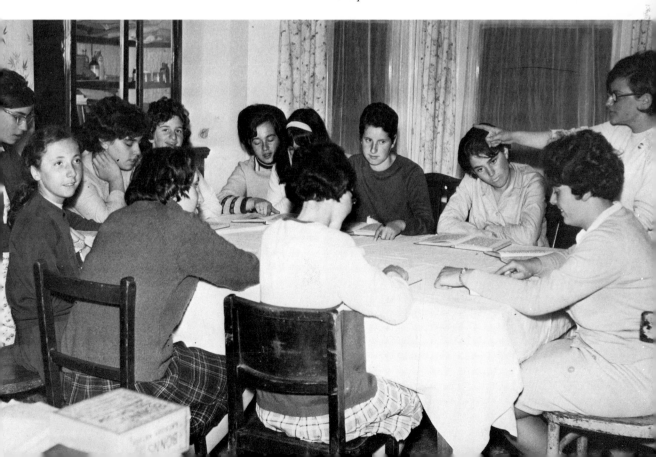

Lubavitch revive Mill House

Ever since its creation over two hundred years ago, the *Chassidic* movement has been a revivifying and pioneering force in Jewish life, and Lubavitch has been a kind of "ginger group" within *Chassidism*, the activists who are always in the van of positive Judaism.

It was, therefore, entirely in character for the Lubavitch Foundation to take over an empty house in 1964, adapt and renovate it, bulldoze away obstructions and erect additional buildings, and then initiate a programme of youth activities to attract young people from outlying communities who would in all probability have no other contact with things Jewish. In addition, they have restored regular Divine service to a lovely synagogue, only infrequently used for very many years.

It was no ordinary building that the Lubavitch Foundation acquired in 1964 from the Sir Moses Montefiore Endowment Committee of the Spanish and Portuguese Jews' Congregation.

It is the name of the Committee which gives the first clue. The house the Lubavitch Foundation acquired is Mill House, Ramsgate, part of the Sir Moses Montefiore estate.

Mill House stands next to the magnificently appointed synagogue built in the last century by Sir Moses, and to the mausoleum he modelled on the Tomb of Rachel in the Land of Israel, which he visited so many times.

Sir Moses Montefiore, the devout and scholarly *Sephardi* philanthropist and man of action, whose memory is revered by the whole of Anglo-Jewry, *Ashkenazim* and *Sephardim* alike, spared nothing to ensure that his synagogue should be a beautiful building, and that all its appurtenances should match up to its appearance. The *Sifrei Torah* in the splendid Ark

Montefiore Synagogue in Ramsgate

are priceless. He commissioned his own scribes to write them for him.

Nor did he flinch from the more difficult aspects of practising the precepts of Judaism publicly and completely. When this great figure in Anglo-Jewry was invited to dine with Queen Victoria at Buckingham Palace, he calmly brought with him his own food, dishes and utensils.

Sir Moses' devotion to prayer and the worship of G–d have been perpetuated in Ramsgate. One of the conditions on which the lease of Mill House was granted to the Lubavitch Foundation was that the Foundation should fulfil all the *mitzvos* in Sir Moses' will, including the recital of *Kaddish* and prayers on notable dates which occurred in his lifetime.

There could be no more fitting tenants of the Montefiore estate than Lubavitch. Gone are the desolation and the silence, the long, slow decline into eventual abandonment and oblivion. Now, youthful voices are heard in the grounds and buildings, as young Jews from all over Britain come and spend their week-ends at seminars, summer schools and in other activities.

The eight bedrooms of Mill House were clearly not enough to accommodate all the young people the Lubavitch Foundation knew would want to come. For this reason, the bulldozers moved in almost as soon as the ink was dry on the lease, clearing a space round Mill House for Lubavitch movement members to lay the concrete foundations for a number of wooden buildings to serve as additional accommodation.

The lease of twenty-one years at a peppercorn rent, granted to Lubavitch, is not just a legal document. It has proved to be a new lease of life for Mill House. The home of Sir Moses Montefiore has had its Jewish character and atmosphere restored, and is a testimony to the positive work of Lubavitch.

Lag b'Omer parades

Lag b'Omer, the thirty-third day of the *Sefirah*, between the festivals of *Pesach* and *Shovuos*, stands out as a day of special significance.

This date in the Jewish calendar has strong associations with the great Sage, Rabbi Shimon ben Yochai, who taught that no matter where a Jew is and no matter how difficult life may be for him, G–d is with him and gives him strength and courage to live a *Torah*-true life.

In keeping with the spirit of these teachings, the *Lag b'Omer* parades organised by the Lubavitch movement are made up of children from a very wide diversity of backgrounds fused together in a massive demonstration of solidarity. Thus, the time-honoured unity of all Jews throughout their generations is affirmed through a familiar contemporary idiom, the mass public demonstration.

The young participants, together with their parents who are also affected by the occasion, are thus involved in a corporate experience in which religious bashfulness where it exists, is banished. A heightened feeling of oneness with their fellow-Jews results, and the devotion of all those involved, including the organisers, to *Torah* living is thereby strengthened.

The parades can only be held when *Lag b'Omer* falls on a Sunday. In 1967 the *Lag b'Omer* parade in London saw a record turnout of more than a thousand young people from over thirty centres in the Metropolis, only about one-third of them from Lubavitch schools. The remainder were pupils of synagogue religious instruction classes and representative groups from Jewish youth organisations.

After the opening ceremony at Lubavitch House, the parade marched along Stamford Hill to board coaches, which took them to picnic grounds where lunch and refreshments were served. Organised games and tournaments followed, before the participants were returned to their centres at the end of an exciting and enjoyable day.

What purpose is served by these parades organised by Lubavitch in London and throughout the world? In general terms, they have a unique character as occasions which fuse together young members of a community, no matter how diverse their backgrounds and standards of religious observance.

In more precise terms, they enable youth to commemorate the anniversary of a great Sage; and to see how the observance of simple everyday *mitzvos*, e.g. the wearing of a head-covering, the ritual washing of the

Lag b'Omer parade

hands, grace before and after eating, form part of a Jew's everyday life. They also engender the feeling of unity continually fostered by the Lubavitch movement, with its traditional cardinal conviction that all Jews are essentially one family.

Are they successful? Time has shown that these young people return each year and bring their friends with them. They are some of the "new faces" who appear at other Lubavitch activities, and some of them have already become the leaders of these activities.

Lubavitch council for universities and colleges

Visits to universities and colleges have long formed an important part of the activities of the Lubavitch movement in Britain.

It is a sad reflection on us as a community that so many of our young people receiving the highest secular education have had only a meagre Jewish education and little authentic experience of Judaism.

In the experience of Lubavitch, it is this Jewish illiteracy which is a prime cause of the apathetic and negative attitude of so many of our brethren. Their lack of interest, which has been given so many fancy names, is often rooted in plain ignorance of our faith.

It is to redress this woeful neglect of the spiritual welfare of our young people at universities, who are often tomorrow's leaders in many spheres of the life of their country, that Lubavitch members make regular informal visits to Jewish students societies and other Jewish student groups.

A particularly valuable means of encounter, it has been found, is the "*Shabbaton*", where members of the Lubavitch movement spend a *Shabbos* with students at their university or college, thereby offering these young people a sample of *Chassidic* life and an opportunity to experience the teachings of *Chabad*.

Naturally, no attempt is made to force these teachings on these sophisticated young people, but they are given, as they must be given, the chance to experience the roots of their faith from an authentic source.

These visits are not intended to demonstrate a *Shabbos*, but to enable the students to experience and live a *Shabbos* in the *Chabad* manner. The day therefore provides, in addition to services, meals and a *farbrengen*, ample opportunity for discussions, which are usually lively and stimulating. They are designed to encourage a continued interest.

Arrangements are made for the many students who wish to taste more of *Chassidic* life to stay with Lubavitch families over other *Shabbosos* or

Top pictures and centre left: University students gathering at the new Community Centre. ▶
Centre right: One of the regular shiurim *for university students and below: The Chief Rabbi*
addressing students at a celebration marking the completion of a tractate of the Talmud

Yomim Tovim. They are then able to see the practical application of what they have learned from the visiting Lubavitch speakers at their university or college.

However, the programme of the Lubavitch Council for Universities and Colleges is wider than this. There are evening and afternoon discussion groups for local students, all designed to awaken and stimulate an interest in Judaism. The Council also supplies religious publications and the physical necessities for the observance of *mitzvos*, such as hand-baked *matzos* at *Pesach* and *arba minim* at *Succos*.

In January 1969, with the facilities which the Community Centre now makes available, it was possible for the first time to arrange a long desired extension of the Universities programme. Students from the Universities visited by Lubavitch were invited to participate in a *Pegisha*—An Encounter—with Lubavitch at Stamford Hill. The number of students who accepted the invitation was gratifying, and they were accommodated for the week-end with Lubavitch families locally. The students were thus able to experience a typical *Chassidic Shabbos* with their hosts and to meet together at the Community Centre during the week-end for prayers, talks and discussions and for a lively *melava malka* on *motzei Shabbos*.

The Encounter gave the students a practical insight into authentic Judaism, permeated by the warmth of *Chassidus*, a forum for the interchange of views with Lubavitch and with students from other Universities and Colleges, and an opportunity to pose, and, we hope, to receive fundamental answers to, many of the questions which exercise the minds of thinking young Jews.

There may be a chasm between the Jewish intellectual and Judaism, but Lubavitch has found, and is proving daily, that this chasm can be bridged, not by the watering down of precepts and observance, but by sincere and honest endeavour to teach the *Chabad* approach to a living authentic Judaism.

adult education

The adult in search of Jewish education will find the Lubavitch movement more than adequate to his needs, whether he has, through force of circumstances, little or no knowledge of Jewish learning, or whether he already has some grounding in *Torah*-learning. Whatever the level, it is catered for in the adult education programme at the new Lubavitch Community Centre.

Visiting Jewish blind at Succos

Shiurim *for ladies* . . .

. . . *and men*

Tefillin *campaign*

Visiting the blind at Succos

For those who have special needs, individual instruction can be provided at all levels, but one of the courses in the adult education group programme, with the advantages it offers of discussion with other participants will usually be found suitable.

There are regular study groups and lectures in Jewish law, ethics, and *Chassidic* philosophy at both advanced and elementary levels. When circumstances justify it, as with the recent influx of immigrants from Aden, courses using *Ivrit* and other languages as the medium of instruction can be provided.

The needs of young married people are met by regular *shiurim* on *Taharas Hamishpocho*, as are the needs of young women requiring instruction in the laws of *kashrus* and domestic Jewish law regarding *Shabbos* and the *Yomim Tovim*.

A new publication, *What's on at Lubavitch*, gives a fuller picture of these activities, which are constantly being amended and expanded.

The activities of Lubavitch in the field of adult education are not, however, restricted to the many people who visit the new Community Centre in search of it.

A very extensive speakers' programme, which provides speakers for a wide variety of Jewish groups is, judging by the number of invitations received, very popular.

Participation in symposiums at Jews' College and similar institutions plays its part in the programme, as do visits to preach, by invitation, from the pulpits of synagogues on *Shabbosos* and *Yomim Tovim*.

The Lubavitch adult education programme also includes such activities as visiting the Jewish blind, who require special assistance to enable them to participate in the reading of the *Megillah* at *Purim* and other *mitzvos* like that of the *lulav* and *esrog* at *Succos*.

Rosh Hashonoh sees groups of Lubavitch members visiting hospitals to blow the *shofar* for those who are unfortunately unable to attend services, and *Pesach* sees the distribution of hand-baked *matzos*.

It is a cornerstone of *Chabad* philosophy that wherever possible its activities must include a practical element, for Judaism is a living religion.

Lubavitch women's organisation

One of the paramount factors in Judaism is the important part played by women in so many aspects of its development.

The home, *kashrus*, the upbringing of children, influencing their spiritual and material development and their education are but a few of women's contributions to the Jewish scene.

In consonance with this vital role, the women's organisations of the Lubavitch movement are in the forefront of the drive towards spreading authentic Judaism in Britain. This drive is centred on the Agudas Neshei u'Bnos Chabad, or Neshei, as it is often briefly termed. Its primary aim is the dissemination of *Yiddishkeit* in its fullest and widest sense.

The British Neshei Chabad has now been striving for this lofty aim for fourteen years. Its activities, including discussion groups, lectures on Jewish law and social evenings are by now well known to the wide circle of membership, whose mutual influence has been a big factor in spreading true Jewish values among the women of Anglo-Jewry.

Parallel activities are conducted by the Bnos Chabad for girls under eighteen, while the Lubavitch Parents' Association organises fund-raising entertainments, such as concerts and bazaars, for the financing of projects for the Lubavitch Day Schools and Kindergarten.

The British Neshei Chabad also actively concerns itself with the less fortunate members of the community by giving *Chanukah* gifts to children in hospitals and orphanages, sending *shalach monos* to sick people at *Purim* and providing extra food for the needy at *Pesach*.

All the activities of the Lubavitch women's organisations are a strong force for effectively spreading their influence to other women who are not yet members of the Lubavitch family.

The facilities at the new Community Centre will, it is hoped, aid their efforts to bring many more Jewish women into contact with the living and life-giving sources of *Yiddishkeit*, permeated with the inner warmth of *Chassidic* teachings and way of life.

Lubavitch publications

The dynamic, outward-looking character of the Lubavitch movement is well reflected in the publications emanating from the Lubavitch publications department of the Merkos L'Inyonei Chinuch (Central Organisation for Jewish Education).

Here is yet another example of the motto of the movement, "*Ooforatzto*" ("You shall spread forth . . ."), translated into action. About 20,000,000 copies of various publications cater for the religious needs of Jews throughout the diaspora and testify to the concern of the Lubavitch movement for the spiritual and educational welfare of the whole of world Jewry.

Left: A section of the bookshop which offers a wide selection of Jewish and religious works in many languages. Right: Taking publications to the People of the Book

The general policy of Lubavitch publications is not to duplicate the efforts of other Jewish publishing houses, but rather to concentrate on works of a unique nature and religious authenticity which, either by virtue of restricted readership or high publishing costs, would otherwise be denied to the majority of world Jewry.

Of course a publishing policy like this requires these publications to have a non-profit making basis, and they are invariably subsidised by private individuals, or published entirely free of charge.

Lubavitch publications have another unique feature—they are designed to meet the reading needs of Jews of all standards of religious education, from those well versed in *Torah* and Jewish knowledge to the great mass of the Jewish public who, in our generation, have an urgent need for explanation and interpretation of the basic teachings of authentic Judaism.

The publications, which are fully described in detailed catalogues obtainable from the Lubavitch Foundation, fall into three main classes: Educational material including textbooks, periodicals, fiction and non-fiction books in Hebrew, Yiddish, English, French, Spanish, Russian, Italian, Persian, Danish and Dutch; publications in the *Otzar HaChassidim* (*Treasury of the Chassidim*) series, dealing with *Chabad* philosophy, ethics and Jewish law, many of them works by the great leaders of the *Chabad* movement since its inception, including a great many by the former

Lubavitcher Rebbe, Rabbi Joseph I. Schneersohn; as well as rather more specialised publications outside the scope of the previous categories, including, for instance, works such as the famous *Halachic* encyclopedia *Sedei Chemed*.

Among the more popular publications deserving of special mention is *Talks and Tales*, a monthly magazine, published in about a dozen languages, which has acquired great popularity among children, parents, teachers and students and now has 50,000 subscribers; *Our People*, an authentic Jewish history book for the young, firmly based on traditional sources, of which three volumes have appeared to date, taking the reader up to the destruction of the Second Temple; the newly launched *Lubavitch News Letter*, which keeps many thousands of British friends of the Lubavitch movement informed of the latest news and developments; and *Jewish Home*, a quarterly for the Jewish woman.

In addition to the foregoing, Lubavitch publishes visual teaching aids, including maps and charts. Also available are long-playing records of *Chabad* music and songs and aids to learning *Tanya*.

In Britain a new service has just been launched to assist in disseminating Lubavitch publications and Jewish knowledge. This is the Bookmobile—a caravan specially fitted to serve as a mobile bookshop, showroom, and *Tefillin* booth. Based on the successful experience gained in the use of these mobile facilities in the U.S.A., the Bookmobile is touring Jewish communities in England.

The Lubavitch publishing activities in Britain now have their headquarters in the more spacious premises of the new Lubavitch Community Centre at Stamford Hill, London. Here, there are a reference library, reading room, and a showroom in which the complete range of publications may be inspected by visitors.

The high standards set by Lubavitch publications in their manifold and polyglot variety, are eloquent testimony to the vision and initiative of that department's founder, the late Lubavitcher Rebbe, Rabbi Joseph I. Schneersohn, and to the manner in which it has been controlled and expanded by the present Rebbe, Rabbi Menachem M. Schneerson. שליט״א

The results achieved in the past have demonstrated overwhelmingly that these publications meet, in the broadest sense, the great and urgent needs of Jewish education throughout the world. In the future, as in the past, the Lubavitch movement will continue to strive, with G–d's help, to satisfy the thirst for knowledge for which our people, the People of the Book, has been renowned throughout all its generations.

Lubavitch in Manchester

The opening of the new Youth Centre at 62 Singleton Road, Manchester, so soon after the new Community Centre in London, is proof of the success of Lubavitch activities in that area and is a tribute to a small band of people, whose untiring efforts in the cause of Lubavitch over the past two decades have made the Centre first a necessity and then a reality.

Lubavitch is not new to Manchester. Since early in this century there have been synagogues with strong Lubavitch affiliations there. Founded originally by immigrants from Russia, who had studied at Lubavitch *yeshivos* or whose families had been followers of the Lubavitcher Rebbes, they grew into flourishing congregations.

As these congregations increased, *Chassidus* was taught to interested congregants by the spiritual leaders of Lubavitch in Manchester, but it was mainly localised, and no extensive impact was made on the large Jewish community in Manchester as a whole.

The arrival in England, in the late 1940s, of Rabbi Szemtov, brought a change in this attitude. Lubavitch was to become a more dynamic force in the community, and bring its message of love of G-d, love of Israel and love of the *Torah* to the widest possible section of the community, particularly to the children.

A committee was soon set up to implement the new programme. Its first purpose was to raise funds to assist the establishment of the Lubavitch Foundation in London and then to commence its own activities in Manchester and the surrounding area.

This committee, whose enthusiastic and energetic approach soon won support from the community, was the forerunner of the present Manchester branch of the Lubavitch Foundation. From a small beginning there has grown an organisation which now requires a full-time organising secretary. All the Lubavitch institutions in Manchester are affiliated to it.

In the intervening period, too, a number of young men from Manchester have studied at the Lubavitch Yeshivah in Brooklyn, some receiving their Rabbinical diplomas there. Together with others, they have been guided and advised by the present Lubavitcher Rebbe and are now leaders of many Lubavitch activities in Manchester, imparting their knowledge to children, teenagers and even adults.

The new Youth Centre, financed by funds raised locally, now enables most of the activities of the Lubavitch Foundation in Manchester to be concentrated under one roof.

Dayan Weiss and Rabbi Dubov affixing a Mezuzah *at the opening of the new Lubavitch Youth Centre in Manchester*

Some of the varied activities at the Youth Centre

Mr Zalmon Jaffe addressing the participants at the opening of the Youth Centre

Two Manchester girls attended the first Lubavitch summer camp for girls in 1962. They were so impressed by what they saw and experienced that when they returned, they set up the first girls' group in Manchester, which met once a week in the hall of the *Talmud Torah*. By the summer of 1963 there were three separate groups meeting at different locations and catering for all age groups.

In the following five years, about 300 girls have attended these groups. Some of them have been encouraged to attend seminaries and on their return have become the leaders of the very comprehensive programme in which the girls' groups now participate.

A small number of Manchester boys attended the first boys' summer camp in 1961, but it was only after the following year's camp, when the Manchester contingent consisted of sixteen boys and leaders, that the boys' group in Manchester was established. By the winter of that year, when the camp reunion was held in the city, the boys' group had some fifty members, and it has grown steadily in numbers since that time.

The first group met in private homes, and a year later a second group began to meet in the hall of the local synagogue.

The groups now meet at the new Centre on *Shabbos*, Sunday and Thursday of each week, and have a varied programme with both secular and religious content. Many of the 350 boys who have attended the boys' groups have gone on to *yeshivos*, both in England and abroad.

The girls' and boys' groups have their own committees. Group activities are planned by the committees together with group leaders. Boys and girls attend the camps and reunions that are held in conjunction with the Lubavitch Foundation in London.

Day camps were first introduced by Lubavitch in Manchester in 1964, and they have proved a great success. They operate during school holidays and provide a variety of interesting, instructional pursuits. In addition, children are taken to the seaside and places of interest around Manchester. All the activities, which are conducted against a traditional Jewish background, are designed to impress upon the young people that Judaism is quite consistent with a normal, healthy and useful life.

A very active and flourishing women's group participates in regular social and cultural events. A fortnightly *shiur* is a well-attended feature. This group arranges fund-raising functions, and part of the proceeds is used to meet the cost of sending girls to seminaries.

Manchester Lubavitch arranged *Lag b'Omer* parades in 1966 and 1967 in which hundreds of children from schools, *chadorim* and youth clubs in Manchester, Leeds and Liverpool participated.

The Lubavitch Youth Organisation in Manchester provides all the services with which Lubavitch Youth Organisations throughout the world have become identified, and for which they have been acclaimed.

It has a university and college visitation programme; members visit hospitals and old-age homes, particularly at *Succos* and on *Rosh Hashonoh*, to enable the sick and aged to perform the *mitzvah* of *lulav* and *esrog* and hear the *shofar* being blown; hand-baked *shemura matzos* are distributed to young and old at *Pesach*; special literature and publications are printed and distributed at frequent intervals, especially before festivals.

The first charter flight from England to see the Rebbe in Brooklyn was arranged in 1961 and left from Manchester. One hundred and eighteen passengers, including twelve Rabbis, made the journey and were received by the Rebbe on their arrival. These flights have now become an annual affair, and through this medium hundreds of people have made personal contact with the Rebbe.

Shiurim at various levels are held each week. One of these is given by Rabbi Dubov, the oldest of the Lubavitch *Chassidim* in Manchester. These together with *melava malkas* which are held each *motzei Shabbos*, and, *farbrengens* which are held on special days in the Lubavitch calendar, all add to the warmth for which Lubavitch is renowned. They provide a real Jewish stimulus for a growing band of adherents, and an inspiration to the many people who are constantly finding in Lubavitch the true Jewish appeal that *Chassidus* provides.

forward . . .

At first glance it may seem that Anglo-Jewry has some particular background which separates it from Jews elsewhere. Many would like to believe that the English Jew differs from his co-religionists in America and Europe and is more sophisticated than they. This is a wrong assumption and a harmful one, and the cause of communal lethargy.

The golden era of the British Empire still plays an important part in the attitude of the Englishman to foreigners. In addition to the usual national pride, which is acceptable to an extent, there is a feeling that England is entitled to a special position in the world because of her past greatness and deeds. Slowly, this frame of mind is being replaced by a more pragmatic approach which is awakening us to realities.

The Jewish community in this country was formed in the same way as communities in other lands. Its rapid integration and assimilation into the Western mode of life follows a very ordinary pattern.

During the late nineteenth century, following the persecution and pogroms in Eastern and later in Western Europe, the Jews came here to seek a haven. Their total preoccupation with securing their material needs allowed little thought for spiritual matters.

True, synagogues and *Talmud Torahs* sprang up in Jewish districts, but they were staffed by untrained *Yiddish*-speaking teachers, who were no match for their colleagues in the English schools. The greatly inferior amenities offered by the religious institutions as compared with the secular ones immediately discouraged the children, and any sincere interest in Jewish studies was lost to secular advancement.

Eventually, the best brains went into the professions and other callings as they became open, and most were eventually lost to Judaism. Even those who remained were often basically ignorant of Judaism and largely indifferent to everything it stood for.

Today, a great number of our youth are born into affluence, but they cannot look at their material paradise as their own achievement. The creative urge in many of them has been directed, for want of Jewish education and training, into secular arts, whilst others have made a lasting mark on the professions, commerce and industry. Yet, settled and established though they may be, they complain, when approached, that something is missing. Although their wealth, charm, intelligence and industry open doors which were hitherto locked, this does not help them to find the object of their quest.

Lubavitch, with its unique *Chabad* philosophy, believes that it has what many thoughtful Jews are looking for. Such questions as belief, the relation between G–d and the Jews, creation, *Torah* and Divine inspiration are dealt with at length in the numerous Lubavitch volumes, many of them in English. The movement's *Chassidic* warmth and its pragmatic approach to the concept of "loving one's fellow-Jew" delight the hearts of everyone who experiences them.

Lubavitch members are as observant as the most religious section of the community, yet differ from it, because their consciences are constantly challenging their exclusiveness, questioning their narrowness. They understand how much a dialogue with the non-religious Jew could benefit the community. It is here, through its contacts with all segments of Jewry, that Lubavitch shows the observant community how Judaism can be awakened in the rest. It stresses what we all have in common, instead of what divides, and tries to get away from old controversies and recriminations. Lubavitch rises above petty parochialisms, for thus, and only thus, can unity be achieved.

Lubavitch is a movement of action rather than of theory, and has already made its mark in this country. With its full range of educational media it strives to provide guidance to every Jew at every level. It begins with a full-time kindergarten and continues with boys' and girls' primary and secondary schools, where Jewish and secular instruction are fairly equally divided. Aware of the fact that many parents are not yet prepared to give their children such an education, evening classes supported by extra curricular activities are held daily after school. The acquisition of the Montefiore Estate in Ramsgate has given a new boost to these efforts.

Lubavitch is not content to wait for people to come to it, but goes out to them, with regular visits to universities and youth clubs of all shades of religious affiliation, and none. It performs a vital service for the community through the dissemination of religious textbooks and other literature which, incidentally, have been adopted in many Jewish schools and *Talmud Torahs* throughout the country.

The inspiration for all these and other activities stems directly from the Lubavitcher Rebbe, who is today acknowledged as the most influential religious leader of our time. His pronouncements on major issues are eagerly awaited by Rabbis and laymen alike. His messages through the *Lubavitch News Service* are a deep source of encouragement to many.

Obviously, this is not a field where results can be measured and weighed, but the greater awareness of Judaism as a living force and the wider interest it has aroused is in good part due to his patient concern for the spiritual welfare of all his brethren, no matter how far they may have strayed from Judaism.

Lubavitch, by giving new force to our ancient traditions, by reasserting the message of our Prophets, can instil hope where despair once reigned.

"America is not different", the previous Lubavitcher Rebbe declared on arriving in New York in 1940. Neither is Britain. This country offers much that is missing elsewhere; peace, stability, humaneness, concern for the welfare of others and leisure. Yet there is still room for a full Jewish life which does not diminish any of these things but, on the contrary, adds another dimension to existence.

the European Bureau of Lubavitch
in Paris

aid for refugees and community rehabilitation

historical background

The Central Lubavitch Office in Paris was founded by the late Lubavitcher Rebbe immediately after the cessation of hostilities of the Second World War (1945).

Founded primarily for the purpose of rendering aid to Jewish refugees and war victims, it still bears the name Lishko Eiropis l'Ezras Pleitim v'Sidurom—"European Bureau for Refugee Aid and Rehabilitation". However, its crash programmes for refugee aid soon extended to long-term projects for community rehabilitation on a broad front, so that this Bureau became the fountainhead of almost all Lubavitch activities in post-war Europe and far beyond.

Rabbi Benjamin Gorodetzki, an able administrator and indefatigable public servant, was named Director General of the European Bureau, whose sphere of activity also included North Africa and Israel.

To give an adequate description of the work of this Bureau since its creation almost a quarter of a century ago, would require a voluminous tome. All that can be done in this space is to give a brief review and some chapter headings.

work in the camps

After the holocaust of the war, the surviving refugees requiring immediate aid were of two categories: survivors of the concentration camps and, a

Above: Beth Rivkah Girls' School near Paris
Below: Students in Morocco learning the art of making Tefillin

little later, a wave of refugees from East European countries who made their way westward. The American Joint Distribution Committee, Hias, UNRRA, and similar relief organisations came to the rescue. But these were concerned mainly with the material and physical needs of the displaced persons. There was a vast field of activity to meet the religious and spiritual needs of these war victims, for the majority of them were remnants of East European Jewry, long known for their religious fervour and *Talmudic* learning. It was, therefore, one of the first tasks of the Lubavitch Bureau in Paris to organise religious and educational facilities in the D.P. camps. The Lubavitch *Chassidim* among the refugees were mobilized to conduct religious services, study-classes on various levels for children and adults, and generally take charge of the religious life in the camps. It was also necessary to provide them with religious articles (*Tefillin*, *taleisim*, etc.), sacred books (*Siddurim*, *Chumashim*, *Gemorros*, etc.).

refugee resettlement

With the total destruction of the flourishing Jewish communities in Eastern Europe, most of the surviving Jews wished to escape from the charred ruins. The European Bureau helped many of them to make their way to D.P. camps. During 1946 and 1947 the Bureau succeeded in settling a number of refugees in France. This was no easy task, for it was necessary to provide them with documents, entrance visas and shelter. At one time the Bureau operated five large buildings serving as absorption centres for refugees. Considering the desperate economic situation in France after the war, with shortages in housing, food, clothing, etc., it can readily be seen how difficult and complicated this work was in those years.

training for religious calling

At the same time the European Bureau embarked upon a project of training a selected group of refugees for various religious callings, particularly as Rabbis, *shochetim*, *mohelim* and teachers. The gain was to be twofold. They would be provided with a means of livelihood, and they would fill a pressing need for these services in the communities where they would eventually settle. Indeed, many of these trainees are still serving in these capacities in various Jewish communities in France, England, the U.S.A., Canada, Australia and other places.

A Talmud Shiur *in Istanbul*

community rehabilitation

The Lubavitch Office in Paris never lost sight of the spiritual needs of the Jewish communities in post-war Europe. When it concerned such important matters as the supply of *shemura matzos*, kosher meat, religious articles and religious functionaries, it was the Lubavitch Bureau in Europe to whom everybody turned. It was the focal point, *the* address, for all religious matters, on the individual as well as communal level.

operation kosher meat

One of the outstanding services rendered by the European Bureau was the Kosher Meat Operation of 1948 and 1949, when **three** million pounds of kosher meat, generously supplied by the Government of Eire for Jewish refugees in the camps and in Israel, was processed by some fifty Lubavitch-trained *shochetim*. After the conclusion of that operation, a number of *shochetim* remained in Ireland and England to help alleviate the shortage of *shochetim* there; others found ready employment elsewhere.

Sefer-Torah operation

The *Sefer-Torah* operation is another interesting vignette in the work of the European Office. Some 1200 *Sifrei Torah* which had been salvaged in Germany were placed at the disposal of the American Joint. Most of them were mutilated, damaged and spoiled—war casualties like the refugees themselves. The Joint turned them over to the Lubavitch Bureau for repair and eventual distribution to Jewish communities.

kosher kitchen in Madrid

A further example of Lubavitch pioneer work under the auspices of the European Bureau was the establishment in 1951 of kosher dining room facilities for Jewish students in Madrid. There had been a substantial increase in the number of Jewish students from Spanish Morocco and elsewhere studying in Madrid. They turned to the European Bureau for help, and they were not disappointed. Thus, for the first time since the expulsion from Spain in 1492, Jews were enjoying the freedom of religious practice in that country. The kosher dining room and other religious facilities in the University of Madrid lasted for three years. Thereafter, the number of Jewish students dwindled.

deployment of Lubavitch manpower

In the late forties there began the resettlement of many Lubavitch refugees from France to other countries. Some one hundred families were sent to Israel to establish the now famed *Chabad* Village (Kfar Chabad). A group of some ten families were helped to emigrate to Australia. Their impact upon the Jewish community of Australia is mentioned elsewhere in this publication. Other families settled in England, Italy, Belgium and various other countries in the New and Old worlds. Wherever these Lubavitchers came, they breathed new life into the Jewish communities through their dynamic efforts to strengthen and spread *Yiddishkeit*.

Lubavitch educational work in post-war Europe

Yeshivah in Brunoy

Concurrently with its crash programmes and long-term projects for refugee aid and community rehabilitation, the European Bureau of Lubavitch in Paris concentrated also on the vital problem of Jewish education. It has been instrumental in establishing and operating a whole network of educational institutions: *Talmud Torahs*, *Yeshivos*, Girls' Schools and Teachers' Seminaries, which have changed the entire complexion of many a Jewish community.

One of the first institutions to be established by the European Bureau after the war (1945) was the Lubavitch Yeshivah Tomchei Tmimim at Brunoy, in the vicinity of Paris. It has become one of the finest *yeshivos* in post-war Europe. Originally established primarily for refugee children, it has since attracted students from many parts of the continent and from North Africa. Many of its graduates now serve as Rabbis, principals and Hebrew teachers in various parts of the world.

girls' school and seminary

At about the same time, the Beth Rivkah Girls' School at Yerres, a suburb of Paris, was established. It was the forerunner of similar girls' schools in other countries, to which reference will be made later.

Realising the pressing need for women teachers, even for its own girls' schools, the European Bureau established in 1958 the Beth Rivkah Teachers' Seminary in Yerres. It is now housed in a magnificent building specially built for it, with the most modern educational facilities. It offers a three years' course of teacher-training and higher education. Last year fifteen students graduated with distinction from the seminary, as fully qualified teachers, bringing the total number of graduates to date to about 50. The seminary commands the highest respect and recognition and its graduates are eagerly sought after by various schools. Some senior students are enlisted as teachers even before graduation. The seminary has been a boon for eligible bachelors of similar training and background. The young Lubavitch couples, where the husband is a Rabbi, *shochet*, or teacher, and

Girls Teacher's Seminary in France

the wife a trained educator, have been eagerly sought after, for they are a great asset to any community.

The seminary at Yerres has made such remarkable progress that it has recently been found necessary to add a third floor to the building.

Both the Beth Rivkah Girls' School and Teachers' Seminary at Yerres are residential schools, with dormitories, dining room and other facilities for the students. The same is true of the Lubavitch Yeshivah in Brunoy.

other educational institutions

Among the various educational institutions which it has been instrumental in establishing, the European Bureau takes particular pride in the day-school in Lyons, which it recently established with the co-operation of the local community and its Chief Rabbi, Rabbi Kling. A graduate of the Teachers' Seminary is in charge of the Hebrew department of the school.

With the influx into France of refugees from North Africa, especially Algiers, the Lubavitch Bureau in Paris intensified its efforts to establish new *Talmud Torahs* and expand the existing ones.

A further important activity has been the establishment of a system of visiting teachers for children who, for one reason or another, did not attend *Talmud Torahs* or day schools.

Lubavitch work in North Africa

The remarkable work of Lubavitch in North Africa deserves a great deal more space than is here available. But even this scanty report will indicate its extraordinary scope and achievement.

The programme was set in motion by the late Lubavitcher Rebbe shortly before his demise in 1950. At first, attention was concentrated on the transition camps in Marseilles, where there was a steady influx of refugees from Morocco, whose ultimate destination was Israel. Soon, this Lubavitch activity was transferred to Morocco itself. Insofar as organised religious education was concerned it was virgin soil. The problems were many. However, with the reputation that preceded Lubavitch, and with the warm response of the local religious and lay leadership, the Lubavitch programme began to unfold very rapidly. In due course, Lubavitch had established and was operating some 70 educational institutions, from primary schools to *yeshivos* and teachers' seminaries. There were separate schools for boys and for girls. From 5000 to 6000 students attended these

Lubavitch schools, which bore the name "Oholei Yosef Yitzchak Lubavitz" (after the late Lubavitcher Rebbe). Many more boys and girls were involved in summer camps and other youth activities conducted by the Lubavitch establishment in Morocco.

A special school for *sofrim* was established in Morocco, similar to the one in Paris. Here, young men were trained not only to become *sofrim* "*STaM*" (*Sifrei-Torah, Tefillin, Mezuzos*), but they were also taught the entire process of preparing the parchment, *battim* (the leather "houses" for the *Tefillin* scrolls), etc. It was a useful trade, filling a sacred need.

A *yeshivah* was also established in Tunisia. It is now housed in its own building. A school and seminary for girls was established there too. Some 300 students attend these institutions.

In the historic community of Djerba, the offshore island near the coast of Tunisia, another *yeshivah* was established. About 200 boys benefit from the Lubavitch educational programme in this ancient Jewish community.

Wherever Lubavitch is active, adult education is not neglected. Evening courses for working people were arranged in *Talmud* and various Hebrew subjects.

Although some of the Lubavitch work in North Africa has now been curtailed due to the considerable emigration of Jews from those Arab countries, much of the activity is still carried on with undiminished vigour. At this time, for instance, there are still 2000 children in the Lubavitch educational institutions in Morocco alone.

publications

Realizing the acute need for Jewish religious and educational literature in the French language, the Lubavitch Bureau in Paris assumed the task of publishing a French translation of many of the popular educational books already published by the Central Office of the Merkos L'Inyonei Chinuch in New York in Hebrew, Yiddish and English.

In 1954 the Bureau began to publish the *Talks and Tales* monthly, under the title *Conversations avec les Jeunes*, which have appeared uninterruptedly ever since, and are now in their 15th year of publication. (In New York, the *Talks and Tales* and its Yiddish companion monthly *Shmuessen* began to appear in 1941.) The impact of this unique monthly publication on its French-speaking readers and subscribers has been far-reaching. It is avidly read not only by the younger generation, but also by their parents. For many of them it is the only literary source of knowledge of Jewish history, biography, *Midrash*, Jewish ethics, etc., which constitute regular features of this monthly publication. Many are the unsolicited testimonials on file which have been received from prominent educators and grateful readers and subscribers, about the influence and inspiration which this monthly journal has brought into their homes.

The Bureau has also published the *Complete Festival Series* (2 vols.) by the well-known educator and author Dr. Nissan Mindel; *The Memoirs of the late Lubavitcher Rebbe* (2 vols. in one tome); *The Commandments*; Dr. M. Lehmann's novelettes and Commentary on *Pirkei Ovos*. Last but not least is the French translation of the *Chabad* classic, the *Tanya*, of which two parts have already appeared and the rest is in preparation.

credits

In conclusion, mention must be made of the consistent co-operation and substantial financial support which the European Bureau of Lubavitch has received from the American Joint Distribution Committee and the Memorial Foundation for Jewish Culture. The leaders of these great philanthropic and cultural organisations have always shown much interest and understanding in regard to the vital public services rendered by the Lubavitch movement, whose activities are personally directed by the Lubavitcher Rebbe. From their direct contact with the Lubavitch representatives and field workers, they have known and appreciated the selflessness and dedication of the Lubavitchers in carrying out their assigned tasks. Many of the Lubavitch projects could not have been implemented, and many Lubavitch institutions could not have been maintained, without the annual grants and subsidies from these sources. The late Charles Jordan, Director General of the American Joint, had on every occasion shown genuine interest and understanding of the religious and educational needs which the European Bureau of Lubavitch brought to his attention, and strained every means to meet these needs. One of his last acts, before his tragic and premature passing, was the approval of the building expansion of the Beth Rivkah Seminary in Yerres, mentioned previously. Fortunately, his successors at the helm of these bodies have maintained the same high standards.

Mention must also be made of the interest and support of the Central British Fund, which participated in the Seminary building, and whose annual grant towards Lubavitch work in North Africa is both helpful and encouraging.

Some day, hopefully, a comprehensive and documented history will be written about the Lubavitch rôle in the rehabilitation of post-war European Jewry. Only then will it be possible to fully assess the vitalising force which the Lubavitch movement has provided for many a Jewish community in all parts of the world.

President Shazar of Israel visiting the Lubavitcher Rebbe in New York

Chabad in Israel

Chabad started its activities in the Holy Land long before the establishment of the State of Israel in 1948, and since that date its work there has grown considerably.

During the time of Rabbi Shneur Zalman, the founder of *Chabad*, several of his colleagues and many *Chassidim* emigrated to *Eretz Yisroel*. Rabbi Shneur Zalman raised money to support the newly established *Chassidic* communities in the Holy Land, and his successors were at all times interested in aiding the *yishuv* there.

In the *Chabad* view, moral and financial support from afar, while important in itself, is no substitute for practical participation wherever possible. Thus, in 1868, *Chabad* initiated what was later to become a network of varied activities in the Holy Land; the establishment of the Kolel Chabad in Jerusalem.

In the century that followed, *Chabad*, as will be seen in the following pages, extended this one organisation and made its influence felt in every facet of life in Israel.

From its small beginnings the Kolel Chabad is now responsible, in Jerusalem, for a *Talmud Torah*, a kindergarten, the Beth Chanah Girls' School, and the Tzemach Tzedek and Medrash Shmuel Yeshivos, thus covering the education of youth of all ages.

It also administers funds for the initial support of new immigrants in the *Chabad* settlements in Israel, for help to the sick and needy and for the provision of interest-free loans to those requiring assistance.

The headquarters of *Chabad* activities in Jerusalem is now the

Shikun Chabad, which also provides flats for young people in Jerusalem.

Also in Jerusalem is the oldest Lubavitch *yeshivah* in Israel, the Yeshivah Toras Emes. Originally founded in Hebron in 1912, this *yeshivah* later moved to Jerusalem, where it provides advanced studies for both resident and non-resident students.

In 1938, *Chabad* established the Yeshivos Achei Tmimim in Tel Aviv, and in 1946 expanded its departments to cater for advanced studies.

It has never been the aim of *Chabad* to confine its activities to a particular group, but to spread the message of *Torah* on the widest possible scale. To this purpose the Agudas Chassidei Chabad, with headquarters in Tel Aviv, was founded in 1941. The purpose of this body is to unite all *Chassidei Chabad* for the intensified dissemination of *Torah* and *Chassidus* in cities and settlements throughout Israel.

As a result of the efforts of Agudas Chassidei Chabad and its associated groups, *Chabad* has become a household word in Israel and is renowned for its work in bringing *Torah* to the country's inhabitants.

It is not unusual to read articles in the press headlined: "Lubavitchers received with open arms by non-observant kibbutzniks, *Sabras*." *Chabad* headquarters, inundated with requests for groups of young *Chassidim* to visit settlements and villages, is not slow to comply. The type of kibbutz does not matter to *Chabad*; it recognises only two types of Jews—those who are observant and those who are not yet observant—and its aim is gradually to make the second group part of the first.

In the spirit of true *Torah* workers, the *Chassidim* who carry out this aspect of *Chabad's* work in Israel are mainly volunteers, devoting their evenings and week-ends to this important task.

Chabad's insistence on work as the natural adjunct to *Torah* is nowhere better illustrated than in the story of Kfar Chabad.

In 1948, with the first *aliyah* of Russian Jews, Kfar Chabad, was established in the Lod Valley, on the Jerusalem–Tel Aviv road. Founded as the result of a directive from the late Lubavitcher Rebbe, Rabbi Joseph Isaac Schneersohn, the village was to be the home of these Russian immigrants, who came to Israel empty-handed. Their attitude to the difficulties they encountered and how they overcame them is succinctly described in the following extract from the *Jewish Observer and Middle East Review* (of July 3, 1959).

KFAR CHABAD: WHERE CHASSIDIM AND J.N.F. WORK TOGETHER
The story was being told in Israel last week of the quiet devotion of a group of *Chabad Chassidim*—that sect of zealous Jews which lived for 30 years under

Soviet rule, stubbornly keeping to the tenets of their faith, and when the opportunity came in 1949, sent 74 families from among their adherents to settle in Israel.

Refused help: There were several noteworthy aspects of this *aliyah*. The *Chabad* members refused all offers of help from religious and political organisations; they insisted upon going on the land; they adapted themselves to modern agricultural methods while at the same time scorning modern kibbutznik dress.

The Jewish National Fund allotted them 600 acres half-way between Tel Aviv and Lod. It was tough going, but the word *Chabad* is an abbreviation for *Chochmoh, Binoh, Daas* (wisdom, understanding, knowledge). And to them it was a point of honour to live as they taught. This meant subsisting only on what they earned by their own toil.

Four years ago, *fedayeen* raiders penetrated the village and killed five children and their teacher in the schoolroom. Still the *Chabad* stuck it out. When the Sinai war came, their young men waived their religious right of exemption (they were ordained as Rabbis) and joined up, seeing service in the Mitla Pass.

Branching out: Now, after ten years of development, the *Chabad Chassidim* are branching out. A second *Chabad* village has been set up near the first by the sons of the original settlers, who have completed their army service, and a third village is in the planning stage.

Much assistance has been given to these *Chassidim* by the Jewish National Fund, which cleared the land and built the villagers' roads and trained the inexperienced newcomers in agricultural methods. Relations between the J.N.F. and the Kfar Chabad villagers are very close. The J.N.F. instructors admire the *Chabad Chassidim* for their hard work and modesty and eagerness to learn and to help. On their side the *Chassidim* like the J.N.F. because, as Rabbi Shlomo Maidentshek, their leader, says: "J.N.F. is not interested in politics or vote-catching, it does not work for profit or for any gain other than the development of the Jewish State."

But that was just a beginning for the *Chabad* village: the Russian immigrants were augmented by families from North Africa and these, too, have been totally integrated. Now the village has grown into a small town of some 250 families. New dwellings and roads have been added, as well as a dairy farm; other civic necessities are in the course of being provided.

A centre known as the "House of the President" (marking the association of President Shazar with Kfar Chabad) has recently been completed, and will be used as a community centre for the youth of the village and the neighbouring settlements.

A feature of Kfar Chabad which has won universal acclaim is its vocational schools. Here, students living in the village, most of them

*Students receiving vocational
instruction at Kfar Chabad*

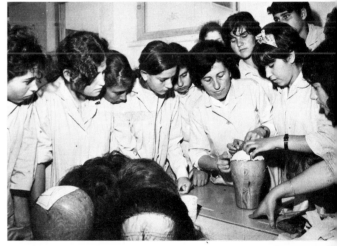
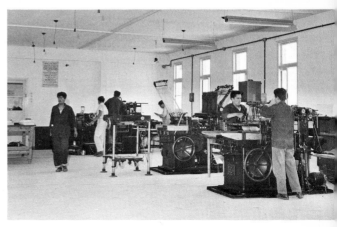

A Gemorrah Shiur *in progress*

immigrants, are taught a useful trade, spending half of each day in study and the second half in practical instruction.

The first of these schools, for carpentry and woodwork, was established in 1954. It has received considerable aid from ORT, and is equipped with the latest woodworking machinery. Instruction is by qualified *Chabad* craftsmen-teachers. Graduates of the school are qualified craftsmen much in demand in Israel. The furniture manufactured at the school can be seen in many settlements in Israel, particularly Kfar Chabad. All the carpentry work, including the pews, in the new synagogue in the village has been carried out by the students. In 1964 a tool shop was added to the school, and students are now trained in modern tool-making techniques.

In 1955 the first of the agricultural schools was established and, in the succeeding years, in collaboration with Aliyat Hanoar, other schools have been added. Modern agricultural techniques particularly relevant to the climatic and soil conditions of Israel are taught. Among their other activities the schools breed turkeys and geese, and have even built up an export trade of goose livers to France.

The year 1955 also saw the opening of the Gan-Israel summer camps, which provide holiday accommodation for children from all over Israel.

A teachers' seminary for girls was opened in 1956, followed by the Beth Rivkah Girls' High School and Girls' Vocational Schools. Here, girls with academic ability are trained as teachers, and others are taught suitable trades and crafts. Hundreds of girls have now passed through these schools, which possess modern premises and the most up-to-date equipment.

Chabad has never forgotten the five students and their teacher murdered by Arab marauders in 1955, while at evening prayers.

This tragedy, referred to earlier, shocked the entire Jewish world, but the Lubavitcher Rebbe, Rabbi Menachem Mendel Schneerson, was determined that it should not discourage the *Chabad* community but, rather, should inspire them to greater efforts. With his help and guidance, Yad Hachamisha printing schools, dedicated to the memory of the murdered students, were established in 1958. These schools have elicited much praise. Equipped with the most modern plant and machinery, they now produce not only prayer books and a variety of Lubavitch publications and literature for both local and overseas needs, but compete successfully for orders from industry and commerce. Their work is of a high standard, and graduates of the schools are fully qualified in their particular branches of the printing industry.

In 1950, Kfar Chabad also set up boarding schools which now have a total of 150 students from all parts of Israel. They provide an eight-class course of religious and secular education.

In addition, some 500 students, including both *sabras* and immigrants, attend the *yeshivos* in Kfar Chabad. They are accommodated in comfortable dormitories and receive all their material necessities. These *yeshivos* have both intermediate and senior departments of learning, and by the time they have completed their courses, the students are qualified teachers. Some students carry on to the advanced institutions of learning established in 1964 at the direction of the Lubavitcher Rebbe. These especially gifted young men advance their studies in preparation for the Rabbinate and other communal activities.

All these institutions, both academic and vocational, have been success-ful in raising a generation of students who, in addition to their advance-ment in *Torah* and *mitzvos*, are able to perform useful occupations and earn

Yeshivah *and synagogue at Kfar Chabad*

an honourable living. They are encouraged on graduation to settle in towns and settlements throughout Israel. In this way they contribute to the growing economy of the country and help with the voluntary duty of every Lubavitcher—the spreading of *Torah, mitzvos* and *Chassidic* philosophy and teachings.

Many of the graduates of the seminary and *yeshivos* become teachers in the network of Lubavitch schools throughout Israel. These schools, in Jerusalem, Jaffa, Kfar Saba, Lod, Zarnugar, Rehovot, Teanach, Brosh, Sdos Micha, Cholon, Kiryat Gat, Nes Tziyono, Bat Yam and elsewhere, provide a secular and Orthodox Jewish education for over 6,000 children of varying ages. The schools are State-aided, but remain under the control of *Chabad*.

These are not the only *Chabad* activities in Israel. The Lubavitch Youth Organisation, founded in 1952 with its centre in Tel Aviv, has established education courses and study groups in all aspects of *Torah*. It also arranges public meetings and lectures throughout Israel and on the radio.

On the practical religious level the Youth Organisation promotes such activities as *Lag b'Omer* gatherings, action for *Esrog* and *Lulav*, *Tefillin* campaigns and so on.

It also produces a monthly magazine, *In the Vineyards of Chabad*, and *Chabad Bulletin*. Both publications have a wide circulation.

Anniversaries of special events in the *Chabad* calendar are commemorated by exhibitions and displays which excite great interest and at the same time enlighten the public as to *Chabad*'s aims and work. Tens of thousands of Israelis received *shalach monos* at *Purim*, with a special message from the Lubavitcher Rebbe.

A festival of music in Caesarea devoted one evening to *Chabad* music and dances. An audience of some 3,000—including President and

Girls' orchestra—Kfar Chabad

Mrs Shazar—were enthralled by a performance both artistic and inspiring.

The list could be extended ad infinitum, but the message is already clear. With its kindergartens, schools, *yeshivos*, vocational schools, youth work and adult education, *Chabad* provides facilities for all.

Just before the outbreak of the Six-Day War, the Lubavitcher Rebbe instructed the Lubavitch Youth Organisation in Israel and throughout the world to initiate an active *Tefillin* campaign, to see that Jews observe the *mitzvah* of *Tefillin* as a means of ensuring Divine protection against Israel's enemies.

As soon as the Western Wall was liberated, a cable arrived from the Rebbe with instructions to intensify "Action *Tefillin*" throughout Israel and to establish immediately a *Tefillin* booth near the Wall, where even those who did not regularly observe the *mitzvah* of *Tefillin* be given the opportunity to do so.

President Shazar visits book exhibition

The positive response to this spiritual campaign has been unbelievably overwhelming. More than 500,000 visitors to the Western Wall since the Six-Day War have observed the *mitzvah* of *Tefillin* and the campaign initiated by the Rebbe has since won the support of all leading Rabbis in Israel.

The inauguration of the *Tefillin* campaign in those worrying days preceding the fighting in June, 1967 was immediately followed by the Rebbe advising his followers to ignore the advice given by many neutral countries to their nationals to leave Israel. The Rebbe observed: "Israel's Guardian is surely not asleep."

Not unusual, too, in those difficult days was the following report from the Negev, which appeared at that time in the *Jewish Chronicle*: "Among the tankmen is a *Chabad Chassid* who, until his mobilisation, was studying in the *yeshivah* at Kfar Chabad. . . . . His job is to load the guns on the

Mrs Golda Meir, Prime Minister of Israel, at Kfar Chabad

David Ben Gurion at a Lubavitch Book Exhibition in Israel

Sir Isaac Wolfson inspects new equipment in the machine shop

President Shazar visits the printing school at Kfar Chabad

At the opening of the "House of the President"—Kfar Chabad

tanks with ammunition. His *Tefillin* bag lies close to his ammunition supplies."

The tankman referred to in that report returned, thank G–d, to Kfar Chabad to continue his studies. Not all of his fellow students who served were as fortunate. The story of one who did not return is perhaps significant.

David Golombovitz went through the fighting on the southern front. During that time his tank was destroyed and so were his *Tefillin*, but David was unhurt. Shortly after the fighting ceased, David was given leave to attend the circumcision of his son at Kfar Chabad. This he did, returning afterwards to his post by the Suez Canal, complete with new *Tefillin*. Almost immediately after his return he was, unfortunately, killed in one of the incidents which occurred in that area. His comrades, as soon as they were able to, visited his widow and gave his belongings, including his *Tefillin*, to her. His widow thanked them for their visit and asked them to keep the *Tefillin* and to use them regularly. This they promised to do.

The Rebbe in one of his talks—which was especially for women— proposed that every woman should donate a pair of *Tefillin* to the campaign undertaken by the Chabad Youth Organisation. Mrs Shifra Golombovitz, the widow of the young soldier, took charge of the fund for this cause, arranged by the Chabad Women's Organisation. After her husband's death she received 800 Israeli pounds, which she used to purchase *Tefillin* in furtherance of the campaign.

She visited her late husband's division in Givaat Brennar taking with her seventeen pairs of *Tefillin*, enough for almost half the men in his platoon who promised to put them on each morning.

At the unveiling of a memorial to the men of the platoon who fell, an officer paid tribute to the great influence that David Golombovitz had exercised on his comrades, and said that during the fighting, he had begun carrying out the Rebbe's instructions, by giving his comrades the opportunity of practising the *mitzvah* of *Tefillin*.

The *Tefillin* campaign has, since the cessation of hostilities, been extended throughout Israel and is a great success. The Chaplaincy Corps has even provided a helicopter to enable emissaries to visit army camps in Sinai, and scores of officers and men have donned *Tefillin* for the first time in their lives.

Apart from the *mitzvah* being performed by Israelis, many Rabbis in other countries have spoken favourably of the *Tefillin* campaigns being

Left: General Arik Sharon performs the Mitzvah *of* Tefillin *after the Six-Day War.*
Right: Tefillin *campaign at the Wall*

Eightieth birthday of President Shazar

Left: Twentieth anniversary of founding of Kfar Chabad. Right: President Shazar celebrates his eightieth birthday at the Lubavitch Synagogue, Old City, Jerusalem

carried on by *Chabad Chassidim* in those countries, largely prompted by news and photographs of the campaign in Israel and of its reception there.

In England, for example, the Lubavitch Foundation in conjunction with the Chief Rabbi inaugurated a National *Tefillin* Week. Over sixty thousand pamphlets and booklets on *Tefillin*, printed by Lubavitch, were distributed by synagogues throughout the country. Many synagogues held special services. As a result of this campaign in England there was a marked increase in the observance of this *mitzvah*, which was reflected by a temporary shortage of *Tefillin*.

Israel's victory in the Six-Day War brought joy and exhilaration to the Jewish people throughout the world. Inevitably, it also brought tragedy to hundreds of Israeli children, whose fathers died in action so that Israel might survive.

The Rebbe immediately wrote to his *Chassidim* instructing them that, while the Israeli Government supported these children within the framework of legislation, it was necessary that someone be found to fill the place of their fathers in spiritual matters, as all this now devolved on their busy mothers. "One must find the approach", the Rebbe wrote, "to teach these widows and orphans and to occupy oneself with them."

An immediate request was made to the Ministry of Defence for the

General Dayan and Israeli generals attending joint Barmitzvah *celebration for Israeli war orphans held at Kfar Chabad*

addresses of all war widows and orphans. The Ministry was, quite naturally, reluctant at first, but the reputation of *Chabad* in Israel is such that the addresses were given to a committee formed especially by *Chabad* to attend to the financial and administrative aspects of the project, and to which the Ministry of Defence nominated a representative.

The financial backing for the enterprise was to be supplied by the setting up of committees in countries where *Chabad* was represented.

Mrs Shifra Golombovitz wrote to those who had been similarly bereaved and many of them have had meetings in Jerusalem. Plans are being made to care for the war orphans' education, to provide them with clothes, holidays and toys, and to provide assistance at *Barmitzvahs* and weddings. While it is hoped that these orphans will be brought close to religious observance, the first task of the committee is to provide practical material help to those widows and their children who require it.

By personal example and teaching, *Chabad* in Israel, as in the rest of the world, endeavours to show that *Yiddishkeit* must permeate the whole life of every Jew, and that the observance of *mitzvos* need not be a penance, but a wonderful and joyous experience.

Joint Barmitzvah *celebration, held at Kfar Chabad, Sept. 1969. Israeli war orphans participate in* Chassidic *dance*

Australia's most Jewish city

Compared with Europe, or even the United States, Australia's Jewish community is a young one. The first organised Jewish life in the vast, under-populated continent with a desert heart that is Australia, began as recently as 1817. In that year, twenty Jews in New South Wales formed a burial society, the beginnings of the flourishing community of 70,000 or so in Australia today.

The history of the Lubavitch movement in Australia is very much younger—just twenty years. Nevertheless, during this brief span, the Lubavitch movement has accomplished more in the field of Jewish education and positive Judaism than anyone could have imagined, even taking into account the dynamism and record of achievement of the *Chassidic* movement.

Melbourne, capital of the state of Victoria, is the hub of Lubavitch activity in Australia, and every year, at *Succos*, the Lubavitch Yeshivah College in the city builds the largest *succah* in the world, holding 550 children.

But let us begin at the beginning, and go back twenty years, to the time when the Lubavitch movement first "discovered" the Jews of "down under" and decided to revivify their Judaism and Jewish education in Australia.

Although many thousands of miles from the larger Jewish centres of the world—London is some 10,000 miles distant—Melbourne is itself the chief centre of Jewish life in Australia. So it was natural for the Lubavitch movement to set up its headquarters there.

The beginnings were modest enough—a small building housing a handful of boys, some from Eastern Europe, others Australian-born. As with all Lubavitch institutions of learning, the staff and pupils soon began to acquire a reputation for diligent scholarship.

Soon the number of enrolments began to snowball, and today, Melbourne's Yeshivah College, in the suburb of St Kilda, provides complete elementary and secondary school education up to matriculation and university standard for some 350 boys. The Beth Rivkah Girls' School which is part of the Lubavitch school system in Australia, does the same for more than 300 girls. These schools together with the Lubavitch kindergartens form the largest Orthodox educational system not only in Australia, but in the entire Southern Hemisphere.

In addition, Yeshivah College has, within the last eighteen months, opened a department that is unique in Australian Jewish history—a full-time *yeshivah gedoloh*, where twenty or more young men devote a number of years to full-time *Torah* study. The Lubavitcher Rebbe, Rabbi Menachem M. Schneerson שליט״א has sent six American-born young men from the New York *yeshivah* to the Melbourne *yeshivah* to strengthen it in its work.

The *yeshivah's Beis Hemedrash* is full every *Shabbos*, and more than a hundred people take part in *shalosh seudos*, listening attentively to *Chassidic* discourses given originally by the Lubavitcher Rebbe.

The Beth Rivkah Girls' School now has an annexe which houses a teachers' seminary, the only full-time institute for training Jewish teachers in Australia.

At this point it is worth emphasising that the outstanding examination results and the number of scholarships gained by Lubavitch pupils give the lie once and for all to those who maintain that it is impossible to combine a thorough Jewish education with a more than adequate secular education.

Here is what the Victoria State Inspector of Schools had to say about Yeshivah College: "There are several definite indications that the school is really developing. The school is to be congratulated on the excellent examination results."

In addition to the high quality of the teaching staff, the very modern school buildings and up-to-date equipment undoubtedly also play their part in helping the Lubavitch schools to maintain their fine scholastic record.

Of course, physical education is not neglected. There is no shortage of

Left: Rabbi Dr Sir Israel Brodie visiting Lubavitch Day School in Melbourne
Right: Beth Rivkah Ladies College, Melbourne

Outings . . .   *. . . and sports*

A section of the world's largest succah

The new Yeshivah College

sports, games and other facilities. Cricket and association football are regularly played as are the quieter forms of recreation, such as chess.

In addition, the schools arrange for visiting speakers to talk to pupils and staff about a variety of subjects; there are excursions to places of interest, drama nights, art exhibitions and inter-house competitions of many kinds.

The schools also take good care that contact with parents is closely maintained at all times. Parent-teacher meetings, some at the school, others in private homes, are a regular feature of the school year, and the Parents' Association takes an active part in providing all kinds of extra facilities at the schools.

And *tzedoko* is not forgotten. Every pupil at the schools makes a regular weekly contribution for charitable purposes, the collection being made by the older pupils. Local and Israeli charities benefit.

Lubavitch in Australia has had as great an impact on Jewish education as it has on Australian Jewish life generally. How big this impact is, can be gauged from the activities of the Zeirei Agudas Chabad, known locally as "Yeshivah Youth".

This Lubavitch youth organisation arranges summer camps for boys and girls; initiates trips and excursions for them throughout the year; distributes *matzos* for *Pesach*, and disseminates Jewish literature. 1967 saw the highly successful organisation and implementation of Melbourne's first *Lag b'Omer* parade and outing, which was attended by many hundreds of Jewish children.

Weekly *shiurim* and a variety of smooth-running social functions are provided by Neshei Chabad, the Melbourne branch of the world-wide Lubavitch Women's Organisation. Naturally, its Australian members are also very active in Lubavitch school affairs. Doubtless, too, they have had more than a small say in the decision to build a new *mikvah*, needed because existing facilities, though modern, are now inadequate for the community's needs.

Thanks to the Lubavitch movement, Melbourne, the capital of the state of Victoria in the Commonwealth of Australia, can truly claim the title of the most Jewish city in the world's largest island and smallest continent and, indeed, in the entire Southern Hemisphere.

Chabad in Italy

The photograph reproduced here shows the front page of a brochure giving details of the activities of the Beth Chana schools in Milan. The caption reads: "Here at last is the opportunity you have been searching for."

Looking back over the years since 1959, the Ohel Jacov congregation in Milan and, indeed, the city's entire Jewish community, would readily agree that this phrase applies equally well to the appointment of their *Rav*.

It was in that year that this small Orthodox congregation of some seventy-five families asked the Lubavitcher Rebbe to suggest a suitable candidate for the vacant position of *Rav*. The congregation had no Lubavitch affiliation, but their *shochet* was a Lubavitch *Chassid*. Also, one of their Joint Presidents had met the Rebbe on a number of occasions and, impressed with these meetings and what he knew of *Chabad*, had suggested taking this step.

The Rebbe recommended a young member of an old Lubavitch family, Rabbi G. M. Garelik, a graduate of Lubavitch *yeshivos* in Israel and New York. Accompanied by his wife, Rabbi Garelik arrived in Milan to take up his appointment in December 1959.

Milan was to realise very quickly that the new *Rav* was not content merely to minister to his flock and conduct the daily *shiurim* he had arranged.

There were language difficulties, for neither the *Rav* nor his wife spoke Italian, but this was no deterrent. The house which the congregation had provided for them soon became a hive of communal activity, and Mrs

Garelik lost no time in starting a kindergarten there. On *Yud Tes Kislev*, just a few weeks after his arrival, the first *farbrengen* was held to mark the anniversary of the *Alter Rebbe*'s release from prison.

Neither the kindergarten nor the *farbrengen* was limited to his own congregants—they were both open to every Jew who wanted to participate. This was the pattern for all future activities, too. The friendly welcome, the warm atmosphere, soon became a byword, and more and more people attended the frequent gatherings.

At this time, too, the newcomers established in Milan a branch of Merkos L'Inyonei Chinuch, thereby making available, for the first time in Italy, publications and literature supplied from the central office in New York.

Some three months later, at a particularly well-attended gathering to celebrate *Purim*, Rabbi Garelik produced a draft copy of *Talks and Tales* in Italian, and suggested that it be sent as a *shalach monos* to the Lubavitcher Rebbe in New York for his approval before publication. Some weeks later the draft was returned from New York, amended and corrected in Italian in the Rebbe's own hand. This was the first indication that the Rebbe knew the Italian language. For the past nine years, *Talks and Tales* has been published regularly in Italian by the Merkos L'Inyonei Chinuch office in Milan and has attracted a growing readership.

The year 1960 also saw the first Jewish summer camp—Gan Israel—in Italy. It was organised on a site near Lugano, bought specially for the purpose by the Joint Presidents of the congregation.

Fully supported in every way by the leaders of the community, these activities have continued to grow, and the Lubavitcher Rebbe has sent other graduates from the Lubavitch *yeshivos*, with their families, to organise and assist in the work. They have all been carefully chosen so that their individual talents might be used to the best advantage, and include scholars, educationalists, welfare workers and two Rabbis of *Sephardi* origin and their families, since they are best able to integrate Milan's *Sephardi* congregation.

So far, eight such families have been sent to Milan by the Rebbe. They are young men, working with their wives as a team, eager to play an important part in the exciting achievements of the last nine years—and to plan and work for the fulfilment of future projects.

Rabbi Garelik is quick to point out that his share of the changes is no greater than theirs.

Things have certainly changed since 1959! The kindergarten now has

Rabbi Nissim, Sephardi *Chief Rabbi of Israel, visits the summer camp in Italy*

A girls' class at the day school in Milan

Mr C. Zippel, a President of the Milan Congregation, visits the new Community Centre in London

its own premises and caters for children between the ages of three and six; the Beth Chana day school (named after the Rebbe's late mother) provides secular and religious education for children between the ages of six and ten; religious instruction classes are held in the afternoon for boys and girls between the ages of ten and eighteen, and are well attended; the summer camp has outgrown its original site and has become a celebrated venue not only for Italian children, but for groups from other European countries too.

A residential *yeshivah* has been opened for boys between the ages of thirteen and eighteen and a number of students are engaged in full-time studies in well-equipped and comfortable surroundings. It is hoped that this *yeshivah* will soon develop into a centre of learning for students from other countries in Europe.

Recently the Merkos published the *Tanya* in Italian, the first of many books planned to be published by them in that language.

Requests for help and advice pour in from other cities and towns— many for the personal attention of the Lubavitcher Rebbe.

But some things have not changed. The *farbrengens* are still held regularly, the *shiurim* are still held daily, and the warmth and enthusiasm are as abundant as ever.

The record of these years in Milan is an indication of what can be done —is being done—by groups of dedicated Jews trained in the tradition of service to, and love for, their fellow Jews, working under the direction of a man who is the personification of this tradition, the Lubavitcher Rebbe.

Proud as they are of their achievements, the talk in Milan is of the future rather than of the past. Of the many, many things still to be accomplished on the Italian Jewish scene. Of the time when the students at present in the schools and the *yeshivah* will graduate and be ready to play their part there—or wherever the Rebbe may send them. For their experience has made them more aware than ever of the challenge still to be met in Italy and elsewhere.

Merkos in Minnesota

The face of Jewish education in many parts of the world has undergone a veritable rejuvenation since the Merkos L'Inyonei Chinuch, the educational section of the Lubavitch movement, began its activities in 1942.

Founded by the late Lubavitcher Rebbe, Rabbi Joseph I. Schneersohn, whose pioneering efforts and farsightedness in the field of Jewish education are now generally recognised, the Merkos L'Inyonei Chinuch was from the outset under the overall direction of the present Lubavitcher Rebbe, Rabbi Menachem Mendel Schneerson. שליט״א

From the beginning, the aim of the Merkos has been to promote Jewish education among the younger generation—regardless of background—in the spirit of authentic *Torah*-true Judaism. In order to accomplish this monumental task, Merkos set out to improve the existing Jewish educational institutions; to create new ones; to establish contact with Jewish youth unoriented to the basic knowledge of their heritage; to provide a multilingual library of textbooks and educational literature for school and home; to stimulate active interest in Jewish education at its various levels; and to promote religious observance as a daily experience.

The Merkos quickly grew and developed into a highly departmentalised organisation—a most progressive and dynamic force in the world of Jewish education.

Since 1950, even new dimensions have been added to the organisation by the expansion of its services to Jewish communities around the globe. Through members of Lubavitch's unique "Peace Corps", Merkos opened regional offices in more than a dozen countries. The directors of these

Havdalah *service at week-end retreat, Minneapolis*

Lubavitch supervises putting on Tefillin *by 250 youths attending Bnei Brith Convention*

branches have had years of extensive training in diverse fields of Jewish education and welfare, and each heads a staff of dedicated personnel.

A typical and most successful example of these branches is the Merkos Upper Midwest regional offices in Minneapolis, U.S.A. Started in 1962, it has grown into a vibrant entity during the short period of its existence. Among its many and varied activities it has established education classes for children and adults in outlying Jewish communities; adult education classes, and a network of *Shabbos* parties in the twin cities of Minneapolis and St Paul; a programme of literature dissemination; a summer day camp and *yeshivah*; and a weekly radio programme. In addition, it participates actively in the educational programmes of existing synagogues and Jewish educational institutions in the area.

In order to enhance and expand these programmes and to introduce new programmes geared to *Torah* study and observance, the Merkos

Mike Epstein,
Washington
baseball star,
putting on Tefillin

purchased, towards the end of 1965, a ten-acre estate on Lake Elmo in Washington County, Minnesota. Funds for this project were raised locally. The estate is now fully operative as a Jewish education centre, providing facilities for young people in a healthy and picturesque environment.

This office of Merkos, under its regional director, Rabbi Moshe Feller, continues to flourish and grow, always seeking some new way to further the aims of the organisation. A most unusual project conducted by this Merkos office is a programme of retreats called "Live and Learn". Young people from various Jewish groups spend *Shabbos* and Sunday at the estate, where in addition to prayers, singing, dancing and recreational activities they participate in seminars. "Jewish education", says Rabbi Feller, "means to live Judaism, and we feel that our week-end retreats can endear Jewish living to our youth."

Girls receiving instruction in making Challoh

The purpose and success of the Merkos is well summarised in the following extract from a journal published by this local office:

In addition to our work amongst groups of Jews, Merkos spends a great deal of time with individuals. It is proud of its reputation of increasing and intensifying the *Torah* commitment of the individuals to whom it administers. It is this concern for the individual that is perhaps the most unique and most praiseworthy feature of the Merkos. The Merkos is as concerned with a Jewish serviceman or ballplayer having a pair of *Tefillin*, as it is with Jewish children spending their summer in a proper Jewish environment. The spiritual welfare of a single paralysed grandmother is as important to the Merkos as is Jewish information flowing into hundreds of Jewish homes over the airwaves. While the Merkos conducts classes in *Talmud* for academically advanced teen-age boys, it does not overlook the spiritual welfare of a teen-age girl in a remote Jewish community. The spiritual welfare of every Jew is important, and its enhancement is the goal of Merkos.

Rabbi M. Feller with students at Carleton College, Northfield, Minnesota, where he has been appointed to give an accredited course on Chassidism

To enable outlying Jewish communities to experience "An Evening with Chassidim", the Merkos office in Minneapolis now uses a charter plane. The picture shows from left to right, Rabbi M. Feller, Dr V. W. Greene, Rabbi A. Zeilingold and Mr F. Gordon about to undertake such a trip to La Crosse, Wisconsin

Zeirei Agudas Chabad—
Lubavitch Youth Organisation

The important rôle played by Zeirei Agudas Chabad—the Lubavitch Youth Organisation—in the world-wide activities of *Chabad* has been mentioned only briefly in CHALLENGE.

Founded in 1955 by the Lubavitcher Rebbe, it concerns itself with the spiritual needs of young Jews, and strives ceaselessly to familiarise these young people with the basic concepts and practices of Judaism.

The criterion of "youth" for membership is not age but spirit. The Organisation seeks to help Jewish youth find the road towards fulfilment of the commitment that exists in every Jewish soul, by encouraging them to observe the precepts of our heritage and by stimulating an intellectual and emotional interest in our faith.

To achieve this, the Lubavitch Youth Organisation interests itself in children, teenagers and young adults, and reaches into congregations, fraternal groups, camps, schools, colleges and universities, the armed forces—wherever Jewish young people are to be found.

With its centre in the U.S.A., Zeirei Agudas Chabad functions also in Argentina, Australia, Brazil, Canada, Denmark, England, France, Holland, Israel, Italy and South Africa.

Through its various departments, which include also the visiting of the sick and aged, it is the instrument by which the various "action" campaigns, such as the *Tefillin* Campaign, are carried out.

The Lubavitch Youth Organisation is unique among youth organisations, because it recognises its obligations not only to assist fellow Jews spiritually and materially, but also to encourage in its own members a

Lubavitch "action" campaigns

continuous striving for self-improvement, as taught to every Jew by the *Torah* and practised in daily life through *Chassidic* enthusiasm and inspiration.

The striking characteristic of a creative and undiluted approach to Jewish youth is one of the major ingredients of its great success in re-kindling the spark of Jewish consciousness in the hearts and minds of thousands of our youth.

Members of the College and University Council of the Lubavitch Youth Organisation in U.S.A. prepare packages of Shemura Matzos *for use during Passover at armed forces bases and on college campuses. A special shipment of these* Matzos *had been despatched for Jewish servicemen in Vietnam*

what Chabad says...

*Over the centuries, Chabad philosophy
has proved a most fascinating study
not only to Chabad Chassidim but
to people from all walks of life. It has
constantly been stressed, however,
that the most important aspect of this
study is its application in our daily lives.
It is hoped that the following selection
of articles will serve for many as an
introduction to Chabad Thought and
will cause the reader to seek further in
the vast treasury of Chabad literature.*

Ahavas Yisroel

One of the basic commandments in the *Torah* is that of loving one's fellow Jew (Leviticus, 19:18). It is not only one of the 248 positive commands in the *Torah*, it is also a cardinal principle of Judaism. There are, however, many questions that can be asked about this commandment. One seldom finds these questions discussed, and there is a tendency to accept this injunction as a truism or a cliché that is taken for granted.

One of the interesting things about *Chabad* literature on this topic is that it reaches to a deeper understanding of this command by probing some of these questions. We will attempt to give here a short résumé of some of these discussions, whereby *Chabad* attains its own special insight into this fundamental pillar of Judaism.

Many traditional commentators take the positive form of this command found in the Bible to be identical with the exhortation of Hillel to the would-be proselyte in the justly famous passage in the *Talmud, Shabbos* 31a. When the Bible says: "You shall love your neighbour as yourself" (Leviticus 19:18), what is meant is the same as Hillel said to the proselyte: "That which is hateful to yourself, do not do to your friend. This is the entire *Torah*; the rest is only an explanation—go and study." The questions we shall now raise centre on equating these two apparently different precepts. How could they mean the same thing?

One is a positive command and the other negative. As one might refrain from harming someone without ever feeling love for that person, one could perform the second without necessarily performing the first. Again, the first command is related to how one should feel towards another person, while the other is concerned with how one should act. These are two totally different norms. How then can Hillel's advice to the proselyte be construed as expressing the same command as the Biblical injunction in Leviticus?

In addition to these questions relating to the comparison of the Biblical command with the story of Hillel and the proselyte in *Gemorrah Shabbos*, there is another more general question that can be raised about this commandment. Why does Hillel say it is the "entire *Torah*"?

In general it is said that there are two kinds of commandments in the *Torah*; one group relates man to G–d, as for instance *Tefillin*, *Shabbos* and *kashrus*, while the other group comprises ethical commands relating man to his fellow-man, such as the prohibitions against theft and murder.

One can understand how the command to love your neighbour as yourself might be the foundation of the ethical commands, but how is it fundamental to the commandments relating man to G–d? How is it the entire *Torah*?

Let us first deal with the questions concerning the equation of the Biblical command with the story about Hillel, and we will then turn to the latter more general question.

The *Tzemach Tzedek* (grandson of the *Alter Rebbe* and third in line of succession) provides an answer to the first question in his *Derech Mitzvosecha*. He explains the negative command of Hillel in the following way. What is hateful to oneself? First and foremost, the revelation of one's own faults to another person who, one knows, will condemn one for them. Everyone has failings that could be remedied. However, because of self-love, one usually finds a way of justifying one's faults to oneself. As it is said, "love blinds the eye" — in this case, self-love blinds the eye. This does not mean that a person fails to notice his own faults, but that one is prepared to overlook them or understand them in a light that does not call for censure.

Similarly, we do not mind so much revealing our backslidings to friends who are sympathetic and understanding. What is abhorrent is that someone ill-disposed should find a fault in us, so that he can use this to justify his condemnation of us. At this point, Hillel's command is applicable: "That which is hateful to yourself, do not do to another." Just as you do not desire the reproach of others when they see your faults, so you should refrain from condemning others when you see their faults. You should be as quick to justify the mistakes of a fellow-Jew because of your love for him, as you would be to justify your own because of self-love.

We can now answer some of the questions we asked previously. On the one hand, the negative injunction of Hillel speaks to the emotions, as does the Biblical command. On the other, this negative expression turns out to be a deeper and more probing analysis of the positive, Biblical command. You cannot obey one without fulfilling the other. You cannot come to forgive the bad side of another person until you first come to love that person to a degree similar to the kind of love you have for yourself. The positive and negative expressions of the command are different ways of saying one and the same thing.

In answer to the general question of how the *mitzvah* of *ahavas Yisroel* is the entire *Torah*, it would be helpful to mention another point. Some modern readers have sometimes asked and, indeed, the *Ramban* in his interpretation of Leviticus 19:18 does ask: Is it not unnatural and perhaps abnormal to inculcate in oneself love for another person as strong as one has for oneself? Are human mortals capable of such love? The *Alter Rebbe* discusses this in Chapter 32 of the *Tanya*, and in so doing provides an answer to the more general question.

Here, the *Alter Rebbe* describes the impossibility of attaining true *ahavas Yisroel* as long as one pursues the pleasures of the body and thinks only in terms of physical success. One must orient one's thinking away from the body to the soul. The real life of a Jew does not lie in the attainment of physical success and comfort. *Torah* and *mitzvos* are the only authentic life of the Jew. If the Jew thinks in terms of his soul and pursues that which strengthens the spirit over the flesh he will ultimately come to realise that all Jews are spiritual brothers.

Our souls all come from one Heavenly Father and have one source. Since we were all "bound together" at our source in the one G–d, our souls still partake of one another, in spite of the fact that our physical bodies separate us from one another. There is a part of every Jew in every other Jew. When one Jew harbours ill-feeling for another, it is as if he banishes a piece of himself. A Jew can be whole only when he has attained the true fulfilment of the *mitzvah* of *ahavas Yisroel*—of loving each and every Jew without exception as he loves himself. Instead of this being an unnatural state, it is the only condition in which a Jew can attain complete self-realisation.

How is it possible, one may ask, to attain such a high level of the triumph of the spirit over the body? The answer is the *Torah* itself. Through study of *Torah* and performance of *mitzvos* a degree of spirituality can be attained which makes genuine *ahavas Yisroel* possible. That is the reason why *ahavas Yisroel* is the entire *Torah*. For it is only a concerted, whole-hearted devotion to *Torah* that enables one to achieve ascendancy of the soul, which is the sway of the spirit and holiness over the forces of egoism and selfishness which are the source of evil. The Jew can emerge victorious in this internal struggle between the body and the soul only through a life of *Torah* and *mitzvos* and through no other means. Such a life culminates in a feeling of love for all Israel, and this is the *mitzvah* of *ahavas Yisroel*. This, therefore, is the entire *Torah*, for it is the goal and the final fruition of a life of *Torah*.

living in our element

The convention of placing the burden of responsibility for success or failure solely upon a leader has provided a convenient excuse for most people, leaving their consciences unscathed instead of impelling them to face up to self-examination. This has been true of those living under a tyrant's yoke, and it has been equally true in a democracy, where public acclaim and condemnation fall alternately to the leader's lot, while the people exercise the judge's prerogative from the polling booth.

In the realm of religious life, such escapist views are ruled out. Leadership may be acknowledged, zealously followed, or arbitrarily rejected, but personal responsibility remains the core of Judaism. As a nation we have been appointed to a special task, to act as a "kingdom of priests and a holy nation". No longer is it the leader who assumes the sole responsibility. The *mitzvah* of: "Thou shalt rebuke thy neighbour", and the injunction to "glorify His Holy Name", are the heritage of every individual.

Every father has the obligation to instruct his son or see that he receives the proper education and training. Every mother must provide the positive example and environment for the complete and unhampered development of her child so that he can become receptive to the precepts and concepts of the *Torah*. Every Jew, in the final analysis, stands at a cross-roads. He is the mentor of those around him, Jew and non-Jew alike, with all the opportunities and dangers that the *mitzvah* of *kiddush Hashem* imposes.

Moreover, no neutral position is possible, for any action or non-action creates waves of influence which reverberate throughout each man's world, turning, according to the will of the Creator, this person in one direction or that one in another.

The Sages remind us that, in the delicate balance in which the fate of the world hangs, a deed of merit on the part of one individual may become the deciding factor. When each man realises that even taking no sides carries a deadweight force as a definite action, he must answer the modern version of the eternal question—where exactly do I stand? If a Jew can arrive at a realistic self-portrait, he will have acquired a valuable asset in determining his future course of conduct as compared to his past mode of behaviour.

In the long, dark corridor of centuries that led from the destruction of the Second Temple to the annihilation of European Jewry by the Nazis, the Jews have performed many functions on the world scene. We have been the scapegoats of power-mad dictators, as well as of over-zealous, fanatical religious leaders of the nations of the world who, with inquisitorial wrath and under the benevolent guise of saving souls or with the ruthless brutality of making the world "*Judenrein*", have de-humanised their followers to perpetrate deeds of unimaginable cruelty and terror.

We have been the whipping-boys of the frustrated, the misdirected and the vainglorious, who vented their bitterness and hatred on defenceless minorities and received the plaudits and help of the masses for ignoble actions. We have served in the minds of the more enlightened and liberal as the barometer of humanity's level of compassion and tolerance; a fulfilment of G–d's blessing to Abraham: "And in you will all the families of the earth be blessed."

Yet all these purposes are negative in character, ignoring the positive function of the Jew. They present what others have done to us or see in us, but shed no light on the obvious question of what we are or what we must be in fact and deed for the world; the purpose of our creation.

After the Nazi Holocaust and the establishment of Israel, surely it is time to reject the debilitated, emasculated view of Judaism that seeks to find its image in the eyes of others. Socrates' counsel to "know thyself" is more pertinent and conducive to a proper understanding of our duties than the preoccupation with what we are or may seem to be to others.

The answer, as so often, is implicit in the problem. The Jew must adopt the vigorous approach, take the positive step. We have been placed here not to be acted upon, but to act; not to react to others, but to take action ourselves; not to be driven by desperation to the realisation of our duties or our identity, but to "serve G–d in joy", to re-shape our image for ourselves. The Jew must rid himself of the stultifying habit of vacillation and compromise, assume his full obligations, which are to observe, to do, and to fulfil.

A foremost example of this healthier progressive attitude can be seen in the far-flung activities of Lubavitch. Flourishing *yeshivos* have been established in cities and towns throughout the world. Lubavitch brings the concept of *Torah* and a special brand of *Chassidus* to areas that were formerly barren of *Yiddishkeit*.

This double rôle of dissemination of *Torah* and the proliferation of an active Jewish laity give the lie to those who have called Judaism an outmoded way of life, an effete anachronism. For here is traditional Judaism in the modern world, garbed in symbols and manners that may not at first be understood or fully appreciated, yet are alive, vibrant, growing, achieving and prospering. Here is an approach that may possibly raise the eyebrows of the curious, uninformed Jew, but will yet ultimately bring him to acknowledge its positive accomplishments.

Let none gainsay it. It is not the constant concession and compromise, the yielding inch by inch of all that is holy and sacred in our heritage that is responsible for the Jewish renaissance insofar as it exists. It is rather the realisation on the part of the middle-of-the-road individual, the apologist, that it is more and more necessary to stop the sham of believing that the less obvious or different his Judaism appears in the eyes of his Gentile neighbours, the better chance he has for survival.

This ostrich philosophy of burying one's treasure and not using it oneself in the hopes that the plunderers of the world will also forget it is there, cannot apply to Judaism. For while Judaism can live—has lived—when suppressed from without, it cannot live when it is suffocated from within. Such defeatism is equivalent to the "better Red than dead" doctrine on a religious plane. Lubavitch has proved that we need be neither "Red nor dead" to survive. The sainted Rabbi Akiva, in his famous parable of the fish and the fox, taught that we cannot expect to live out of our element— *Torah*—"for it is our life and the length of our days".

The dedicated performance of *mitzvos*, the drawing from the well of inspiration provided by *Torah* study, the probing deep into our collective conscience for the courage and resolution to meet the challenge of the latter-day obstructionists who come in the guise of open enemies, false friends, even well-meaning do-gooders—these are the new-old frontiers that must be conquered; the divine heritage that must be re-won by each generation and by each person.

It might even be argued that the times and currents of today are more propitious than ever before for this task. When Jews lived in continual terror of expulsion, forced conversion or death, the unanswered question may have formed on the lips of the sorely tried. When Jews lived only by the grace of a bloodthirsty or at best indifferent nobleman, and security or life depended on the whim of a "benevolent" bishop, the anxiety and trepidations of the oppressed might be understood. When, in the days of the grandeur that was Rome, Jews existed at the sufferance of an Emperor, or when in the Middle Ages they were hounded from country to country, denied what today we call fundamental human rights and forced to live on the political and economic outskirts of world society, the difficulties facing the faithful could be appreciated.

But in free countries today, how can we excuse the sleazy, shoddy attempts to dam or dilute the mighty stream of Jewish life that springs ever fresh and invigorating from its eternal source? How, except by repeating the words of the *Torah*: "ye waxed fat, and thick and gross". Granted that in some places we are still beset by flagrant violations of minority rights and the unabashed abuses and abrogations of liberties for those "outside the pale". Yet the general trend is one of growing tolerance. Inch by inch, the liberals are pushing back the adherents of an attitude that all recognise as archaic. Within this relatively bright picture, nothing should prevent the energetic pursuit of the *mitzvos* which have been our mainstay throughout the generations.

We survived the buffeting of changes from the nomadic life to the agricultural, and then the industrial revolution. We will survive the turbulence that ushers in the age of automation and nuclear physics. True, the winds of change are ever blowing. Those who do not detect the underlying truths, who do not see the firm bedrock beneath the swirling waters, may shift chaotically from one bank to the other or even be drawn into the whirlpool to perish.

But those who remain steadfast to the principle of *kiddush Hashem* will see in it all only an opportunity for the fulfilment of our purpose to become "a kingdom of priests and a holy nation".

a Chassidic gathering

Two of the features which characterise the *Chassidic* way of life are warmth and vitality in the service of G–d and in all aspects of living.

"Serve G–d in joy", wrote the Psalmist, and this is one of the basic doctrines of *Chassidism*. There are two kinds of joy in serving G–d. The higher, sublime joy pulsating through every fibre of the *Chassid*'s being as he binds himself to the Al–ty in the fervour of ecstatic prayer, and the simpler joy born of perfect faith, in which the *Chassid* seeks the presence of G–d in his daily behaviour.

The *farbrengen*, or informal gathering of *Chassidim*, has played an important rôle in regenerating and perpetuating this important factor in the *Chassidic* approach.

It is at the *farbrengen* that a *Chassid* is made. Here, he receives guidance, encouragement and, when necessary, chiding. Here, he drinks from the waters of *Chassidic* wisdom—not the wisdom to be found merely by reading books, for it is at the *farbrengen* that the books come to life. Here, these books speak through the voices of the men who order their lives according to their pages.

On the surface, the *farbrengen* appears to be no more than a simple gathering of men of various ages, grouped around a table; some seated, others standing; all of them eating or having a drink. One or two may be holding forth while the rest listen. Occasionally they break into song, often without words. Then another drink and more discourse.

To the uninitiated observer, no doubt there would be nothing spiritual or uplifting in the proceedings. But to the participants and to those who understand the *Chassidic* way of life and are sensitive to spiritual values, the *farbrengen* is far from being the unedifying occasion it may outwardly appear.

The people gathered at the table are alert and purposeful. The *mashke*, taken in small quantities, removes the burdens of material cares, and makes the participants more receptive to the ideas thrown out by the speakers. The melodies are melodies of the soul, unencumbered by limiting words. Melodies charged with emotion, expressing all the yearning of the *Chassid*'s soul and its desire to be united with the Al–ty.

No atmosphere could be more conducive to listening—not only with the ear and with the mind, but also with the soul.

At a *farbrengen*, a *Chassid* listens; sometimes to others, sometimes to himself, but always with the same object in view—to receive knowledge, to apply it and to elevate himself.

Farbrengens fall into two categories. One is the *farbrengen* of the *yeshivah*, where the *mashpiah* is surrounded by his pupils; the *mashpiah* has come to instruct, and the pupils to learn from him. The other type is the informal gathering of older *Chassidim*, where the purpose is mutual gain.

At the former type of *farbrengen* the *mashpiah* alone speaks. He is a man with a deep understanding of human nature, quick to recognise the requirements of others and experienced in influencing people. His every word is weighed with precision, and he will encourage, criticise, praise and rebuke.

His is no cold, ethical discourse or vague philosophising on correct behaviour. The youthful listeners are uplifted to a level where they live ethics and become so receptive to what is right and what is wrong, that the message is absorbed into their very being. Here, purposeless boys are moulded into purposeful men.

The *farbrengen* of older *Chassidim* is of a somewhat different character. At times an elderly *Chassid* may have something specific to say but the proceedings may often open with a general discussion on a specific element in *Chassidic* teachings, or a completely spontaneous remark. A story may be told, perhaps a personal anecdote. One *Chassid* may rebuke another or he may even rebuke himself.

Remarkable results have been achieved at such gatherings. Some men have been fired with enthusiasm, others have become chastened and penitent; souls have been laid bare, and whole patterns of life have been changed.

The Rebbes and *Chassidic* leaders attached great importance to the *farbrengens*. Rabbi Menachem Mendel, the *Tzemach Tzedek*, gave up a considerable amount of time in order to participate in *Chassidic* gatherings. For five years he participated as an ordinary *Chassid*, and later when he assumed leadership, he commented that the *farbrengen* had laid the foundation of all his subsequent *Torah* study.

The place of the *farbrengen* in *Chassidic* life is an important one, for everything about it is vital—alive. The words of the *farbrengen* are living words and its instruction is living instruction. Conducted in the right spirit, and in the warmth of brotherly love, the *farbrengen* has for generations been an instrument which has made *Chassidism* a living force in Judaism.

שָׁלֹשׁ תְּנוּעוֹת

מהבעש"ט , המגיד ממעזריטש ורבנו הגדול נשמתם עדן

Chabad melody—the pen of the soul

Music and song are as old as man himself. They are as much part of his life as sunrise and sunset, summer and winter, youth and old age. Even before G–d made his covenant with Abraham, men were singing songs of praise, hunting songs, mourning dirges. Women sang their children to sleep and children sang as they played.

In the *Torah*, music has a particular significance. Repeated reference is made to it in the *Tenach*, *Talmud* and books of *Kaballah*, Ethics and *Chassidic* study.

When the Red Sea engulfed the chariots of Pharaoh, "Then sang Moses and the children of Israel this song unto the L–rd, and spoke, saying, 'I will sing unto the L–rd, for He is highly exalted.' " This is one of the most famous *Tenach* references to song, and springs easily to mind, but there are many others, including the lyric masterpiece, *Shir Hashirim*. They all bear witness to the power of music and melody and demonstrate their importance in religion, in praising the Al–ty and in elevating the soul of man.

The significance of instrumental music, too, is demonstrated in *Talmudic* discussions. The purpose of the instruments played by the Levites in the Temple was to elevate the spiritual state of mankind; to sanctify and refine it. In our own day, as during the millennia of Jewish history, music and song are an intrinsic part of Jewish worship.

The particular achievement of *Chassidism* in the sphere of music has been to broaden and deepen it, and make it part of a way of life—the *Chassidic* way of life. The aim of this life is to achieve a communion with the Al–ty in order to banish gloom and despair, so that good should triumph over evil and the soul should search for perfection and purity in its ascent of the ladder to the Throne of Glory. Through song and melody any Jew—every Jew—can rise above the material limitations that restrict him, thereby revealing the G–dliness in his soul. While the melody lasts, while the song is being sung, the singer rises, by degrees, to new levels of inspiration, purity and adherence to the *Torah*.

Since song is so integral a part of *Chassidism*, not only did the early *Chassidim* compose melodies themselves, but they encouraged others to do so as well. These *Chassidic* pioneers were eclectic. If they detected a "holy spark" in the folk songs of the areas in which they lived, they incorporated the themes into their own melodies, or *nigunim*, as they are called. The result can be heard in songs like "Nye Zhuritze Chloptzi", which is sung in Russian.

An even more obvious example is "Napoleon's March", a *Chabad Chassidic* song without words, which is an adaptation of martial music played by Napoleon's troops when they invaded Russia in 1812. It was adopted as a victory song by Rabbi Shneur Zalman of Ladi, founder of *Chabad Chassidism*, and symbolises the victory of the Jewish people over Satan. Lubavitch *Chassidim* traditionally sing it at the conclusion of the *Ne'ilah* service on *Yom Kippur*, before the *shofar* is blown. Your prayers have been accepted, the melody declares, and you will all have a happy New Year.

Just as *Chabad* threw a new light on *Chassidic* thought, so it contributed also to *Chassidic* melody and developed still further the part played by melody in *Chassidic* life.

It has been said that while the *Baal Shem Tov* had brought new significance to song in Jewish living, the *Alter Rebbe* revealed the very soul of *Chassidic* melody.

"The tongue is the pen of the heart, but melody is the pen of the soul", he declared, giving the reason why so many *Chabad* melodies have no words. *Chabad* music differs greatly from other *Chassidic* melody. True, it is often joyous and ecstatic, but it is also mystical and reflective, pensive and yearning.

Chabad songs reflect the inner state of the singer's soul, but without set forms or rules. Indeed, *Chabad* seeks to free melody from rigid formulae and rules. Feeling, the outpouring of the heart and mind, is the inner core of *Chabad* melody, so there is little need for words.

Words, indeed, can sometimes limit pure melody, whereas, without them, melody can soar into the infinite. That which defies expression in words can and should, according to *Chabad* philosophy, be conveyed by melody. Words may express an idea, but they also transpose it from the spiritual world to the material. Melody does quite the opposite. This indeed was what the *Alter Rebbe*, whose famous "Ten melodies" are the archetype of all *Chabad* songs, meant when he said: "The tongue is the pen of the heart, but melody is the pen of the soul."

The sixth Lubavitcher Rebbe, the late Rabbi Joseph Isaac Schneersohn, underlined the vital significance of melody in *Chassidic*, indeed in Jewish, life, when he said: "A melody should be sung with the same correctness that one would employ in citing a commentary on the *Torah* learnt from one's teacher or Rabbi."

Over the years, *Chassidic* songs and melodies have grown and multiplied as they have been handed down through the generations. They have spread far beyond the confines of *Chassidism* to Jews all over the world.

The invention of the record player and tape recorder has meant that Rabbi Joseph Isaac's dictum can more easily be obeyed, for now, *Chassidim* do not have to rely only on their memories, or even on musical notation. They can hear for themselves these melodies being sung and played, and can learn them correctly. New compositions can be recorded for posterity, to be heard exactly as they were written, down to the finest nuance and sweetest cadence.

For this purpose the Nichoach Society was founded by Rabbi Joseph Isaac Schneersohn. Its task is to collect *Chabad nigunim* from various sources and determine their authentic versions. After this they are notated and preserved in book form and in recordings. The present Lubavitcher Rebbe has also given strong encouragement to the work of the Nichoach Society, which has so far published two printed volumes and issued several series of recordings of *Chabad* melodies.

Each new generation finds new meaning in *Chabad* melody. If some of the *nigunim* are applied to parts of the liturgy and the Psalms, as has been the case with some of the "Ten melodies" of the *Alter Rebbe*, who is to say that this should not be so? For even if "The tongue is the pen of the heart", while "melody is the pen of the soul", a Jew's heart and soul can still mingle in ecstasy, reflection and mysticism in their ascent of the ladder of perfection to the *Kisei Hakovod*.

...WITH ALL THE PRIVILEGES & OBLIGATIONS THERETO APPERTAINING...

an insight to teshuvah

Anyone who has experienced an encounter with *Chabad* must at one time or another have asked himself, "What do they really want?" Whether the encounter occurs at a university in England or in casual discussion with one of the Lubavitch emissaries, or during a *pegisha* in Crown Heights—any sensitive and thinking person must wonder about their standpoint and their aims.

After all, in our community, one is exposed to all types of appeals. Sooner or later a demand is made. Sometimes a cheque, sometimes a petition, sometimes an application form, sometimes a request for personal help.

It is no surprise, therefore, to discover that the *Chabad Chassidim* are also interested in some type of commitment from the Jews whom they encounter. The commitment can be paid off in instalments—such as one new *mitzvah* at a time. But, remarkably, the ultimate objective of Lubavitch is nothing less than *teshuvah*, nothing less than the desire to revolutionise completely and irrevocably the life of the modern Jew.

Since the word "*teshuvah*" is usually translated as "repentance", there is a certain unfortunate but understandable tendency to equate the Lubavitch movement with the familiar and classical missionaries (*lehavdil*) who exhort sinners to become penitents. Indeed, the Lubavitch emissaries around the world have been termed "Jewish Missionaries" by those whose thinking is oriented only to the history of Western civilisation and who are unfamiliar with the inner meaning of *Chassidus*.

The objective of Lubavitch in promoting *teshuvah* among Jews is based on "return"—the true and literal meaning of the word. The Rebbe explains the significant difference between the two concepts:

> Repentance implies turning over a new leaf. A person regrets that he committed an evil act or did not commit a good one, and he wants to conduct himself in a new fashion.
>
> *Teshuvah* emphasises return. A Jew is inherently good and wishes to do good; it is only because of various reasons for which he is either not responsible or only partially responsible that he committed an evil act. But inherently he is good.
>
> And this is the essence of *teshuvah*, to return to one's source and origin, to one's inner self, and to reveal one's inner self so that it will be the proprietor of one's life.
>
> This is why *teshuvah* is applicable to all, even to the righteous. It means that the *Tzaddik* is also constantly trying to return to his inner self and to reveal it. And *teshuvah* is equally pertinent to the sinner, because no matter how low he has fallen he always has recourse to *teshuvah* since he does not have to create anything new but only to return to his innermost self.

It is apparent, therefore, that the performance of *teshuvah* involves considerably more than a simple feeling of regret (even though heartfelt) or a "New Year resolution" (even though sincere). *Teshuvah* in the classical Jewish sense means continual introspection and continual striving to return to G–d's instruction as revealed in our *Torah*. It means the re-orientation of one's will and desire in order to conform to Divine law. It means a total revolution (albeit a gradual one) in one's personal life; a yearning to cleave to G–d.

Perhaps for one raised in a traditional Jewish home, for one oriented from infancy to *Torah* and *mitzvos*, the path of return would be a short one and a familiar one. But for those of us whose Jewish background is somewhat skimpy, or who have always equated Judaism with a theoretical "ethical monotheism" or a "randomly evolving civilisation"—the path of return is not only unfamiliar, but is actually littered with obstacles. The obstacles may include our own families, who think of the *kashrus* laws as mediaeval. They may take the form of habit, like the enjoyment of a Saturday afternoon football game (in the best English tradition), or they may consist of philosophical speculation which fragments religion into "ritual" and "ethics" (in the best Greek tradition).

Indeed there are any number of rationalisations and appetites and desires and excuses that may be interposed on the path of the *baal teshuvah*.

Perhaps that is why the scholars of the *Talmud* said: "Where the *baal teshuvah* stands, even the completely righteous cannot stand." On the one hand, the *baal teshuvah*, or one who returns, has to put forth a greater effort to subdue his passions and his familiar appetites—he has more obstacles to overcome to reach this level. On the other hand, not only must he reach it, he has to "stand" on that level, despite the memories and old passions, despite the criticism and pointing fingers.

One cannot avoid the question: "Is it worth the effort?" After all, the "burdens" one assumes as a *baal teshuvah* are so real, the "denials" are so inconvenient, the "rewards" are so tenuous and abstract. Ultimately, the only person who can answer the question is the *baal teshuvah* himself.

Others can describe the warmth of a real *Shabbos*, the joy of a real *Simchas Torah*, the meaningfulness of sincere *tefillah*. Still others can offer testimony about a deep transformation within a family when the wife started observing the *mitzvah* of family purity, and *kashrus* is observed. But the real evaluation must be a personal one—a recognition that reality and significance in a Jew's life become apparent only when he becomes one with the G–d of Israel, the people of Israel and the *Torah* of Israel.

At this stage, one no longer thinks in terms of burdens and rewards. If you can stand the analogy, it is not dissimilar to election to a fellowship in a professional society, or being awarded a meritorious degree. On many of the certificates and diplomas accompanying these awards one finds the following in small print: " . . . with all the privileges and obligations thereto appertaining . . .", but one never really enumerates the privileges and obligations literally. One is a doctor or a fellow, obviously there are privileges. Equally obviously there are obligations.

There is a beautiful parable about a man climbing a hill with a heavy load. If the sack contains rocks, they are considered a real burden, and the climb a difficult chore. There is certainly no desire to pick up another rock—indeed there is a great tendency to empty the sack when no one is looking.

Alternatively, if the sack contains diamonds and precious stones, the sack is not a burden, but a treasure. The climb is not a chore but a meaningful mission. Not only will the man guard his treasure with care, but when he finds other diamonds on the path, he will add them to his load.

Is the game worth the candle? It is, indeed, when you are entrusted with a treasure and a mission. It is, indeed, for those who seek reality and meaning. It is, indeed, when *teshuvah* means return to G–d and *Torah*.

In fairness, it should be said that the path of *teshuvah* is not guaranteed to accomplish any miraculous overnight transformations. Even if you are carrying diamonds, the path is usually long, often difficult, and sometimes lonely. Even potential champions must practise the skill of weight-lifting by degrees, starting with lighter weights and working up to Olympic records. That is why our Sages tell us that one *mitzvah* leads to another. That is why Maimonides cautioned us to teach mystic truth little by little, and to train by easy stages.

But the essence lies in the doing. No one has ever won any game just by reading the rules—no matter how well he has learnt them. No surgeon has ever removed a growth by just studying anatomy—he had to start with an incision. And no Jew has ever become a *baal teshuvah* by reading essays—he had to start with at least one *mitzvah*.

Rabbi Tarfon said: "The day is short, the task is great, the labourers are idle, and the wage is great, and the Master is urgent. It is not your duty to complete the task, but you are not free to desist from it altogether."

the significance of Chassidic dancing

It has been said that the face mirrors the heart. Inner feelings are portrayed in facial expression. It is no coincidence that the Hebrew word for "face"—*ponim*—also means "inwardness". All feelings like pleasure, joy, anger, surprise, disappointment and the like, have their own unmistakable facial expressions which are spontaneous and involuntary, and hard to repress or control.

Stronger emotions call forth additional manifestations, laughter, shouting, clapping the hands and so on. In the case of intense joy, even the feet are stimulated. People "dance for joy". Thus, dancing for joy is the highest manifestation of the most intense feeling of inner happiness, a feeling which permeates the entire body, from head to foot.

Chassidic dancing, that is to say dancing as defined in *Chassidic* terminology and concept, is the outward manifestation of a most intense feeling of religious joy and ecstasy. *Chassidic* dancing is always done by males separately, as mixed (or social) dancing is prohibited by Jewish law.

Chassidic style dancing is not a new development. There are many references to dancing in the *Tenach*. Miriam the Prophetess danced and sang praises to G–d after the miraculous crossing of the Red Sea; King David whirled and skipped before the Ark of the Covenant. Most festivals, and particularly that of *Succos*, were accompanied by dancing from most ancient times. The Hebrew word for festival—*chag*—connotes circle dancing, and it is significant that the most joyous festival of all—*Succos*—was called, simply, "the *Chag*".

There are two frequently used terms in Hebrew for dancing: *mochol* and *rikkud*. The first means circle dance, the second—jumping or skipping up and down. *Chassidic* dance includes both varieties, each having a significance of its own, as will be explained later. However, since the circle dance may also include hopping and skipping, the *rikkud* is generic and includes all varieties of *Chassidic* dancing.

The *Chassidic* circle dance is done in a closed circle, with one hand, or both, resting on the shoulders of the dancer in front. It usually, though not necessarily, moves counter-clockwise. There is no limitation on the number of participants.

The up-and-down dance is more often done in crowded quarters, where there is no room for a massive circle dance. Individual *Chassidim* may perform a solo whirling or hopping dance, or it may be performed by two or more individuals. There is no set pattern of body movements in a solo or duet, though a duet usually involves "approach and retreat", and the locking and unlocking of arms.

The dancing is done to the rhythm or beat of a lively *Chassidic* tune or melody. Certain tunes and melodies are particularly popular on certain occasions and festivals. Both tunes (without words) and melodies (with words) are significant, not only in the rhythm and movements they call forth, but also in their variety of inspiration. Usually, an animated *Chassidic* tune without words will stimulate a higher degree of ecstasy. Wordless tunes are considered in *Chassidus* to be on a higher plane of religious expression, since words are essentially limiting. (A person overcome by emotion is "speechless".) Some tunes may inspire *teshuvah*, others—a longing or yearning for the mystic union of the soul with its Source.

Chassidic dancing is usually accompanied by hand clapping from the bystanders, who join in the singing with gusto.

Chassidic dancing is practised (at any rate by Lubavitch-*Chabad Chassidim*) on special occasions—*Chassidic* gatherings, *farbrengens* (*hisvaadus* in Hebrew). These take place among Lubavitch *Chassidim* at the conclusion of the major festivals, and also on *Purim*; at the special *Chassidic* historic anniversaries (*Kislev* 19, *Tammuz* 12–13, etc.); at festive celebrations, such as weddings; on the arrival or departure of visiting *Chassidic* groups. *Chassidim* hardly ever dance during prayer, except during the Festival of Rejoicing (*Shemini Atzeres* and *Simchas Torah*, particularly during *Hakofos*, when dancing with the scrolls of the *Torah*).

The history of *Chassidic* dance recalls a controversy in the early period of the *Chassidic* movement. In the late 1760s, when the movement flourished under the leadership of Rabbi Dovber, the Maggid of Meseritch, some of the *Maggid's* disciples came to have their own large *Chassidic* followings, eventually giving rise to various branches of *Chassidus*.

One of the *Maggid's* disciples was Rabbi Abraham of Kalisk, who was of a sensitive, emotional nature. He was particularly responsive to that aspect of *Chassidus* which stressed religious feeling ("G–d desires the heart"), and made this the mainspring of his *Chassidic* philosophy and manner of Divine service, indoctrinating his followers accordingly.

To be sure, *Chassidic* doctrine recognises that the mind—"cold reason"—is intrinsically too limited to serve as the exclusive vehicle of communion with G–d. Religious fervour, joy and ecstasy, transcend rational limitations; hence, they offer a much more gratifying vehicle of religious expression.

Moreover, a purely rational approach to religion and religious experience, apart from the paradox inherent in such an approach—trying to grasp rationally that which is essentially above and beyond human reason—is, at best, limited to intellectuals. But they, too, must realise sooner or later that human reason often functions as a "brake" rather than an "accelerator" to religious fulfilment.

Be this as it may, the *Baal Shem Tov* wished to rehabilitate the ordinary Jew, as well as the scholarly, insofar as Divine service was concerned. Accordingly, he emphasised qualities like sincerity, humility and joy as basic ingredients of true Divine service. In this way he breathed new "life" into the practice of the repetitious daily *mitzvos*, so that they should be fulfilled not as a matter of habit, but as a meaningful religious experience. Of course, this too was no innovation. To "serve G–d with joy" was an important element in Lurianic *Kabbalah*, on which *Chassidus* is based and, in fact, has its origin in the *Torah* itself.

However, as already noted, Rabbi Abraham Kalisker and his *Chassidic* followers exaggerated the point. In order to create the proper mood for daily prayer, they felt the need of a lengthy period of inspirational preparation through dancing and singing. They were thus given to excessive emotional outbursts of religious fervour, such as exaggerated gesticulation, dancing in their stockinged feet and even turning somersaults in the street.

These strange displays reached their height in 1770. They added fuel to the already smouldering opposition to the *Chassidic* movement which was unjustly suspected of deviationist tendencies that might estrange Jews from Orthodox Judaism.

Whatever reservations one may have about *Chassidus*, no one will now suspect *Chassidim* or *Chassidus* of heterodoxy; on the contrary, *Chassidim* are now universally regarded as "ultra-Orthodox". But in those early days, when the movement was young and largely unknown, it was the suspicion of heterodoxy that fed the opposition to *Chassidus*, and the highly charged emotionalism of the Kalisker *Chassidim* was not calculated to allay the suspicion, unwarranted as it was.

However, even among the *Chassidim* themselves, though they could better appreciate the religious feelings which prompted these excesses, many frowned upon the Kalisker school, and the *Maggid* himself rebuked his disciple for his lack of self-control. He pointed out to him that dancing should not become an end in itself, and that self-discipline was a sine qua non of *Chassidus*.

While the excessive emotionalism of the Kalisker *Chassidim* eventually waned, and the whole episode turned out to be no more than a passing phase in the early development of the *Chassidic* movement, the doctrine "serve G–d with joy" has remained germane to *Chassidus*, and religious fervour and enthusiasm are still characteristic aspects of *Chassidus*. Nevertheless, a distinction is sometimes made between *Chabad* (*Chochmoh*, *Binoh*, *Daas*, hence "intellectual") *Chassidim* and *Chagat* (*Chesed*, *Gevurah*, *Tiferes*, hence "emotional") *Chassidim*, by reason of the varying emphasis on the relative place of these faculties in the *Chassidic* philosophy and way of life.

In *Chabad*, reason and emotion are blended into a unified system, where the mind rules the heart. One of the doctrines of the elaborate psychology of *Chabad*, as outlined in the *Tanya*, is that the mind is intrinsically and by nature stronger than the heart. Consequently, it is possible, by conscious effort, to assert its mastery over the emotions. The *Chabad Chassid* is not taught to suppress feeling, but to use it sparingly and calculatedly. What most characterises the true *Chabad Chassid* in his daily con-duct, is his complete mastery of himself; all outward manifestations are measured and calculated; everything has its time and place, and every human capacity must be fully placed in the service of G–d. But the emphasis is generally on inwardness. Even dancing, while obviously an external manifestation, has in *Chabad* a profound inner, even esoteric, quality.

In the vast literature of *Chabad*, which embraces every aspect of human conduct and deals with the esoteric as well as the exoteric, the significance of *Chassidic* dance also receives attention. Indeed, it is closely related to some very basic doctrines of *Chassidus* itself.

It would take us too far afield to discuss at length the various aspects of *Chassidic* dance in all their implications for the *Chassid*. Only salient points can be mentioned here, and they will at once strike a familiar note for anyone who knows *Chassidic* literature.

It is explained in *Chabad* that everything in the physical world has its counterpart in the spiritual realm.

In dancing the entire body moves. The whole body from head to foot is absorbed in the joy and exhilaration of the dance. However, it is the legs, of course, which play the principal part. The concept of "head" and "foot" is to be found not only in the physical body, but also in the soul. Moreover, this concept is found also in regard to the entire Jewish people, and in the *Shechinah* itself.

In the physical body the head is supreme, both in position and in quality, while the feet are the lowest part of the body. Yet there is a superiority in the feet over the head, in that the feet serve as a base for the whole body and carry it about from place to place. The head may decide where it wants to go, but it is the legs which must carry it to the desired destination. Without the power of locomotion which lies in the legs, the whole body, including the head, would be severely handicapped. Moreover, should the feet stumble even slightly, the whole body, including the head, could crash down and be seriously hurt.

The analogy, as applied to the soul, is that the soul also possesses a "head" and "feet". The "head" of the soul is that aspect of it which has to do with the intellectual qualities, while the "feet" are represented by that quality of the soul which is the source of simple faith. It is simple faith which is the basis of the Jew's entire spiritual life. This is true of every Jew, without exception. Hence, *Chassidic* dance emphasises the great quality of simple faith which, like the feet of the body, can lift the whole body with the head.

As far as the Jewish people is concerned it, too, constitutes a single organism. The *Torah* scholars, Rabbis and Sages, are the "heads" of the people; the ordinary Jew—the "legs". Obviously the legs cannot be separated from the head, nor the head from the rest of the body. There must be complete unity and harmony within the organism. So must there be complete unity and harmony among all Jews if the Jewish people is to be one healthy organism. Thus, *Chassidic* dance exemplifies this unity. For, in the dance all *Chassidim* participate and are linked together, both those who are the "heads" and those who are the "feet".

As for the *Shechinah*—G–d's manifestation in the world—there is also "head" and "legs", as it were, termed in *Chassidic* literature "*sovev*" and "*memaleh*". The former is the transcendental aspect of G–d; the latter—the immanent. Both are, of course, completely unified in the unity of G–d. The distinction is only valid in our human concept, not in reality. It is we who distinguish between the Divine attribute as manifest in nature and that which is over and above nature. In other words, there are aspects of Divine manifestation which we can comprehend in some degree, and those which are beyond the concept of man or angel.

In professing the unity of G–d, as we Jews do daily and repeatedly, we have to understand, as far as this is possible, what this unity means, and in doing so, we cause the *or ein sof* to irradiate our person, our soul, and the world about us. This is a profound and abstruse subject which is fully discussed in *Chabad* literature. But let it be said here that the unity of G–d is symbolically represented by the circle, which has no beginning or end, though we can speak of the "upper" part of the circle and the "lower" part of it.

The "mystic cycle" also recalls the famous saying of the founder of *Chabad*: "G–d converts the spiritual into the material, and the Jew converts the material into the spiritual." In other words, creation is a "descent" of the spiritual into the material, while Divine service, particularly the fulfilment of the *mitzvos* with material objects (*tzitzis*—wool; *Tefillin*—leather; *esrog*—fruit, etc.), constitutes the "elevation" of the material into the realm of the spiritual and holy. Jews complete this "cycle" in the scheme of creation, and make the unity of G–d a reality in our own experience. Here, again, we have further significant meaning in the *Chassidic* circle dance.

The "advance and retreat" feature of the *Chassidic* dance is, of course, symbolic of the fundamental aspect of Divine service—a well-known and basic doctrine in *Chabad*, as in *Kabbalah*.

The rhythm of the dance and the beat to which the dance is attuned, also have their particular significance in emphasising the pulsating vitality that must animate Divine service.

The foregoing by no means exhausts all that can be said about the significance of *Chassidic* dance, at any rate to *Chabad Chassidim*. The inspirational quality of *Chassidic* dance has been greatly emphasised by the heads of *Chabad*, since its inception. Though the occasions for *Chassidic* dance are few and far between in the course of the year, their inspirational effect is a lasting one, and their influence is felt in the daily life of the *Chassid* throughout the year.

who needs Torah?

Who needs *Torah?* Why appeal to this ancient code when our human instincts of elemental justice are adequate guides? Many Jewish young men and women are troubled, uneasy in their Jewish commitment, because of these questions. They pose a challenge to *Torah*-life in our day.

There is a remarkable interest in things Jewish among young men and women with little in the way of a formal Jewish background. Their secular education is formidable; they are people of culture, highly literate, successful in their professions and occupations, Jewish nominally and to a degree emotionally, yet uncomfortable. Being Jewish is too much an accident of birth, and not enough a matter of conviction.

They are frequently liberal in their approach to political and social matters, with active social consciences, and they wonder what Jewishness can contribute to their lives. Their ideals of social betterment and their personal standards are largely based on ideals drawn from the *Torah* in any case. How, then, are they different, not ethnically but in ideals, from their liberal, ethical, non-Jewish friends? Is there any real difference between a "good Jew" and a "good man"?

Torah has undergone refinement of purpose in modern times. It can be used for a variety of irrelevant purposes, while its primary objective and function, its ultimate raison d'être, is obscured and overlooked. "Refinement" means that in our day the irrelevancies are relegated (not necessarily dismissed) to their proper sphere, become peripheral, and that the indispensability of *Torah* is clarified.

Reading the Hebrew Bible, we encounter history and narrative, poetry, the biography of men and of mankind. For millennia, *Torah* provided drama, literature, a sense of history and continuity when these were hardly available elsewhere. Contemporary man, curious about his antecedents and origins, has access to many and expanding sources. Archaeology is a new discipline that literally and figuratively uncovers yesterday's secrets. The tools of the anthropologist and historian provide material for the interested. *Torah's* function as the sole historical source is an anachronism today.

Man's environment, the processes of nature, were mysterious to pre-scientific man. Natural phenomena were regarded as supernatural, neither to be understood nor controlled by mere mortals. Weather, disease, earthquakes—these were beyond man's ken. Only "religion", appeals to powers transcending man's, could "explain" calamities or good fortune. Religion provided a framework that made some sort of sense of an unfathomable world. It is obvious that contemporary man will not look to "religion" for such enlightenment. Science, to use an inclusive term, has successfully assumed the function of explaining the processes of nature.

We could go on citing areas where only religion (or *Torah*) could guide man. Civil legislation, for example, and quarantine of those with infectious diseases, gained currency, if they did not originate, in *Torah*.

But today, man's human resources are sufficient for all those needs. He does not require recourse to revelation, indeed he spurns the suggestion, when his competence is so vast. He invented the sciences and can speculate plausibly on the origin of the cosmos. He can find cures for deadly diseases and can order his society with its economy and legal system, quite by himself thank you, without reference to the supernatural. To present the Bible as a guiding text in these areas is to make the Bible a redundancy and worse.

Interestingly, one area of *Torah* teaching has always been regarded as within man's grasp—morality. The social laws were self-evident moral truths (stealing and killing are indisputably evil) and the only possible problem is —why should the *Torah* bother with such obvious matters. Good and evil, right and wrong, these words are part of the universal lexicon. Oh, we may quibble about trivia, fine points of definition, but the basic validity of the concepts, their broad application, were beyond cavil.

As man's scientific competence expanded, it also became defined. In its own framework, it is potentially infinite. Observable phenomena and measurable quantities are raw material for the scientist—or "man", if you will. It soon became evident that some "things" are not readily observable or subject to quantitative measurement. The scientist can deal with "what" happens and "how". "Why" is beyond his purview. Right and wrong cannot be tested or observed or measured by any of his instruments, not even by the philosopher's intellect. The scientist concludes that as a scientist he cannot make "value judgements", for as a scientist good and evil do not "exist" for him.

Values persist, moral decisions continue to be made (if negatively through default), but the laboratory does not give its guidance, nor does the philosopher's seminar. Today's professional philosopher does not concern himself with the classic problems of good and evil, not because he is uninterested or because the problems have been settled, but because his philosopher's tools are inadequate. The concepts and terms are outside his realm.

Man, in other words, does not possess the human resources to define or even justify morality as morality. Unhappily, the problem of morality remains, for the scientist may be a father, besides being a scientist. He is hardly prepared to rear his children without these concepts of decency and humanity, even though the most sophisticated computer cannot handle them. We do want our children to be honest and clean.

Goodness and morality were recognised as distinct from prudence and effectiveness. The latter terms, whatever they might describe, and whatever attractiveness they may possess, do not entail morality. It may be prudent to be honest. Prudence may conceivably prescribe larceny.

As so many erstwhile physical truths came under the scrutiny of the challenge: Is it true? The challenge extended to moral truths as well. Remember, revelation has been repudiated, scripture cannot justify moral statements. Why then should we not steal under safe circumstances?

Since mores—and morals—are so commonly ascribed to their societies, "society" determines morals. What then shall we make of an Eichmann, that paragon of his society's virtues? Shall consensus determine morality? Does that mean that if "everybody does it", then "it" is proper? And which "society's" dictates is one bound to observe—the beatnik's or Babbitt's? And granted that violating these dictates may be highly imprudent, are they "immoral"?

Here *Torah* comes into its own. Man's resources are inadequate, but he is not limited to his resources. We do appeal to revelation, to the "supernatural", if you insist, not to explain a drought, but to show us how

204

to live. On our own we could not know. Man can logically, rationally, scientifically, produce Nazi Germany, as he actually did.

Whatever history or narrative, biography or poetry, *Torah* possesses, their purpose is to instruct, no less than the *mitzvos* and prohibitions. If in the process we do learn about some Egyptian dynasty, or Near-Eastern pre-history, all to the good. But how to live, this is *Torah*'s intention and purpose.

This is the refinement of *Torah*'s purpose, man's heightened perception of that communication between the Divine and the mortal. *Torah* is a work of instruction, teaching, guidance. Its purpose is to show man how to live, what is his human potential, what "superhuman" element resides within him.

on Mitzvos and meaning

Mitzvos are not all of one type, and the varying names describing them emphasise their individual characteristics. Let us discuss the various types, and then attempt to learn their significance to the contemporary Jew.

Mishpatim are the "justice" *mitzvos*. They are logical; their meaning is self-evident, and no one questions the need or desirability of such laws. They lubricate the wheels of society, and make it possible for men to live together without destroying each other. The *mishpatim* include prohibitions against murder and robbery, *mitzvos* like honouring one's parents, establishing courts of law. Many of them would exist and be accepted by society even without the teachings and sanction of *Torah*.

Edos are another class of *mitzvos*, testimonial and memorial observances. They would probably not have been invented by man, but since the *Torah* has established them, any reasonable person would find them perfectly acceptable.

Some examples are the Festivals: Our ancestors, with attendant wonders and noteworthy occurrences, left Egypt on *Nissan* 15 some millennia ago. We commemorate their deliverance and mark those days (of *Pesach*) by ridding our homes of *chometz* and by using *matzos* and *morror*, etc. They have historical and didactic value and there should be no objections to them.

But the *Torah* is not content with only these *mitzvos* of justice and commemoration. There is another group, the *chukim*, the fiats of G–d, His decrees. Our Sages refer to them as the *mitzvos* that the "nations and the Jew's *yetzer hara* ridicule".

These *mitzvos* have no rationale, they cannot be explained. When one asks "Why?", one usually receives a frustrating and thoroughly unsatisfying shrug in reply. Examples of this class are *pora adumoh*, *shatnez* and, interestingly, the prohibition against *chazir*.

Present-day Jews are fond of asking questions about Judaism, particularly the reasons for *mitzvos*. One of their favourites is: Why does the *Torah* prohibit the eating of certain meats? After all, these questioners will explain, in the "olden days" (they invariably use these words) when there was no sanitation, government inspection or refrigeration, the laws of *kashrus* made sense. But today, are they not out of date?

The ordinary layman may be excused for not knowing. After all, he makes no serious pretensions to scholarship. But too often, those who should know better parrot the same argument. Their ignorance is inexcusable. Centuries before there was any kind of inspection, Rashi's commentary on the *Chumash* clearly and repeatedly declared that the prohibition on *chazir* was unexplainable and that the reason for it could not be adequately and reasonably understood. He could easily have included it under the *mishpatim*, as a health measure for instance, yet he insisted that hygiene was not the explanation. It is one of the group of *chukim*, commandments we cannot rationalise.

This third group, *chukim*, deserves some attention. Why is there no explanation for them? Why should the *Torah* teach us *mitzvos* that defy understanding? What is the place of *chukim* in the total pattern of *Yiddishkeit* — what do they contribute and what is missing without them? Here we must understand the place of understanding in the scheme of *mitzvos* and rationales proposed for any *mitzvah*.

Observers of human behaviour attempt to explain human conduct, motives and values, even subconscious ones. (The validity of their explanations is not the point here; we are now concerned only with their degree of competence to evaluate human behaviour.) The psychologist's subjects are human, like himself. They have similar cultural backgrounds—or at least the psychologist must be familiar with his subject's background, and the measure of his familiarity will affect his judgements. Their common ground is essential to enable him to explain his subject's conduct. What he is saying in effect is: "Why would I behave like that?"

If the subject under study comes from a totally unfamiliar background, and the observer cannot draw on his experience of apparently universal human traits, it would be futile to attempt to understand, let alone explain, the reasons for his conduct and his values.

We must remember that there is an infinite and unbridgeable gulf between man's intelligence and G–d's. "For your thoughts are not like my thoughts", the prophet declares.

The human mind and experience are limited. No one mind can encompass the totality of human knowledge, so there is much that is unknown to any one person. Human knowledge in its totality is certainly imperfect—there is an infinite and growing world of the unknown. The human capacity for thinking is limited by dimensions, by time and place. We cannot picture the existence of a being not limited by "here" and "there", who is everywhere equally. Nor can we imagine a being for whom past, present and future do not exist, for whom there is no time. The limitations of mortal intellect need not be laboured here. The point is simply that the workings of the human mind are not and can never be comparable to the "processes" of G–d's thoughts.

In attempting a rationale of the *Torah* and *mitzvos*, what man says in effect is: "Why should man propose such ordinances? What meaning have they for us?" The inadequacy of this approach is simply that it is not man who proposed the *mitzvos*, nor can man's mind grasp the reason for them. G–d's reason for issuing *mitzvos* is beyond our powers of divination. His reasons are constant, for He is unchanging. Only man's subjective appreciation varies.

In a sense, *chukim* alone are the ultimate test of *emunah*. After all, one may refrain from stealing, even without accepting G–d and the *Torah*. Not all honest men are necessarily devout.

This will help us to understand why one must observe *mishpatim* with the same devotion as we observe *chukim*. We have no logic supporting *chukim*; reason does not impel us to keep them. Our observance is based completely on accepting them as G–d's teaching, as the will and understanding of His mind. We do not pretend to understand why we must refrain from wearing *shatnez* or eating pork. We are simply His servants. Even those *mitzvos* we do "understand" and accept as reasonable and logical, should be kept not because they promote human welfare or are rational, but because G–d so commanded, and we, His servants, obey. We recognise that even when we do understand, our grasp is imperfect.

One might have some reason other than *emunah* for observing *edos*. The *Pesach Seder*, for example, does have a powerful sentimental attraction. It is in the area where understanding is insufficient, where one cannot answer why, where the purpose of *mitzvos* eludes us, that our only reason for keeping *mitzvos* is that G–d gave them.

An observation I find interesting is that young Jews wonder why their elderly parents could never explain why, for instance, they kept *kashrus* or *Shabbos*. The older people could only stammer inarticulately: "It says so in the *Torah*." This seemed to their children to be rather naïve, simple. Perhaps, though, the parents were instinctively more enlightened than their sophisticated children. They sensed something about the origin of *mitzvos*, about the capacities of man's mind in contrast to G–d's mind. They kept even *mitzvos* that have obvious explanations because G–d gave them, not because of what they understood. They recognised the element that no one can ever properly understand.

This may give us an insight into the pattern of *mitzvos*. *Chukim*, and by extension all *mitzvos*, lie beyond the scope of our minds; we cannot define why they were given. The *Torah* was given to show how the *mitzvah* is to be performed, how the Jew is to live and conduct himself. Our motive for observance is that G–d gave them to us. By observing them, a bond is created between man and the Creator. By neglect or violation, a barrier is erected; man is demeaned, corrupted. If observance brings social benefits or personal satisfactions or cultural advances—wonderful. But these should not be our motives for observing the *Torah* and *mitzvos*.

Only *chukim* emphasise this so clearly. There can be no other reason than *emunah*—complete faith—for keeping *chukim*. Through *chukim*, and the significance they reveal in the other *mitzvos*, the way of *mitzvos* is *derech Hashem*, the way to G–d. Even acting charitably and righteously, doing justice and kindness, must be endowed with G–dly qualities. It is more than just another social convention.

Emunah—the faith of Israel

The problem of faith has returned to torment many who had been certain of their immunity to such concerns. They are hardly confident in their lack of religious belief and are disturbed by this nagging half-belief, as it were.

What upset their composure, their rather cavalier dismissal of religious faith? Possibly disillusionment with faiths other than religious—the political or economic panaceas that would bring brave new worlds in their wake. Perhaps because the militant non-faiths of an earlier generation proved to be illusory.

Now man realises that he can probably never plumb mysteries that seemed all but in his grasp just yesterday. Some Jews had dreams of some universal humanity transcending nation and descent, a world where Jewishness could be cheerfully jettisoned—but these dreams, too, have dissipated in harsh realities. Who can be blamed for being cynical today about the inevitable perfectibility of man?

Thankfully, Jews of whatever station accept their Jewishness in the main, and are prepared for the next question—what to do about it. Virtually illiterate in the formal teachings of their faith and totally unfamiliar with the practices of Judaism, they explore—gingerly and tentatively—the trove bequeathed them by centuries and generations.

Mitzvos, Torah—tell me more about them. How do you use these *Tefillin*, and may I do such and so on the Sabbath? I cannot read Hebrew—how am I to worship? And when these questions are answered to their satisfaction they pull themselves up short—wait a minute, but if I do not have faith in all this, what then?

They are concerned with what is obviously a fundamental consideration that must be resolved before they can proceed in good conscience, without condemning themselves as hypocrites. The question of faith disturbs the Jew groping his way back. How can he move if he does not believe?

Our first task should be that of placing faith in its proper position in the hierarchy of *mitzvos*, and we might understand better by using contrast as well as direct description. The Western Jew—and obviously we have been discussing him with all his Western-ness in culture, outlook, and values and inverse poverty in Jewish learning and living—has absorbed the surrounding culture. Lacking any contrast, he accepts its unarticulated attitudes uncritically and unconsciously.

Specifically, we mean faith—its definition and necessity. To Western man, personally religious or atheist, what he calls "religion" rests solidly on a foundation of faith, if it does not actually consist in the main of that faith. The critical question, the factor that sets apart the "religious" from the irreligious, is: "Do you believe?" His total religious experience is valid or false according to his answer.

The Jew reflects this approach to his own ancestral faith, and when he examines the state of his belief and acceptance of doctrine he is alarmed. In despair at the unanswerable challenge, he is ready to give up and seek himself elsewhere than as a Jew. But, while the difficulty may be decisive for others, it may be only an apparent one to the Jew.

Let us analyse some aspects of faith. The *Talmud* speaks of the burglar praying before breaking into a home. If he prays, how can he steal? If he steals, how can he pray? We can, of course, dismiss the thief as a superficial hypocrite, who mouths a formula without meaning to him. We shall then feel pleasantly superior and spiritual. We shall also lose an opportunity for insight into ourselves and into the nature of faith itself.

Chabad literature describes qualities as pervasive and peripheral. The pervasive make themselves felt; for example, emotions or intellect that suffuse heart or mind. If one's deeds are not in consonance with one's thoughts and feelings, then these latter are deficient. If an inventor's idea is effective on the drawing-board but not in practice, then the idea is faulty. The validity of the thought can be tested.

Faith, however, is of another order, the peripheral. Faith cannot be exposed as deficient if it is ineffective. By its nature, faith may exist on a plane separate from the thoughts, feelings, words and deeds of man. One does not necessarily act in accordance with one's beliefs. To be sure, we cannot respect that person or his faith because of his inconsistencies, but the faith itself is not necessarily illusory.

The prophet speaks of the "righteous living by his faith", and this indeed is the hallmark of the saintly. Dichotomies do not intrude between conviction and performance for such people, and they are properly lauded as "righteous". The *Talmud* comments on this passage by calling it the summation of *Torah*, the one all-inclusive principle, the all-encompassing statement. Faith and life can be compartmentalised, but the saintly person will not permit this. Every phase of his life reflects his faith, and because his faith is pure and selfless and G–dly, so is his life. It is interesting that the prophet does not equate saintliness with faith, but with living by faith. Apparently, one can have faith but not live by it.

While G–d alone can penetrate into the recesses of the soul to evaluate the sincerity of someone's faith, we may indulge the temptation to sit in judgement for a moment. We have seen that a person's life may contradict his professed faith. It could reasonably be argued that this particular individual's faith really is deficient, that he is shallow or a hypocrite. Professing faith and believing are not synonymous. On the other hand, neither is professing atheism necessarily identical with atheism.

That unforgettable day at the Wall bared the soul of avowed atheists, and they prayed and wept with the fervour of the truly devout. Atheists? This spark uncovered so dramatically may be an illustration of a point made repeatedly by Rabbi Shneur Zalman when he was discussing faith in early *Chabad* works.

He declares that every Jew is endowed with faith, a heritage from the Patriarchs and his later forebears. In the course of life this spark may become obscured. (The Lubavitcher Rebbe equates "uncovering faith" with "uncovering soul".) Indeed, the very situation of mortal man in a mundane universe will not inevitably stimulate this spark to blaze forth with a mighty flame.

The close presence of the Creator is not readily evident and the moral imperative of His commands is disputed by the temptations of the moment. This spark of faith can be elicited only through effort. Man must call upon some internal resources of soul to overcome his weakness. The naked eye sees only the delight of the moment; G–d's stricture and displeasure are rather vague and inconsequential at that moment of decision. Man calls upon, arouses, his faith in order to conduct himself as he should. This endowed faith is inherent and capable of being aroused, but it is not the epitome of faith. But first we must define reason and faith.

There is an area of competence for man's mind, and a sphere where his intellect is irrelevant. Man and his mind are dimensioned, limited in terms of time and space. We may use a term like "infinite", but cannot conceive of true infiniteness, if only because our personal existence impinges on infinity—if something is truly infinite, then how can we exist? (This, of course, is a classic problem of theology, and is discussed in *Chabad* literature, but is not our concern at the moment.)

We can understand the dimensioned, however vast, and can constantly extend our comprehension within these limits through study. Naturally, these limits will vary from person to person. Beyond dimension, reason is inoperative.

However, man's inability to comprehend the infinite does not lead to the conclusion that the infinite does not exist. Man can apprehend this state, not through mind but through faith. Faith functions where reason cannot tread. We speak of the infinite, and describe it, at best, in negative terms (He is not limited, etc.). What is this infinite? We do not, cannot, know. But we do believe that He is the ultimate in perfection, the truly unbounded, with no definition or finiteness, transcending mind and understanding. Furthermore—and this is vital—we believe that infinite G–d and insignificant man communicate with each other, that He has revealed His wishes and thoughts to man, and that in turn He cares about man's life and hears man calling Him.

Let us return to our concerned Jew, wanting Judaism, yet oppressed by his inability to believe. How can he overcome the impediment of disbelief? Faith is a *mitzvah*, a cardinal one to be sure, but it is a peer among peers, one of 613. All *mitzvos* must be observed of course, and this includes the *mitzvah* of faith among all the others. It is not the test of piety, nor is it the introduction to Judaism in the sense of progression. For others faith might be the summation of their religion, or it is the indispensable first step. For the Jew, faith is not the beginning but the reward for *Torah* living. One does not begin with faith; faith follows.

Rabbi Shneur Zalman writes about "nourishing faith", but introduces the thought that the word "faith" is the object of the word "nourishing", not the subject. Faith itself needs nourishment, strengthening, vitalisation, growth. He notes the endowed faith of Israel, the heritage, but insists that man must progress far beyond this point. The *mitzvos*, he explains, are bound up with the infinite, for they are His will. By performing a *mitzvah* man is bound up with the infinite. Through the *mitzvah* of *Torah* study, his mind coalesces with the "mind" of G–d; through *mitzvos* of speech his faculty of speech is joined to G–d's; through performing *mitzvos* of action his power of deed is combined with G–d's power of deed.

Performing *mitzvos* brings the reality of G–d into the range of man. The transcendent G–d, beyond all comprehension, illuminates man's soul. He is not distant to man, nor indifferent to insignificant mortals. Does man now understand G–d? His mind is as limited as before, but he apprehends G–d through his faculty of faith, as he could not before.

is woman's rôle in Torah law secondary?

The Jewish woman who patterns her life according to *Torah* law and tradition enjoys the most elevated status among civilised people, yet we have allowed ourselves to be manœuvred into a position where we must defend ourselves against what can, at best, only be called a distorted conception.

Why must we be dogged by the baseless accusation that our rôle in the Jewish scheme of things is always to take second place? Surely it troubles us, or we would not feel called upon to explain and defend our position.

Sadly, the Jewish woman today is prone to discuss her status in Jewish religion in terms of where she sits in the synagogue. Her place behind the *mechitza* is considered the sign of her inferiority and wholly out of date in this era of equality.

To understand the Jewish woman and her rôle in life, one must first understand the source of the rules by which she lives—the *Torah*. The *Torah* has several methods of instruction. There are laws describing duties and prohibitions, such as the Ten Commandments. There are narratives, history, exhortation, and even poetry. All are instructive in their own way.

The *Torah*'s effect, however, is not simply legislative and formal. The *Torah* endeavours to establish and inculcate attitudes. Ultimately, these attitudes give life to the letter of the prescribed law and extend beyond it. They affect the individual's life no less than the law proper. For example, laws fostering respect for another's dignity have a far deeper effect than legal statement might imply or prescribe. Anyone with a rudimentary knowledge of *Torah* law and attitude is aware of the many statutes and sayings concerning the respect and consideration that must be shown to the Jewish woman. Just one example: He who gives honour to his wife more than to himself is especially blessed.

Yet the *Torah* is not an exclusive force of influence. It does not operate in a vacuum. The *Torah* recognises that we live at a certain time in history, within a certain cultural context, and it operates in this framework. While it legislates without equivocation, it need not create isolation.

Moreover, although a large area of human interest is governed by the *Torah*, there is also a large area of option, of decision and of judgement. The bulk of this decision will lie with the community and the individual, though subjected to discipline and control by the *Torah*. The *Torah* has built-in provisions for strengthening its laws if the need arises. So, when the influence of the times and culture demanded it, these built-in safeguards were used.

We are all familiar with most aspects of woman's place in Jewish life, especially as described in the *Tenach*.

Woman's very creation is exalted. As G–d proclaims: "It is not good that man should be alone."

In the midst of paradise, with all his power to conquer the world, man is helpless and joyless without his wife; his life is incomplete.

We learn of Sarah, whom the Rabbis describe as superior to Abraham in prophecy, and Rebeccah, Rachel and Leah the Matriarchs, who are no mere figureheads but each in her own way a paragon of virtue and fore-sight. We have Miriam, the sister of Moses and Aaron, and a whole generation of women in whose merit an entire nation was redeemed. At a crucial time in history it was to Deborah the Judge that strong men turned for counsel. This is hardly the legacy of secondary citizens.

These women and many more like them refute all accusations of inferiority, for their lives extended over a period of centuries, indeed millennia, during which the women of the rest of the world were virtually chattels of their husbands. The rights of women hardly existed, the concept itself was unthinkable. Universal practice gave man a dominance that was not to be infringed by his wife or challenged in any form. With her rights as a woman denied her, little dignity remained.

How ideal must the Jewish woman's life have appeared in contrast. For, at the very outset, our Sages declared that in the union of man and woman, be they rich or poor, simple or educated, there are not only two—another is involved—G–d.

There is hardly a religion or moral declaration in the world that stresses this concept of husband-wife-G–d partnership. It is this concept that defines the rôle of Jewish womanhood today as it did yesterday and will do tomorrow.

For us this does not remain simply a profound thought and a lofty ideal. It is borne out by volumes of detailed laws to the point where this awareness of G–d influences every facet of the relationship of a Jewish man towards his wife. Together with her, he forms a partnership with G–d.

The *Torah*'s restrictions are the Jewish woman's safeguard. For where the *Torah* restricts, it does not demean—it protects and sanctifies.

In a study of Jewish practices, one must clearly understand what is the command and what, in practice, has been affected by prevailing social conditions. For instance, we may regard the old country *shtetl* as the ideal *Torah*-observant community. Yet the emancipated woman looks with horror at that way of life, pointing to the unfair restrictions it placed on women. But were these aspects of their lives derived from *Torah*—or were they rather a reflection of the surrounding culture? Take, for example, their education, or rather lack of education. We must realise that until fairly recently no one, man or woman, received much formal education from the general community. All women's lives were more confined, so this lack was not felt. As our general culture expanded to include women, the Jewish community promptly established excellent institutions to educate girls and women. Any hint of inferior status was not a result of *Torah* law, but a reflection of the times and culture.

Undoubtedly, woman's position in society has radically changed. Opportunities denied her in the past are now commonplace. Barriers are rapidly crumbling and few doors remain closed to the competent woman. In droves, women have left their traditional rôle of motherhood and homemaker ostensibly to broaden their horizons.

Yet, strangely enough, this heady sense of freedom and equality, instead of bringing satisfaction and peace of mind has, as often as not, fostered a spirit of restlessness and bewilderment. The modern woman, with every opportunity to prepare and choose for herself the kind of life she will lead, is faced with a dilemma. Are her talents and costly education being wasted if she chooses to stay at home? If we say "Yes", then are we not ignoring the serious incidence of unhappiness, lack of direction, and even delinquency among children and youth, which are attributed to the lack of maternal guidance? These conflicting views are, as yet, unresolved.

On a completely different, and perhaps more intimate level, where has the modern world's concept of equality finally placed the woman? She has become the most potent instrument of advertising, subjected to every vulgarism, her womanliness crudely exploited to promote sales. Modesty has been set aside as a provincialism, and chastity is considered a shackle rather than a virtue. Thus we find that today's woman, at the peak of her sophistication, has been stripped of her dignity as a human being.

Observing where man's concept of morality has led society, how reassuring are the standards of the *Torah*! It imposes differing demands on men and women because it recognises their quite natural Divinely-given differences. One cannot add up the number of *mitzvos* involving men and women and, by comparing their totals, infer the importance of one over the other. Nor is there a standard by which we can weigh or measure the importance of particular *mitzvos*.

Prohibitive laws—the "Thou shalt nots" apply to both men and women. Positive laws which must be performed at specific times were given only to men. But this may well be an indication of the natural superiority of the Jewish woman over her male counterpart in some respects. For, to the extent that the *mitzvos* constitute an exercise in self-discipline for moral advancement (which is one of the many infinite aspects of the Divine Commandments) it would seem that the Creator has endowed the Jewish woman with a greater measure of such natural self-discipline, since He has exempted her from certain *mitzvos*.

Our Rabbis teach us: "One who is involved in performing a *mitzvah* is exempted from performance of another (positive) *mitzvah* which must be fulfilled at the same time." In exempting her from observance of time-controlled *mitzvos*, the *Torah* has reverently, and with infinite grace, defined for all time the Jewish woman's rôle in life. It has encouraged her natural life-giving instincts and recognises that her primary rôle as the *akeres habayis* is second to none.

Lubavitcher Rebbes have, since the inception of *Chabad Chassidus*, emphasised in all their teachings, the vast potential of Jewish womanhood to contribute to the growth of *Yiddishkeit*. The dimensions of woman's influence are immeasurable; in this rôle the Jewish woman is incomparably first. They have therefore directed and encouraged her to develop and use this vast potential and influence to the ultimate glory of *Torah* and G–d.

divine providence

No man's spiritual path is perfectly straight. Everyone, even the greatest, has his times of spiritual elation and depression, due not necessarily to the weakness and iniquities of man, but to the nature of things.

On each particular level a person is able to achieve harmony between what his intellect understands and what his emotional faculties experience, finding expression in his thoughts, words and deeds. A person should not spend his whole life on one level, however, but must continually strive towards higher attainment. And in all progress, whether purely intellectual or with emotional associations, there is always an intermediate period of regression between one level and another.

In order to acquire new concepts and new depths of understanding, a person must first abandon his previous modes of thought. Unless he does so —unless he empties himself, as it were, of all but the basic fundamentals of knowledge, he will not elevate himself to a higher spiritual plane. No such plane is firmly achieved until the concepts understood with the intellect make themselves felt emotionally.

Once having acquired new vistas of understanding, however, he is no longer inspired or excited by his old ideas; but, on the other hand, he does not yet feel the full implications of his new-found concepts to be affected by them. This is the regressive intermediate stage.

The advice given by *Chassidus* to overcome this is the study of the fundamentals of faith. Not that this will necessarily help the individual to reach a higher level of spiritual attainment, but it provides him with a firm basis to which to return when he feels the need. One who has delved into the principles of faith, and the relationship between man and Creator, will never regress to a level from which he cannot elevate himself. Even though he cannot always achieve unity between his heart and mind, he is able to cleave to certain basic principles.

The many diverse opinions regarding Divine Providence—whether it is of a general or individual nature; whether it affects all mankind individually; or only the Jewish people individually and the rest of the world generally; or whether each created thing is singularly regarded—arise from different concepts of G–dliness.

At first glance it would appear that the deeper and more refined one's conception of G–dliness, the more general must one assume Providence to be. Since the nature of G–dliness is beyond anything that human faculties can comprehend (for even the remoteness between man and the source of Providence cannot be appreciated, and the only knowledge of G–dliness one can have is of a negative quality), how can it be understood that G–d should lower Himself, as it were, to pay attention to the doings of His creatures?

This approach, based though it is on a deep recognition of the greatness of G–d, is not the way of *Chassidus*. *Chassidus* shows a different way of understanding the bonds which exist between G–d and the world. This does not mean that *Chassidus* fails to recognise the profound distance between us and G–d. On the contrary, *Chassidus* emphasises this remoteness; and by means of this comes to a different conclusion.

The philosophical approach, even though it regards the understanding of G–dliness as the very pinnacle of wisdom (as Maimonides often stated, one cannot compare G–dliness to anything within the range of our intellect), nonetheless, tends to impose limitations. A fundamental axiom, which the *MaHaRaL* emphatically declared, however, is that G–dliness can be neither defined nor limited.

Our Sages, of blessed memory, referred to G–d as "The Holy One, blessed be He", since the term "holy" implies something beyond and utterly remote from all confines of definition. Even to consider the understanding of G–dliness as the very highest form of wisdom is to impose limitations upon it, and is hence contrary to the truth. Indeed, it is as materialistic an approach as visualising G–d in physical, corporeal forms, since the highest spiritual planes and gross matter are as one to G–d.

Recognition of the true heights and remoteness of G–dliness does not lead to a negation of individual Divine Providence. If one regards G–dliness purely from an academic standpoint—as a profound and lofty study—

then Providence must of necessity appear to be restricted. But when we understand that the greatness of G–d is beyond all limitations, physical and spiritual, and that the planes of the physical and spiritual are of equal insignificance to Him, then we cannot speak of limitations in the extent of His Providence—for in what way is one level of existence more deserving of individual Providence than another? The greatest man and the lowest earthworm are equally nullified in His Divine light. Space and time are meaningless in respect to G–d; His being engulfs all. All created things are thus equally remote from His essence, and conversely—are all equally near to the all-encompassing Deity outside which nothing can exist.

In the light of this profound understanding, one can interpret the verses: "G–d is high above all nations, upon the heavens is His glory. Who is like the L–rd our G–d who dwells so high. Who descends to look upon the heavens and the earth." (Psalm 113: 4–6.)

Here are mentioned the two approaches and understandings of G–d's Providence. The heathens, from their standpoint, say: "G–d is high above all nations"—G–d is above the world, above human understanding, and so it follows that "upon the heavens is His glory". This is the assertion that G–d is in heaven above, in the realms of the spiritual, but not actually in the world and certainly not associated with the individually created thing. In direct contrast the Jew declares: "Who is like the L–rd our G–d." We, who appreciate the true greatness of G–d, realise that it is only to our limited faculties that He appears to "dwell so high"; and we recognise the fact that He "descends to look upon the heavens and the earth". This, then, is the proclamation that the One Who in His greatness created the world, looks with love upon the heavens and the earth to care for and attend to the needs of every individually created thing.

On the basis of this principle, *Chassidus* has been able to recognise Divine Providence as extending to the minutest details of the Creation. The *Baal Shem Tov* expressed this in very definite terms, stating: "G–d may set in motion a chain of various and strange causes in order to bring about a particular effect in regard to even an insignificant thing. Thus, a storm may occur on a hot and sunny day merely to move a leaf long fallen from a tree and lying in the gutter, or a straw which had for years been part of a thatched roof of a village hut, and place them elsewhere in fulfilment of Divine Providence extending to those particular things." This affirms that Divine Providence is of an individual character, extending to each and every particular thing, even in the inanimate world. Consequently, any denial of individual Providence is similarly a denial of any form of

Providence; and recognition of individual Providence is an acknowledgement of the greatness of G–d.

According to the teaching of the *Baal Shem Tov*, a mighty wind may rage through a forest solely to bring one leaf near to the mouth of a worm. This Providence, then, is such that it is concerned for and attends to the needs of even a tiny worm. Relatively great things occur, without our being aware of the fact, to provide even for the smallest of creatures; for in the final assessment, everything has its plan and purpose in the fulfilment of the Creation and is under Divine Providence at all times.

Various problems, however, arise from this concept of individual Divine Providence. The first and most obvious one is the question of the existence of evils in the world. If the Holy One, blessed be He, pays vigilant attention to every minute detail of each created thing, how is one to understand the existence of evil in the world?

Interwoven with this general problem of the existence of evil are many particular problems, such as, how is evil formed? What is the foundation and secret of its continued existence? How can it be defined in relation to its source? These questions reach the very limits of what is given over to human enquiry and what is not. Particularly since they are derived from and are related to everything that has occurred since the beginning of the world's existence. Nevertheless, one can delve into the nature of evil in the world relative to man's position within the framework of Divine Providence, not merely as a metaphysical exercise, but as a problem with practical consequences in the service of G–d and meditation on one's way of life.

The principal question in all this is similar in form to a saying of our Sages, of blessed memory, that "Evil does not descend from above." In which case it is indeed difficult to explain the existing evils of the world, evils of physical and spiritual suffering. If the Holy One, blessed be He, watches constantly over all his creations, how does evil descend from His hands to our world? The solution once offered was that G–d would mete out punishment to a sinner by withdrawing His Providence from him, leaving him at the mercy of the forces of nature and his own intrinsic evil. According to *Chassidic* doctrine, however, Providence is constant and affects each created thing at all times, so this answer is totally unacceptable.

The question then remains; and those who believe in G–d's Providence must refine their understanding of the subject. It cannot be appreciated by viewing the surface alone; one must delve into the inner meaning of things in order to understand.

The inner qualities of things are expounded in *Chassidus* from many different aspects. Indeed, it presents numerous paths by which one may approach these problems both intellectually and emotionally.

One aspect is the *Baal Shem Tov*'s interpretation of evil as a veil to good. In other words, evil, although a reality, does not function by itself or take any course it wishes, but acts only as an instrument for an ultimate good. This good may be either a direct outcome of evil, or else the evil may cause a person to re-orient himself towards a purpose which is ultimately good. This, however, is not without difficulties, both in its application to human experience and in general recognition of good and evil. There is good of such perfection and sanctity that it has no connection with evil at all, and one would have to lower oneself to undergo the effects of evil.

But again, viewed in this light, each descent, each occasion when evil apparently prevails, is all for a higher purpose. On this point there are many far-reaching explanations—for instance, that evil is a punishment for the wicked, or that it serves to repay the righteous in this world for their occasional wrongdoing—all of which combine to form a complete enunciation of the principle that evil is a preparatory means for achieving good, rather than a contradiction of it. It is the gateway to higher attainment, and as the *Baal Shem Tov* expressed it, the low foundation upon which the fulfilment of good is built.

There is, however, a further and deeper aspect of this question of the world's evils and, when understood more intrinsically, that which appears to us as evil is, in fact, not evil at all. Not only is good the ultimate purpose of all things, but their very essence is also good.

It is because of our limited understanding that we regard certain things as bad. The difference between good and evil in our lives is the difference between obvious and revealed good and the level of good which we do not appreciate and which appears to us as being remote from the positive. It is analogous to the man who speaks kind and benevolent words in a language we do not understand. Even if he were to shower us with all the good wishes in the world, we would gain nothing from it—only annoyance at the time wasted listening to him.

Thus it is with the concealed good of the Holy One, blessed be He; it is related to a loftier purpose which humans are not equipped to recognise or appreciate. On the contrary, it appears to us as something quite undesirable. Were we greater men, we would see G–d's goodness in all things, as was exemplified by Nachum Ish Gamzu, who was known to say of every incident: "*Gam zu letovah*". This was not just a resignation to fate, but a positive declaration that what might have appeared to some as misfortune was in fact something very good.

The criterion, therefore, for distinguishing between good and evil is not the external nature of things, but the degree of concealment from our eyes. We regard many of the things which happen to us in much the same way as small children do.

Because their mental powers are as yet undeveloped, they consider much of the good that is done for them (and which they do not understand) as bad. With mental maturity comes an increased capacity for appreciating the less apparent good.

On a still deeper level of understanding, it can be seen that not only is apparent evil a concealed form of good, but moreover, a higher form of good than the revealed. If we accept that the revealed good is in fact good, this does not signify that it is the highest form of good, only that it is the most obvious; a level that we can appreciate as good. That which we designate as evil, however, is actually a much higher form of good, beyond the scope of our limited powers to realise it as such. Thus, all the manifestations of G–d's power in the world that appear to be of a negative quality constitute a good that is far above us. Viewed in this light, one can appreciate the sayings of our Sages, of blessed memory.

Whether we regard the matter in such a way that we say: "It is a time of trouble for Jacob, and from it salvation will ensue" (that salvation will only come through hardship and trouble); or whether, in the broader sense, as in the words of our Sages: "*Tov*—this is the good inclination, *tov me'od*—this is the evil inclination; *tov*—this is the angel of life, *tov me'od*—this is the angel of death" (that seemingly negative qualities are truly hidden forms of good, and of a higher character), it is only through concealment that an abode for the Holy One, blessed be He, is prepared. The revealed and obvious good, that which we see before us, *alma deisgalyah*, is, therefore, a lower level; *alma deiscasyiah*, provides a medium for a greater manifestation of Divine will, although it is not seen by us.

As in all branches of *Chassidus*, the important factor here is not the abstract doctrine, but the understanding which brings one to practical results, whether it be a change in one's deeds or a change in one's feelings. A deep appreciation of the nature of evil serves as a basis for directing one's emotions properly.

At the first level of understanding, and of associating this understanding to himself personally, the individual finds that he can accept retribution. He realises that his present situation is an instrument for receiving subsequent good, and he no longer objects or becomes embittered. Even though he is suffering now, he is able to bear the trial, trusting with a perfect faith that his affliction is not everlasting and is only a veil to the good which will ultimately be revealed. Thus, he can even praise G–d for it, as the *Mishna* says: "A man is obliged to bless (G–d) for the bad just as he would bless (G–d) for the good."

At a deeper level—the recognition of evil as concealed good—he can attain a still loftier ideal. Not only can he accept retribution when it comes, but he can even rejoice in it. Since he knows that his apparent evil is actually a form of good, he has no reason for being upset. Here, however, a reservation is necessary. A great man, who possesses deeper insight, can truly say: "*Gam zu letovah*". His ability to recognise the hidden good makes it easier for him to bear, and the evil does not cause him as much suffering as a man of lesser stature. What the great man sees, the lesser man believes; and if his faith is perfect, he, too, can say that "evil" does not descend from above, and he, too, can rejoice in his lot.

At the deepest level, appreciating evil as a lofty form of good, he will not only rejoice in his suffering, but will experience abundant happiness. This is only possible for one whose sense of values is perfectly oriented. He can direct himself towards matters of importance—establishing a firm contact with G–d—and can pay no heed to things of little worth. He recognises in his suffering a manifestation of G–d's closeness. Of such a person it is said: "They are insulted but they never insult, they are reviled but do not answer, they act out of love and rejoice in suffering", and also: "But they that love Him be as the sun when he goeth forth in his might." Only one who truly loves G–d can attain this level of rejoicing in suffering.

In this light one can understand the meaning of the *Tzaddik v'tov lo*. For only a *Tzaddik gomur*, who is called "*Tzaddik v'tov lo*", can live a life devoid of evil and in which only good exists. Since his insight and his faith are perfect, he can appreciate all his sufferings in terms of G–dly manifestation, for this is his true desire. To him there is no place for evil, and everything is only complete good.

prayer

"You shall reprove your comrade"[1]—even one hundred times.[2] Therefore I cannot contain myself and refrain from crying out again, in a voice betraying weakness.[3] I plead with you, out of deep compassion have mercy on your souls. Take care, be painstaking to an extreme concerning *Torah* and the service of the heart which is worship[4] with *kavannah*, proper intention. All should begin in unison, as one, word by word, not one here and another elsewhere, one mute and the other idly chatting—may G–d protect us. The main cause and instigator of damage comes from those leading the worship. That office is abandoned to whoever wishes to stride forth and seize the honour, or because not even one desires it. . . .

For this reason, this is the counsel offered, and an amendment established as law not to be violated further, G–d forbid. That is, select specified people fit for this office, by lot or by consent of the majority of the worshippers. These shall be men who worship word by word, moderately, out loud, neither overly prolonging the prayers nor racing intemperately, G–d forbid. Theirs is the duty to lead the prayers, each on his day as determined. He shall assemble close around him all those who worship at least with some voice, not whispering or rushing, G–d forbid. This is amplified in ancient amendments in many cities.

I come now to renew them, to strengthen and invigorate them, never again to be weakened, G–d forbid. (*Gevald! Gevald!*[5]) How long will this be an obstacle for us![6] Have we not sufficient reproofs and troubles that have overtaken us!—may G–d protect and console us with double-fold

[1] Leviticus 19:17.
[2] *Baba Metzia* 31a.
[3] Exodus 32:18.
[4] *Taanis* 2a.
[5] An exclamation of anguish. These two words appeared in the original manuscript written by Rabbi Shneur Zalman.
[6] Exodus 10:7.

salvation,[7] and purify our hearts to serve Him in truth.[8] Strengthen and fortify your hearts, all who hope to G–d.[9]

Also: complete the entire *Talmud* every single year and in every community by apportioning the tractates by lot or by consent. In a city with numerous synagogues, each congregation shall complete [the *Talmud*]. If a congregation is too small to implement [this programme], they shall join to themselves men of some large congregation. This statute shall not be varied or violated. Each of the participants shall individually conclude Psalm 119 weekly.

Since, due to the frailty of the generation, not every one is capable of fasting as he ought,[10] the counsel offered is the declaration of our Sages, of blessed memory, "Whoever observes *Shabbos* according to its *halachah* (law), is forgiven all his sins."[11] Note, according to its law. Therefore it is incumbent upon every individual to master the major laws of *Shabbos*.[12]

Too, be most careful not to indulge in idle chatter, G–d forbid. For it is known to the initiates in the esoteric lore,[13] that in all *mitzvos* there are the internal and the external aspects. The externality of *Shabbos* is the cessation of physical labour, just as G–d ceased making physical heaven and earth. The internal aspect of *Shabbos* is the *kavannah* (intention) in the *Shabbos* prayers and *Torah* study, to cleave to the One G–d, as it is said, "It is *Shabbos* to the L–rd your G–d."[14] This is the state of "Remember".[15] The state of "Observe" in the inwardness [of *Shabbos*] is refraining from speech about material affairs, as G–d ceased from the Ten Utterances[16] through which physical heaven and earth were created. For one parallel to the other. . . .[17]

The foregoing is the last of the essays contained in the fifth part of the *Tanya*, *Kuntres Acharon* (Latest Discourse). The translation of this volume into English by Rabbi Zalman I: Posner was published by "Kehot" Publication Society in 1968.

[7] Cf. Job 11:6.
[8] Prayer-book, Sabbath prayer.
[9] Based on Psalm 31:25.
[10] See *Iggeres Hateshuvah*, chapters 2 and 3.
[11] *Shabbos* 118b.
[12] *Shabbos* 12a. The term is used there in reference to the admonition to examine one's clothing regularly on *Shabbos* to insure against unwittingly carrying.
[13] See "On the Teachings of *Chassidus*".
[14] Exodus 20:10; Deuteronomy 5:14.
[15] "Observe" appears in the Exodus text of the Ten Commandments, and "Remember" in the Deuteronomy text, in the Sabbath commandment.
[16] *Avos* V; see *Tanya* II, chapter 11, and *Iggeres Hateshuvah*, chapter 4ff.
[17] *Koheles* 7:14; see *Likutei Amarim* I, p. 45, note 1.

Torah in the space age

introduction

A fundamental principle of *Chassidus* emphasises the rôle of Divine Providence in every event which occurs, regardless of the event's apparent insignificance. This principle, based on the mastery and eternal involvement of the Creator with His creation, has an important corollary: Everything that is seen and heard is designed to increase a person's awareness of the Al–ty and should teach a Jew how to fulfil the Al–ty's instructions.

It follows that the everyday experiences and observations made even in the lecture room, the laboratory, the academic office, and the science conference room have a deeper meaning. These experiences must be analysed not only for their obvious and external information, but also for the spiritual insights contained therein. In this fashion, they will provide the observer with a practical lesson in his continual attempt to discern and comply with the Divine Will as revealed in *Torah*.

The following anecdotes, based on actual experiences, are selected from an unpublished series of lectures presented by the author on *Torah* and *Mitzvos* in the Space Age.

the space voyage[1]

A few years ago a noted scientist delivered a lecture at a Space Science Conference on the broader aspects of the National Aeronautics and Space Administration Programme. Among other things, the lecturer tried to

[1] Based on a paper by Dr Roger Revelle entitled "Sailing in New and Old Oceans", *American Institute of Biological Sciences Bulletin*, Vol. XII, p. 46, Oct. 1962.

draw a parallel between the problems which will face space explorers in the future and our current condition here on earth.

Using a hypothetical manned voyage to the nearest star, Alpha Centauri, as an example, he emphasised the remarkable engineering, biological and sociological problems that would be encountered during the execution of this enterprise. Since the star is 4·3 light years away, a space ship travelling at 1,000 miles per second (50 times as fast as our current capabilities) would still require more than 800 years to get there and, of course, another 800 years to get back. Thus, any original crew we launched would not survive for even a small fraction of the mission's duration. Instead, we would have to "man" the capsule with men and women who would have children who would then mature in order that they also would have children, and so forth for 1,600 years. Ultimately, after many generations, the remote progeny of the original crew would complete the mission started long before by their ancestors.

(Apropos—the first series of instructions to the crew might be quite similar to the first chronological commandment mentioned in *Torah*: "Be fruitful and multiply"—and replenish the capsule.)

This interstellar space ship would have to be completely self-sustaining and self-supporting. No material of any kind could be wasted. Every generation would be responsible for the next and would be obligated to see that the capsule environment remained conducive to life. Everything would have to be re-used and regenerated: the water, the food, the oxygen, and so forth. Indeed a great deal of work being done by N.A.S.A. scientists today is related directly to these problems: How to avoid polluting our environment; how to convert waste into re-usable raw material; how to regenerate oxygen from carbon dioxide, etc.

The lecturer pointed out the obvious analogy to our earth. "This round ball . . . on which mankind dwells, is a sphere unsupported in space, isolated and complete in itself. . . . A two-billion-man space ship hurtling through the void . . . must be self-supporting and self-contained. We must not, and indeed we cannot, waste anything. . . ."

He then went on to point out that the engineering and technical problems are only one side of the coin. In the interstellar space ship, the crew would have to learn to tolerate each other, generation after generation. Similarly, we on earth must somehow learn to live with each other. On our two-billion-man capsule there are too many fingers on too many emergency "destruct" buttons. We had better learn, and learn quickly, that you don't blow up only "a part of a space ship".

And then the speaker touched on a key topic: Would the fiftieth generation, after a thousand years, still share the aspirations of their pilgrim fathers who set out from earth so long ago? How indeed can you convey to generations still unborn the basic information about where they came from, where they are going, how to get there and how to get back?

To a Jew this story is no mere fantastic flight of the imagination. Three thousand years ago, at Mt Sinai, we were launched with specific instructions and suitable maps. For more than a hundred generations we knew where we came from, where we were going, why we were travelling, who was the Project Officer, and how to get back. And we had no real difficulty in transmitting this intelligence—unbroken from generation to generation —because the *Torah*, our Divine log-book, not only contains cosmic guidance about the overall mission (and how to resolve sociological and political problems, and how to approach the technical question of physical survival and well-being), but also contains the very directions about how it should itself be taught and transmitted to young and old.

And despite all problems and philosophies and explanations and rationalisations, this log-book has met the only real criterion of the empirical scientists—it worked. Our very presence demonstrates that it worked.

But somehow, not too long ago, the complete mission has been endangered. A generation of astronauts arose who decided that they could write a better log-book. They thought the original was old-fashioned, and too restraining, and too complicated, and irrelevant to the problems of "modern times". And if, G–d forbid, the whole space ship doesn't blow up now, it still certainly might be lost—because the children and grandchildren of our modernising generation are untutored in the theory and practice of guidance and control. They have lost their "fix" on the celestial reference points. They know something is wrong, but cannot pinpoint the malfunction and cannot get back on course.

Fortunately, there are some left who have preserved the log-book and who can compute the original Trajectory—who are still in communication with the Immortal Monitor and who tirelessly persevere in their efforts to get the vehicle and its inhabitants back on course. They are few, and the task is staggering—but their enterprise will not, indeed cannot, fail. There is only one true guide to indicate that path—for this generation, for the ones who have preceded us, and for the ones, G–d willing, who will travel after us. It is our basic duty to become familiarised again with this programme.

signal and noise

Not too many people have heard about project "OZMA". This was an attempt by the National Aeronautics and Space Administration to detect the presence of intelligent life on other planets by cosmic communication. A massive radio-telescope, located in West Virginia, was focused towards some predetermined stars, and the operators listened. No one outside the field of cosmic communication is quite sure about what they expected to hear. But we are told that the rationale behind the programme was not as fantastic as it appeared to the layman. If there was intelligent life out there, the argument went, and if their electronic communication apparatus was equal to or better than ours, and if they were as curious about life on earth as we were about life on their planet, they would try to signal us. And it appears that sophisticated electronics people are not inhibited by any language barrier—they communicate by means of numbers. After all, anyone who can build a transmitter would have the same kind of mathematical tools as anyone who could build a receiver. Thus our people listened. They were listening for a signal that was non-random, that was repeated, that had a consistent rhythm or numerical code, and that occurred at specific time periods.

This much is true. The remainder is probably apocryphal, but the story persists. It has been told that only a few months after project "OZMA" was initiated, the operators became very excited. Everything they were listening for was present. At very specific times of the day a faint signal was heard. The signal was quite unintelligible—at least it bore no resemblance to any language or code in the lexicon of the listeners, but it was there. It wasn't ordinary random static or noise, it was repeated with some minor variation at different periods, and it had a definite but somewhat unearthly beat.

Fortunately, before announcing this great discovery to the world, the scientists checked and rechecked their data. They then found that because of a slight aberration in the radio-telescope's focus, they were not communicating with outer space at all, but were picking up a strong signal from a rock-and-roll radio station in Kentucky.

The story has a meaning to those in the Jewish community who are also concerned with a type of cosmic communication. We are also listening intently for some type of signal, and we experience all kinds of frustration and difficulty with our electronics:

—There are those who have the wireless turned off completely and deny that there is any sound at all.

—There are those who are sincerely turned on, but will listen only to what they want to hear and refuse to switch channels.

—There are those whose signal is confused by static or electronic noise, and thus can never gain the full appreciation of the signal itself.

—There are those whose signal is completely drowned out by noise, and they are frustrated because their ears tell them that they are not listening to anything meaningful.

—There are those who have heard only static all their lives and assume that what they hear is a signal. They are quite adamant in refusing when someone wants to help them readjust the set, since they are quite happy with the noise.

—And, fortunately, there are those who by tradition know what to listen for, and by training know how to adjust the set. They can filter out the noise and receive pure signals.

Some people fall into the latter fortunate category by nature. Most of the rest of us have to learn. To learn the difference between signal and noise, and to learn how to tune in properly.

stratospheric samples

Perhaps the most challenging and certainly the most interesting research project I ever worked on dealt with the search for viable microbes in the stratosphere. We had to build large volume air samplers that had never been designed before. We had to sterilise them and learn to handle them aseptically in order to avoid accidental contamination. We had to fly them by huge, unmanned, radio-controlled balloons into the stratosphere, twenty miles high. And we had to learn how to analyse the returned samples with scrupulous care.

The technical, microbiological, and logistic complexities were fantastic. So was the cost. Each flight involved the expenditure of nearly $10,000, and only a small number of the total launchings were recovered without mishap. Little wonder that everyone associated with the project soon started calling the returned samples "precious". They were precious in cost, precious in effort, and precious with respect to the hope we placed in them.

The precious samples were only a few micrograms of dust that had been collected from the stratosphere. Our job was to culture this dust and determine whether it contained any viable microbes. And for this, we had a lot of good advice.

One consultant advised us to use one type of nutrient solution. Another consultant suggested another. One consultant recommended a low temperature of incubation; but another consultant held out for a higher temperature. The advice was all honest. It was good. It was certainly well meant. But the awesome responsibility for making the final decision was our own. And we were concerned for our precious samples not only because of the time and money spent in obtaining them—but, above all, because there was so little sample to work with, only one choice of assay procedure could be used.

Under normal circumstances, when microbiologists are in doubt, they will use a variety of alternative procedures: several nutrients, several temperatures, several assay techniques. But these were truly precious samples. Once committed, there were no others. Once a mistake was made, it was irrevocable.

Consequently, we took a very orthodox approach. On my bookstand near my desk there are a series of volumes with very prosaic titles: *Standard Methods for the Analysis of Water*, *Standard Methods for the Analysis of Dairy Products*, *Standard Methods for the Analysis of Jet Fuels*, and even *Standard Methods for the Microbiological Examination of Spacecraft Hardware*. We chose the *Standard Methods for Microbiological Examination of Soils*. We had no absolute guarantee that they would work. But at the very least, they had worked so well in the past. They had stood the tests of time and experience. And they were based on the accumulated knowledge and insights of every authority who had devoted his professional life to the solution of problems such as ours. . . .

My wife and I think of our children as precious samples. We want to educate them according to *Torah* guidelines, the standard methods for our people. The *Torah* might not be flamboyant or dramatic, but it has withstood the tests of time and experience. *Torah* education is based on the accumulated knowledge and insights of every scholar who has devoted his life to its study. We know that the advice given by some educators is honest. It is certainly well meant. But one wants to experiment this way, and the other, that way. Our precious samples are too few for experimentation. Once committed there is no back-tracking. Once a mistake is made, G–d forbid, the result might be irrevocable. There is no absolute guarantee that the standard methods will work. But the accumulated experience of several thousand years suggests that there is no other way.

the defective instrument

We have a beautiful and expensive new instrument in our laboratory, beautiful because of its complexity and its potential. With equipment like this we can probe even deeper into nature's secrets and perform experiments which might hopefully unlock a puzzle of health and disease. Expensive because of its versatility, this device can help one scientist do the work previously performed by three and can probably do it better.

Quite understandably, anything as beautiful and expensive and as new is treated with a certain amount of deference.

Thus my laboratory technician approached the device one morning not long ago. She had carefully planned the experiment to take full advantage of the instrument's versatility. One might say she had prepared herself mentally for this encounter. Her heart was really in it. And she had also prepared herself physically. Most of the previous day had been spent reading the instruction manual. She knew which knobs to pull, which buttons to push, which dials to twist, and which switches to flick.

But the instrument didn't work.

In cases like this, we call the electronics engineer. He knows all there is to know about devices like these—or at least we pay him to know. The circuitry is his hobby; the complexity is his relaxation. So he pushed the knobs and reset the buttons and did everything a highly trained engineer should do.

But the instrument still didn't work.

It should be noted that this instrument, which cost tens of thousands of dollars, was equipped with a twenty-eight cent plug. And if it wasn't plugged in, it just didn't work. Regardless of the technician's preparation and intention and desire and plan, regardless of the engineer's knowledge and experience and salary, if the instrument is not properly plugged in, the experiment could not start.

A Jew must also be "plugged in" before he can start functioning. Regardless of his complexity and sophistication, regardless of his wealth and learning and occupation and involvement, he must take the first step and connect himself to the Power Supply with the inexpensive plug—his *Tefillin*. He might approach his day with the best intentions, the most careful plans, and even the most sincere preparations—he is not "operational" until he has dedicated his heart, mind and hand to his Creator—according to the instruction manual the Creator provided. It doesn't really matter if he is a brilliant *Tzaddik* or scholar (or engineer) who understands all of the laws about *Tefillin* and plugging in. Similarly, it doesn't matter if he is the youngest, freshest, *Barmitzvah* boy who was honoured with his first *Aliyah* yesterday and is only beginning to read the instruction manual. Both are obligated to fulfil the same *mitzvah*, to perform the same physical act of putting on the *Tefillin*.

In my laboratory, all of the scientific talent, all of the theory, all of the most expensive equipment waited that morning until the twenty-eight cent plug was connected. In our community all of the Jewish commitment, dedication, and philosophy, all of the nice synagogues, the generous donations and the most thought-provoking sermons—nothing proceeds until the *Tefillin* have been put on. When the plug is connected, the power flows, and the "experiment" can start. The instrument is operational.

let's learn some Chassidus

"Let us make a small room, and put therein a bed, and a table, and a chair, and a lamp; and when he comes to us, he shall turn aside there." (*2 Kings 4:10*)

The word "he" refers to an earlier verse: "For a man of G–d, who is holy, passes by us always." The literal reference is to Elisha the Prophet, but the verse can be understood in a more universal sense.

"A man of G–d . . . holy" is the spirit of purity that each of us possesses. It "passes by us always"—this spirit of purity flows to us constantly, as we find: "Whether man or woman . . . according to each person's deeds, does the holy spirit repose on him."

Deborah earned the spirit of prophecy because of the wicks she made for the Sanctuary. The *menorah* there was not meant to provide light for the Sanctuary; the *menorah* light symbolised the light of *Torah* brightening the world through Israel. Deborah made wicks for the *menorah*, thus meriting prophecy for herself and her husband, Lapidos, otherwise a quite ordinary person.

The phrase *"ish Elokim"* describes the nature of the G–dly. *"Ish"* signifies strength of feeling, mastery; while the word *"Elokim"* has the numerical equivalent of the word *"teva"*, nature. *Ish Elokim* is "master of nature"—the one who overcomes nature, and changes it. *"Kodosh"* describes separation, distance, apartness. Since this spirit that constantly "passes by us" is *kodosh*, apart from us, therefore "let us make a small

239

chamber" so that it may settle within us, and enlighten all our worldly affairs.

Let us understand this in terms of *avodah*. The *Zohar* discusses the four articles of this verse at considerable length. Briefly this is the author's point: The furnishings of the chamber of the "man of G–d" are his worship. Each item symbolises a different part of our prayers. "Bed" refers to the evening prayer, *Maariv*; "table" signifies the introductory Psalms in the morning service, *pesukei dezimro*, and the blessings of *Shema*; "chair" is *Shema* proper; "lamp", or *menorah*, is *Shmona Esrei*.

We may wonder, since there are three daily prayers, why *Mincha* is omitted, especially since it is described by the Sages as the paramount prayer. However, the very quality of *Mincha* makes it the climax of the day's prayers, and the four elements of worship symbolised in the four articles of "furniture" are all preparation for *Mincha*.

At the very beginning of the *Torah* we find: "It was evening, and it was morning, one day—*yom echod*." "*Echod*" is the ultimate purpose and goal of serving G–d; that is, that throughout the world (in the four directions and up to the "highest" spiritual stage) there be an awareness of G–d. This is *yom echod*—the revelation of the One. Before this revelation there must be "evening and morning", the light of morning following the service of evening. This means that the beginning of worship, or service, is the evening, *Maariv* in general and particularly the bedtime *Shema*, the last words and thoughts before sleep.

the meaning of the bedtime Shema

Let us understand the meaning of the bedtime *Shema*. It is the occasion for an honest evaluation of the day—what should have been and what actually was. It should have happened that—immediately upon waking—the Jew begins to serve G–d, whether by reciting *Tehillim* or studying *Torah*, according to one's capacities. Then one worships *betzibur*, with a congregation, with all the attendant *mitzvos* and spirit denied one who worships in isolation. Then he conducts his business by *Torah* standards, shunning the faintest deceit, treating others with kindness—all this is what "should have been".

But what actually was? A man may have started his day by attending to his personal affairs; he may have failed to take part in community worship; his prayers themselves have been so hurried that he did not even hear what he was uttering, while his heart was far away in his busy-ness and mundane thoughts. Then, all day he concentrated his mind only on his selfish interests and physical matters. He did not give a thought to the next man's welfare—or for that matter, to his own spiritual welfare.

At night, when assessing the day, the "necessities" of the day have lost their urgency; his schemes were of little help and often hurt him. He realises that he could well have worshipped the required three times with a *minyan*, and he could have designated periods for *Torah* study. He would not have depleted his strength and ruined his health, and besides, through his study and worship he would have fulfilled his purpose in being.

Our Sages tell us that the ultimate purpose in Creation is man, and the ultimate of man is *mitzvos*. In fact, they declare that G–d made a condition with Creation—"If Israel accepts *Torah*, well and good; if not, I will return you to chaos." It is noteworthy that this pact is fulfilled with the individual and with society—when *Torah* is neglected, chaos reigns.

Man must meditate seriously on this. Regardless of what he does, "the counsel of G–d remains". At bedtime *Shema* he resolves firmly: Enough! He will not permit trivia to confuse him any more. He will resolve to "accept the yoke of heaven" in actual practice. For example, he will attend public worship in *shul* morning and evening, where he will worship unhurriedly, so that he will hear what his lips pronounce before the Master of all. He will also establish periods for *Torah* study, that he may know the "deeds they shall perform" in fulfilling the *mitzvos* as they should be—and in even greater measure. He will "excel himself before Him with *mitzvos*"—even beyond his means.

Thus will he create a vessel to receive G–d's blessing, confident that G–d will provide him with adequate sustenance. This, then, is the service of bedtime *Shema*. An analysis of all that occurred during the day, and a determination for the future, both to "turn from evil and to do good". His sleep will be a pleasant one, for then the soul ascends to reap life. When he awakens he will be alert, stimulated to declare with enthusiasm, *modeh ani*, gratefully acknowledging G–d's graciousness in returning his soul refreshed.

the meaning of the morning prayers

When man reflects on this earnestly, he will recognise G–d's kindness in "returning the soul to lifeless bodies", for his own soul has just been returned to him after sleep, which is a foretaste of death; and it has been returned invigorated. Therefore, man's first duty is to serve G–d, whether with the obedience of children to parents, or of servants to their master.

Both relationships are noted in *Torah*: "My son, my first-born, is Israel" and "You are children of G–d." These statements indicate (G–d's) profound affection for the children of Israel, for they were informed that they are the children of G–d. On the other hand, the *Torah* declares: "For to Me are Israel servants, they are My servants." For this reason G–d is called both "Our Father" and "Our King".

Thus stimulated he can recite the Morning Blessings and prepare himself for worship. "One enters into prayer only with earnest feeling"; with the humility that comes from recognition of "Know before Whom you stand" in prayer.

The opening passage of the morning worship is *Hodu*, simultaneously praise and thanksgiving. This acknowledgement is not the same as *modeh ani* recited immediately upon waking. *Modeh ani* is general. It can be compared to one who sees a thing he does not understand, but is aware of its existence, which he readily acknowledges. Man realises that his soul was returned to him, that he is alive again, so he gratefully declares *modeh ani*: "I give thanks to you, eternal King, for mercifully returning my soul. You are indeed faithful!"

Hodu, on the other hand, expresses both thanks and praise, because he has already given at least some attention to G–d's bounty. In the prayers that follow, *Boruch sheomar* and the Psalms, which speak of G–d's greatness and works, he attains a broader and deeper comprehension of the spark of G–d that gives life to all His creatures. This comprehension is such that mortal intellect, the intellect of the animal soul, can grasp it perfectly well. Let us explain.

The animal soul is primarily feeling; emotion, rather than intellect. Its desire is for material things; it wallows in them as a matter of course, and is habituated to physical interests exclusively. It is utterly bound up with worldly concerns. The introductory Psalms serve to chop away this "undergrowth", setting aside one's undesirable elements, and elevating the soul from the morass engulfing it. Similarly, by way of another analogy, a chunk of wood can be shaped into a vessel by chiselling and shaping the outside—external improvement—and by carving the receptacle from the inside—internal development.

The Psalms serve this function. Through spirited worship and enthusiasm, the animal soul is stirred and diverted from evil, at least momentarily. Then there appears a tendency, an inclination to the good, namely the general recognition that G–dliness is good. This is a striking change, because, as we have noted, the natural attitude is that physical gratification is good. Now even the animal soul recognises that G–dliness, spiritual achievement, is good.

the table—transforming the animal soul

The animal soul, as the words indicate, is basically that of the "animal"— undisciplined, subject to natural inclinations, primarily emotional. Still, it does possess a precious quality, for it is prone to be aroused and excited, and this tendency is of great value. We know that some people are stolid, phlegmatic, unexcitable, cold. This is not the result of their intellect. True, in general, the difference between emotion and intellect is that intellect is patient, settled, while emotion is excitement, heartiness.

But patience and calm are not the same as coldness. Coldness, indifference, are not the products of the intellect, but characteristics of an individual's personality. In fact, they are generally a reflection of arrogance and self-adoration. Other people are by nature easily aroused, hotheads who act impulsively, with intense feelings. They frequently perform beyond their ordinary capacities, drawing on apparently untapped powers. Fortunately, they are more apt to be aroused benevolently than not. Indeed, when such a person acts improperly he is remorseful, while if he goes to inordinate trouble or expense to help someone else, he is not troubled by regrets. He might even derive pleasure from such actions, and perhaps he might never have acted, but for the heat of the moment.

When these emotional types study, they are impressionable in a favourable manner. This is especially so if they find themselves in *Torah* surroundings and scholarly company. These conditions help to promote admirable character traits. All this is the result of the tendency to excitability, arousal. The animal soul, as we have noted, possesses this trait.

The introductory Psalms, *pesukei dezimro* and then the blessings of *Shema*, when said with deep meditation on the words and subjects, make a deep impression on the animal soul. Its devotion to physical pleasure is weakened and the soul itself is moved, altered. It is on the way to becoming a vessel for G–dliness. The function of this part of worship is a "carving out" of the animal soul, shaping it into a vessel on the outside and on the inside. The "outside" is improved by rejection of evil, and the "inside" by preparing it to receive G–dliness, an awareness of G–d. The image of the animal soul becomes different. What exactly is this transformation?

The animal soul is desire; an urge and its desires are intense. The *yetzer hara* comes from this lustfulness. The soul expresses itself through its intense desires, channelling these desires into evil imaginings, bodily lusts, despicable character traits. However, the power of desiring is not evil in itself. As the evil image—and imagination—of the animal soul are destroyed, the power of desire is channelled into desirable directions, into an urge to spiritual satisfactions, to worshipping properly, to *Torah* study.

This re-direction of desires, this profound reshaping of the animal soul (not by crushing it, but by controlling it) depends on the person's "table" (his ability to discipline himself in his physical, bodily affairs, so that they conform with *Torah*). The parallels for the "table" in prayer are the introductory Psalms and the blessings of *Shema*.

the chair—Shema Yisroel—the G-dly soul

The "chair" of the "small room", as the *Zohar* explains, refers to *Shema*, which is said seated. "Hear O Israel"—the Jew recognises that "*Hashem* our G-d, *Hashem* is One." The word "Israel" refers to the G-dly soul which is a "part of G-d above" (as distinct from the animal soul). This soul descends into the physical world and physical body, all for the sake of eventual ascent. How does it deserve to ascend? The G-dly soul here below serves G-d through studying *Torah*, fulfilling *mitzvos* by actual performance and through conduct which accords to *Torah* ideals. In this manner man's worldly affairs are purified; they become vessels for G-dliness. How does the soul acquire this ability to transform the material world?

The *Talmud* tells us that before the soul descends into the body it is besworn to "be righteous". This "oath" endows the soul with the ability to "purify" physical beings and worldly matters (by using them for a purpose higher than the physical—parchment for *Tefillin*, wool for *Tzitzis*, money for charity, etc.). The G-dly intelligence (the spiritual perspective, attitude and scale of values) becomes comprehensible, intelligible to the mortal intelligence. The intellect of the G-dly soul calls forth and develops the emotions—the heart feels what the mind comprehends.

Service of G-d must conform with the edicts and spirit of *Torah*, G-d's purpose in Creation. In *Koheles* 7 we learn: "But see only this that I found, that G-d made man straight, and they seek out many reckonings." "Man" refers to the G-dly soul, for the animal soul, needless to say, is called animal. "Straight" ("*yashar*", the first Hebrew letters of *Yisroel*), the fundamental state of the G-dly soul, is made evident when man fulfils the verse: "To do the *yashar* in the eyes of G-d" through *Torah* and *mitzvos*.

However, *Koheles* observes: "They seek out many reckonings." "They" is plural, and cannot refer to the G–dly soul alone. Here he speaks of the G–dly soul in its descent into the body, and the animal soul. They seek out many reckonings—instead of unity, concentration, the soul is scattered, dispersed, flitting among the distracting thoughts that confuse and divert him from serving G–d, straying because of the sort of speech and deeds that "are not G–d's".

For this we recite *Shema*, a word that has meanings beyond "hear". "*Shema*" also means "gather together" and "assemble". Man is called upon to *Shema*—bring together—his thoughts and words and deeds, to make them *yashar*. How? Through meditation on "*Hashem Elokainu*", the source of Creation, and on the fact that even this physical world is not separate from or independent of Him, that nature and its ways stem from Him.

What is the meaning of "*Hashem* is One"? The prophet declares: "I, *Hashem*, have not changed." Creation did not affect Him (as an activity involves and affects the person performing it). *Hashem* is the same, before, during and after Creation, since all of Creation comes from a mere radiance of *Hashem*, not his essence.

The effects of *Shema* would be, then, that man would create the proper vessel that his mortal intellect (which would ordinarily prefer physical good) should accept and submit to the Divine intellect (the realisation that spiritual good is the superior), that G–d's understanding should permeate all his affairs to the point that everything he does will conform with G–d's intelligence.

the Menorah—Shmona Esrei

The *menorah*, as the *Zohar* explains, refers to *Shmona Esrei*, the climax of the service. Note that the *Shmona Esrei* is recited standing, while *Shema* is said seated—respectively they are the "*Amidah*" and the "Seated Prayer". What is the difference?

Shema is meditation on G–d with intellectual comprehension, understanding, for "hearing" implies understanding. In *Shema* the worshipper perceives and understands the greatness and exaltedness of the Infinite. This realisation arouses in his heart an intense feeling of reverence or love, but the feeling is conscious. *Shmona Esrei*, though, is said standing humbly and silently. It is symbolic of complete loss of self, utter nullification, total lack of awareness of self.

We find in Kings 1:19: "After the fire there was a silent voice," Fire is the flames of longing awakened in *Shema*, the aroused love in the stormy, excited heart. The worshipper still "exists", he is conscious of his self, aware of his own being, he desires to satisfy his longing—therefore the excitation. A burning log will crackle noisily in the flames, and is silent only after the wood is consumed—and then the coals have the most intense heat. The blazing yearning of *Shema* testifies that his "being" is not completely lost, he still "exists" as a separate individual being, so his love is consciously excited.

Shmona Esrei, in contrast, is the silent voice, the inaudible prayer, the utter loss of self experienced in the presence of the King. *Menorah* is *Shmona Esrei*. The *Chumash* uses the expression *"maasai hamenorah"*, "making the menorah". Through action, deed, performance of good, one attains the status of *menorah*. This means that only through actual practice of good, with a sense of submission to G-d's "yoke", can one rise to the very highest state. Let us examine the verse about *menorah* a bit more.

"This is the making of the *menorah*: hammered gold, including its stem and its decoration it is hammered." Rabbi Shneur Zalman, founder of *Chabad*, explained: "Whoever wishes to abandon evil, to make himself a *menorah*, must follow this order. 'Hammered'—the unshaped lump is struck with the hammer until the parts are spread. Through the hammering, the top gold goes to the bottom and the bottom gold rises to the top. It is all fused. The earlier shape is lost. So must man do with himself. He must break his traits of character so that they lose their initial form. So our Rabbis teach us: 'Nullify your will before His will.'"

The *menorah* is made from a mass of gold. This formless mass parallels the "raw material" of man's character. Basically the individual might tend towards arrogance and complacency, or to the opposite extreme, dejection and melancholy caused by material concerns. In either case, just as the gold must be moulded into a *menorah* through abolishing and nullifying its previous state, so, too, in terms of human character, one must completely rework his usual traits to conform fully with G-d's will. This is effected through *Mincha*—the afternoon prayer.

Mincha—the unique prayer—the unique time

Mincha has a unique quality unshared by either *Shacharis* or *Maariv*. *Shacharis* is the morning prayer, offered before becoming involved with workaday affairs. This is no spectacular phenomenon. Indeed, how could it be different! A Jew awakes, and of course, the first thing to do is to go to *shul* and *daven* with a *minyan*. *Maariv* comes at the end of the day, when work is over. At the same time, worshipping is not remarkable either. It is only to be expected of every Jew.

But *Mincha*! Here we have something striking. It is in the heart of the day's work, in the middle of the rush of business, while a man is immersed in his occupation. But he stops his work—to pray. This is true service. This is the quality of *Mincha* that marks it off; both the daily *Mincha* worship, and the symbolic *Mincha* as well.

For, the three daily services have parallels in the lifetime of the Jew. *Shacharis*, morning worship, represents childhood and youth; the period of schooldays; "exile to a place of *Torah*"; diligent, undistracted study. This is unremarkable. It is the personal obligation of every Jew to instruct his son in *Torah* and, for that matter, to study *Torah* himself. *Maariv*, the evening worship, stands for the declining and advanced years, when there is leisure for study and observance. Again this is an expected, a normal, occurrence. However, *Mincha* is the prime of life; the active years of intense involvement in worldly concerns; the pursuit of a career; the responsibilities of rearing a family. To discipline and control oneself under these trying circumstances, to adhere to *Torah* under the pressure of these obligations—this is truly serving G–d.

We can now understand that the furniture of the small room—bed, chair, table and lamp—comprising *Shacharis* and *Maariv*, are a preparation and introduction to *Mincha*. Meditation during bedtime *Shema*, proper devotion during the developing stages of the morning worship—these help the worshipper to attain the heights of *Mincha*, through comprehension, fully realised. His human intellect will assent eagerly that he should conduct himself according to *Torah* ideals and direction, both in his daily *Mincha* and in his lifetime *Mincha*. For the *Zohar* declares that *asiya le'ela*, through action and deeds, one attains heights far superior to those that can be achieved purely through intellect and comprehension.

"Let us make a small room, and put therein a bed, a table, a chair, and a *menorah*. . . ." The spirit of purity all Israel possesses must "settle" within the Jew and reveal itself in him. This is brought about through these four elements. "Let us make . . .", for action is supreme. Serving G–d through action, in *ahavas Yisroel* generally and through hospitality in particular—as this entails bodily effort and trouble—brings one to the most exalted levels of worship in all the four phases comprising the prayers. Thus man fulfils G–d's purpose in Creation, to make this world a "dwelling place" for Him, a purified vessel fit to accept His bounteous blessings for children, health and prosperity.

encounters

Chassidus *particularly involves the
totality of Jewish life. Mind and heart,
time and place, young and old, sacred
and secular, men and women, action and
worship, music and art, story and
scholarship—whatever touches upon any
part of any Jew's life can be enriched
with the elixir of* Chassidus, *the
warmth and enthusiasm of* Chassidism.

Herman Wouk at "An evening with Lubavitch", Philadelphia, May 1968

"pictures" *by Herman Wouk*

Transcript of a talk delivered by Herman Wouk at "An Evening with Lubavitch" in Philadelphia, U.S.A., on Sunday, May 19, 1968.

Many of my contemporaries can write easily and eloquently on many subjects. I have a few ideas on a few subjects; and it takes me 500 pages and a couple of years to say what I think about one topic. I must therefore simply chat with you heart to heart, without manuscript or notes.

I will explain what a *Misnagid* is doing at a *Chassidic* gathering, with three pictures.

My wife and I went to the Soviet Union in the summer of 1966. We travelled for a month, and everywhere we went to synagogues and looked for Jews. I will not here tell the tale of Soviet Jewry, which needs another evening or another book.

It was time for *Mincha* on *Shabbos*, in the synagogue in Leningrad, a big, old structure, falling to ruins. As I came there, a busload of American tourists descended outside. One of them took a picture of this wreck of a synagogue, which still has a ruined nobility. He said: "All this will be dead in five years." They climbed back into the bus and drove on.

I went in, and found the usual Soviet *shul* Jews—old, bent, fading Jews, speaking a curiously familiar *Yiddish* (because I'm a Russian Jew and all I know is the *Yiddish* of Minsk), *davening* as I don't hear *davening* any more, no matter where I go. I grew up in the Minsker *shul* in the Bronx.

That's the way they *daven* in the Soviet Union—the old Jews who still *daven*.

In the Leningrad synagogue there was also one young man, good looking, alert, with a trimmed black beard, a Western suit, and a general air of determination and competence. Struck by this apparition in a Soviet *shul*, I went up to him afterwards and said, in effect, "Explain yourself."

He said: "I am a Lubavitcher *Chassid*."

"Are there many like you here?"

"There are others like me."

"Is it hard?"

"It's very hard. I live in Riga. I have three children. I am bringing them up in every respect the way I live. They learn, they know, and they will follow in my path." Then he added: "I know you're going to America. Some day you are bound to encounter the Lubavitcher Rebbe. Tell him that you saw me, that I am well, that my children are well, and that they learn." He told me his name.

In Leningrad, in the summer, it never gets dark at night. So *Shabbos* is really never over. Their custom is to *daven Mincha* and *Maariv* at ten-thirty. By the time I got back to the hotel I had forgotten that man's name. I am giving the Rebbe his message now. The Rebbe surely knows who he is. He is alive and well, his children are growing up as *Chassidim* and he sends the Rebbe his love.

That is my first picture.

My grandfather died in Israel and is buried there. He was a Lubavitcher *Chassid*. I did not visit him the year before he died, but my mother and her sister did. My aunt wanted some pictures of my grandfather. She went into *shul* with him and took colour movies as he put on his *Tefillin*.

He died. When my aunt came back to this country she showed her film, and there was my grandfather in the *shul*, in the morning light of Tel Aviv. It was a very crude piece of photography. My aunt is no expert. It was sheer luck that it came out at all. She just held the camera straight and pointed it at my grandfather. That picture ran for maybe a minute and a half. It had the deepest beauty of any film I have ever seen.

There was a very strong side light. The colours came out rich. My grandfather was a living Rembrandt. There was a light from without and there was a light from within. There was grace in his tying of the *Tefillin* straps, gestures he had been performing for more than eighty years. These few moves were soaked with meaning, with the dignity of the ancient people to which he belonged, with the mystery and the power of this symbol.

That is the second picture.

We had a wonderful *Seder* at my house last year. The nephews all came. Forgive me for boasting, but they included one from Harvard, a Phi Beta Kappa, now studying at the University of Pennsylvania; one from Harvard Medical School; one from Johns Hopkins Medical School; one from Wesleyan University, a licensed aeroplane pilot who speaks a much better Hebrew than I do. They all came. The whole family was there. The *Seder* went on for hours. It tumbled out of the dining room into the living room. We sang and we started to dance.

Now, my two boys are *Misnagdim*. They can learn, they go to *shul*, and they have cool, critical intelligences. *Hislahavus* comes hard to them. So we sang and danced and they watched. At last my younger son began to dance. Then my older son, who is a very cool cat indeed, began to dance too.

My mother, descended from a Lubavitcher family, said, "Look at the *Chassidim*."

My father, a *Misnagid*, was a dancer. But dancing is inherent to *Chassidim*. It is not a form of art, but of worship. "All my bones shall speak the L—rd." When a *Chassid* can no longer express himself in any other way, he uses his body to praise G—d. I think that was what my boys were doing at the *Seder*, with the rest of us.

That is my third picture.

I am not at all sure about anything that relates to Judaism, except that I love my people Israel and I want it to survive. The rest is opinion and guess. My ideas keep changing. But two seem central and stable—that the Land of Israel is the beating heart of Jewry, and that without the Law of Moses we cannot long survive in history.

A movement that brings to a Jew courage of conviction, courage that reaches to the risk of one's life, is a good movement.

A movement which illuminates the beauty of our faith is a good movement. I remember that when my grandfather sat over the *Talmud* with me, and he would explain a difficult commentary of *Tosephos*, his eyes would light up. "Isn't that beautiful? Do you understand, do you see how it fits, what it means?" And I would wearily say "Yes", hoping that the half-hour would be over and he would let me go.

But now I am saying that to my boys. "Don't you see how beautiful this is—what *Rashi* said, what *Tosephos* says, what the disagreement is, what the agreement is; how this ties in to the whole structure of the argument?" And they look at me and say, "No, we don't see it." And I say, "Good. That's what I said when I was your age, and you hold out until I make you see it. Because the beauty is there."

A movement that gives us the dance, that is able to dance in praise of G–d after all our weary history and all our tragic circumstances—and in back of all our prosperity we live in tragedy, distant or close—a movement that can restore the dance to us as a mode of worship is a good movement.

You hear the challenge so often: What relevance does Judaism have to Now? Now is the race riots. Now is the international situation. Now is the Vietnam war. Now is the new Broadway plays. Now is the black humour. Now is mini-skirts. Now is the election. Now is the sense of unease that pervades the United States. Now is the nuclear bomb.

But there is one very rigid limitation on Now. It very, very quickly tends to become Then. The concerns of the moment change so fast. My hair is going from dark to grey. I have lived through many Nows. I have lived through Nows more frightening than the Now we are in. I lived in a Now when the American system seemed on the verge of economic and political collapse. I lived through a Now when it seemed possible that this globe would be ruled by military devils in a thousand-year bloody Byzantium in which Jews would cease to be even a memory.

But through all these Nows there were things that did not change. Out of the things that do not change, I suggest, comes the strength to meet and endure the Nows; comes the faith that bears up the spirit; comes the dedication to long good in Man and long good in History. The support of the Now with the Eternal, is what religion offers and what *Chassidim* teach in their special way.

I have a relative in Washington who does not have long to live, a distinguished radiologist, a patron of the arts. He loves to talk *Yiddish*. He's a *Modzitzer*. He told me that he went back home to Russia fifteen or twenty years ago and he went to the *Baal Shem Tov*'s grave. There he saw two words engraved—*Ohev Yisroel*—a lover of Israel. If that was his message, then I am a follower of the *Baal Shem Tov*. And there is no *Misnagid* in this room who is not in that sense a follower of the *Baal Shem Tov*. To those who walk his ways, and teach his *Torah* as he taught it, the *Chassidim*, and pre-eminently the *Chassidim* of Lubavitch, we owe thanks and love.

HERMAN WOUK

2230 S STREET, N.W.

WASHINGTON, D. C. 20008

ב״ה

September 20, 1967

My maternal grandfather, Rabbi Mendel
Leib Levine, was a Lubavitcher who
studied at the Volozin Yeshiva, in
the Chabad tradition of knowledge
joined with piety. My father, an
active, religious, informed man of
business and charity, was a Mitnagid.
From my grandfather I caught an enthusiasm for learning, and a simple
unashamed love of our faith.

These have been traits of Jewry since
classic times. In the era of the
Enlightenment, it has taken special
dedication to hold to them. Chabad
can inspire that dedication. Therefore
I honor the movement.

Yours sincerely,

Herman Wouk

HW:mhd

the power of Chabad *by Bella Rosen*

I remember how fascinated I was as a child to read the letters my father received concerning the late Lubavitcher Rebbe, Rabbi Joseph Isaac Schneersohn.

Among them was a pamphlet published in England in 1929. It was an appeal for funds to enable the Rebbe to carry on his work for Russian Jewry from Warsaw, where he had moved after his release from prison in Russia, and his banishment.

The pamphlet described the Rebbe and the work he had been doing, and contained a résumé of the aims and ideals of *Chabad*, some impressions of the Rebbe's recent visit to America, and press reports testifying to the remarkable impression he had made upon American Jewry.

I recall Rabbi Yitzchok, the *Masmid*, a personal emissary of the Rebbe— who was by this time in Paris—coming to my parents' home in Cardiff, where an appeal was made for funds for the movement. I remember, too, how I listened spellbound to stories of the stirring heroism of the Russian Jews of that period, and the courage and fearlessness of the Rebbe himself.

Years later, when I married my late husband, who was then a Rabbi in Manchester, I became acquainted with other Lubavitch *Chassidim*. Among the many people, old and young, who came to our home were two elderly Lubavitch *Chassidim*, Rabbi Nemtzov and Mr Gadian, who visited us regularly.

Although they had left Russia many years before, they enjoyed telling my husband the countless stories they remembered from their youth there, and they found in him a ready and attentive listener, eager to hear all they had to relate.

It was many years later that I came to know Rabbi Szemtov. My husband had made his acquaintance shortly after his arrival in England as the Rebbe's emissary and was very drawn to him, both personally and because of my husband's keen interest in the Lubavitch movement.

My husband came from *Chassidic* stock. His father was named after the Radomsker Rebbe, but he had been educated by Lithuanian Rabbis and the influences that moulded him were connected with his years of study at the Etz Chaim Yeshivah in London and the Mir Yeshivah in Poland.

His teachers throughout his youth and early manhood had been products of the *Mussar* movement, a great ethical movement which had a profound influence on the *yeshivos*, and had much that was very commendable in it.

But, as he grew older, my husband felt that although there was much to be admired in the *Mussar* movement, it tended to produce a negative attitude to life. All the introspection and concern for the betterment of one's character, although laudable, had the effect on many people of making them gloomy or self-centred.

He felt that a counterbalance was required, and he found it in *Chassidism*, particularly in its intellectual branch—*Chabad*. This movement concerned itself with the ethical and moral training associated with *Mussar*, but

The late Rabbi Dr Kopul Rosen during a visit to Kfar Chabad

tempered it with its concern for other "souls". Its warm humanity and mission of love appealed to my husband's own nature. He became particularly interested in Kfar Chabad, and spent some time there when he visited Israel.

When he became fatally ill in November, 1961 and knew that his time was limited, he called Rabbi Szemtov. Although he was in the North of England at that time, Rabbi Szemtov immediately hurried to him. He discussed his position, both spiritual and physical, with Rabbi Szemtov and told him that he would like to visit the Lubavitcher Rebbe. Arrangements were swiftly made and my husband left for New York, taking with him as his travelling companion an old friend of his Yeshivah Etz Chaim days and now a militant Lubavitch *Chassid*.

The Rebbe talked to my husband on two successive nights. My husband told me that never before had he been so deeply impressed by any other human being. The Rebbe's appearance, his eyes, his clear, penetrating and kindly look, his sharp perception, his leading questions and his intellectual profundity overwhelmed him. At a time when he was approaching his "heavenly Father", my husband felt he was being assisted by a newly found "spiritual father".

In discussing my husband's approach to life, knowing full well his imminent fate, the Rebbe told him that when soldiers go into battle, they do not concern themselves with their personal position, but with the ultimate objective which they wish to achieve. "You, my dear friend," he said, "are a soldier going into battle."

From that moment my husband no more concerned himself with the probable outcome of his illness, but seemed to be injected with a lively optimism which he maintained until the end. He even influenced the stream of visitors who called on him until he was unable to receive any more.

During this period he kept in close contact with the Rebbe by letter and by telephone, and received constant visits from the Lubavitch *Chassidim* in London. They supported and encouraged him through this difficult period, and comforted me and my family at that time and since. The warmth and concern that they bring into human relations is so rare a product of modern living that it becomes doubly precious when we meet it.

Last year I, too, had the great privilege of talking to the Rebbe, and I was able to judge for myself what my husband meant when he tried to convey to me the deep impression the Rebbe had made upon him.

the man from Lubavitch

"Thank you very much", he said.

The man from Lubavitch had asked to see me at my office. He had told me briefly of the movement's work, plans and needs. I had responded with a modest donation. Yet another school, another *yeshivah*, I thought, each important in itself; each deserving support. Another face to see about once a year. And that was that—or so I thought.

Not the man from Lubavitch.

"And what about you?" he said. "Where do you stand? What is your brand of *Yiddishkeit*?"

Where did I stand, indeed? I suppose I considered myself Orthodox, not madly so, but Orthodox. My wife and I were products of traditionally Jewish homes and we kept one ourselves. We believed strongly in G–d, went to synagogue regularly on *Shabbosos* and *Yomim Tovim*, observed *kashrus* and practised and enjoyed religious ritual.

Our children attended religious education classes, did fairly well and liked them. We drew our own lines in what we observed and salved our consciences over what we did not, by at least admitting it was wrong. We did not try to bend the rules.

"We're fairly Orthodox", I told him proudly, little realising just how wrong I was.

"We need your money, of course," the man said, "but we're interested in your *Yiddishkeit* too."

This was a different approach, perhaps a new gimmick. No other *sheliach* had said this to me before. Perhaps they had been afraid to ask.

This friendly, smiling, young man from Lubavitch did not look as though he was afraid of anything.

"There's always room for improvement", he continued. "There's no limit to improvement and a greater attachment to G–d." "Attachment" was a new word; I little realised how often I was to hear it. Not waiting for my comments, he continued: "I'm sure you can find a little time for learning."

"I'm very busy", I countered. "Perhaps some time later. I'm off on holiday to Israel shortly."

"All right, I'll phone you when you get back. Where are you staying in Israel?" I told him, and after a few pleasantries he took his leave.

That evening I mentioned the encounter to my wife and then forgot all about it.

But the man from Lubavitch didn't.

Chabad in Israel wasted no time in contacting me when I arrived there. My family and I visited Kfar Chabad, the Lubavitch village, and we were tremendously impressed with what we saw. Vocational schools, agriculture; boys and girls from all parts of the globe being taught a trade, and *Yiddish-keit* too.

We spoke of the visit to our friends in Israel, and even the non-religious among them praised *Chabad*'s activities in the State. We heard of how they worked to encourage even a spasmodic interest in Judaism. We were impressed and intrigued—the man from Lubavitch had struck again.

We had not long returned to England when the man 'phoned.

Very staccato. "Did you have a good holiday? I'm in your district this evening speaking to a group. Is it all right if I call in for a few minutes afterwards?"

He did.

We spoke of Israel, Kfar Chabad and other things. "Found any time for learning?" he asked. I do not think he expected a reply. He left some literature and went.

Some time went by with just an occasional phone call. Then came an invitation to visit the schools in Stamford Hill and Hampstead. My appetite whetted by the literature and what I had seen in Israel, I accepted.

The buildings weren't particularly impressive, but what they contained was. I met other men from Lubavitch, each modern in outlook, each dedicated to his task.

I found a little time for learning; just a little. "Another small *mitzvah*", the man from Lubavitch urged—and in time that came too.

What was it that made Lubavitch different? I suppose it was that here was a group of observant Jews who, while not compromising their own standards, were tolerant of the shortcomings of their fellow-Jews. To them life consisted of teaching and encouraging a return to *Torah* Judaism. They were—they are—confident of ultimate success—and made me believe in it too.

Some time later, I visited New York and had the privilege of meeting the Rebbe. For me this completed the enchantment. For there, in Brooklyn, is *the* man from Lubavitch. Like his predecessors over the past two centuries, he is deeply concerned for the welfare, the spiritual and material welfare, of his fellow-Jews—all his fellow-Jews, everywhere.

Ooforatzto

There is no Hillel House at Nottingham University. The level of Jewish observance there is pitifully low, although one or two students are occasionally seen in *shul* on *Shabbos*. However, there is a Jewish society and it normally has Friday evening meetings, called *"onegei Shabbat"*, where students meet and talk, drink coffee and talk some more.

The students are bothered about the problem of Jewish identity—what makes them Jews? They observe nothing, so why does their Jewish identity nag at them? The answers come back in various forms from the various groups: Israel, assimilation and, occasionally, someone mentions keeping the *mitzvos*.

Through social contact or some other way, some members of Lubavitch are invited to Nottingham. What is Lubavitch? Canvassing progresses and people otherwise uninterested in any religious Jewish identity think that they will come and look at the oft-talked-of *Chassidim*. Amid a clutter of paper plates and imported *siddurim*, they arrive and are shepherded to a local hotel. (Their guide feels a little anxious at the reaction of the hoteliers to the behatted *Chassidim*.)

All passes off satisfactorily, and only an hour late we set off for the University. *Lechoo nerannenno*, let us sing; *Shabbos* begins, the Rabbis arrive. We eat, we sing, we ask questions and then we are told a story. Then, when everyone sits back satisfied and full of song and food, it comes—the message. *Mitzvos* on the instalment plan. And you can see that *mitzvos* are not a burden—not just to be performed, but also to be enjoyed, to be lived. So this is *Chassidism*. The songs continue, the chatter goes on, and eventually the party breaks up. Lubavitch is not finished—a little chat with one student before walking back to the hotel.

Shul on *Shabbos*. A very disappointing turnout of students. A little despondency begins to grip the organisers. Has the evident enthusiasm of last night waned away with sobriety, hunger and university breakfast? Only seven expected for lunch. A sermon by Rabbi Lew. I feel that a sermon is not the way Lubavitch can teach us effectively. Actually being with the people themselves would be more effective. However, the Nottingham community is roused, and a lively discussion ensues at the small *kiddush* afterwards.

We walk to lunch. There are fourteen; we are in business again. Lubavitch spirit overflows like the wine in the *kiddush* cup, and once more the feeling hits even the least conscious student that *mitzvos* are not merely prohibitions. There seems to be a positive aspect. Some students become aware of *mitzvos* they have never heard of before.

We know that you are not supposed to work on Saturday, but we did not know you could enjoy yourself like this. A little philosophy comes over with the meal. There are two laws, the natural law and G–d's law, and G–d's law is greater than the natural law. What's that? Well if you do not work on *Shabbos* you will not starve—G–d will look after you. Does this hold water? It is the philosophy of faith; it was not made for water to be poured into it. It is destroyed by water. But the *zemiros* start and the question falls away.

Discussion is lively after the meal. Some of us discover that we have a Jewish background and even possibly a Jewish future. What has happened? Students leave; the hard core remain—the Lubavitch members *daven Mincha*—the synagogue service is too late for their *minhag*. A feeling of holier-than-thou appears for a moment. Why is there a difference in their service, say, for grace from the "normal" Anglo-Jewish *minhag*? And then we all go off to *shul* for *Mincha*.

Is the "bride" a little tipsy on vodka as she leaves? No, but full of good-will and happy. *Shabbos* in Nottingham has never been quite like this.

Sobriety returns. The week begins at midnight when the Lubavitcher leave. What are the problems?

Really, we agree with keeping the *mitzvos*; we know we have to perform them. But do we have to wear a long coat and *gartel*; must we regard women as somehow second-class citizens? A woman's voice shall not be heard. If we accept the *mitzvos*, must we also accept the Lubavitch way of life? Is there an alternative Orthodox society, then? Well, there is not really. The synagogues do not seem to offer the complete answer; and yet association with the community is an essential of Jewish life.

The answer seems to be to create the right sort of community by the same method as Lubavitch—by example. Is this why Lubavitch came? Academicians, politicians, artists, free thinkers will eventually be members, probably influential members, of society—and they have been touched somewhere very deep by the enthusiasm of Lubavitch. Thank you for that, especially, and for the food and your trouble and—everything.

a black hat and a beard
by Velvl W. Greene

Different people encounter Lubavitch in different ways and with different degrees of anticipation and preconception. In my case, the preconception was negative and the anticipation even more so.

In the first place, I was busy—extremely busy. During that winter I was responsible for an extremely important and highly classified scientific project. The final deadline was getting uncomfortably close and every minute was precious and committed. Second, I was becoming very difficult to see. Because of the project, I was isolated from the world by many closed doors, any number of secretaries, and even by armed guards. And third, and above all, I had as much interest in meeting this Rabbi as I had in meeting any other charity collector.

I had seen his picture in the local newspaper and had some vague recollection of a black hat and a beard. Some of them will take $3 and go away; others hold out for $5. But he had been remarkably persistent. When he telephoned some weeks before to make "an appointment" no persuasion on my part was enough to reveal the urgency for such a meeting. I thought, at the time, it would be easier (and perhaps less expensive) to give him ten minutes at 4.30 p.m. than to argue on the phone. But now, as the appointment time approached, I was sorry I had given him even ten minutes.

The outer guard buzzed me, and I passed him through. Then the inner guard, then the receptionists, and finally he was in my office. Much too young to be a real Rabbi, I thought, and much too innocent to be a successful *meshulach*. But he accepted an invitation to sit down and in surprisingly excellent English he explained his mission. (There's something about a black hat and a beard that conditions one to *the* accent. But this boy was obviously as American as the flag.) The incongruity threw me completely off balance—thus I listened before I talked.

The Rabbi's request was simple. He didn't want a cheque, and he didn't invite me to give a speech, and he didn't ask me for a job—all three of which situations covered more than 90 per cent of my routine requests. He wanted my name. Apparently the organisation he was representing wanted to have a banquet, and he was looking for "prominent" people in the Jewish Community to lend their names as sponsors. In retrospect, it was not really an unreasonable request. Though I couldn't see why he considered me as "prominent", I figured that he and his colleagues were so "far out" that even second and third echelon members of the community would be useful, as long as they looked and acted normally.

I tried to tell my visitor that he was wasting his time. I pointed out a whole series of reasons why I couldn't lend him my name. Aside from the fact that Lubavitch and *Chassidus* was an anachronism, aside from the fact that his dress and appearance turned me off, aside from the fact that my modern Jewish point of view was quite incompatible with old-country Orthodoxy, as a Zionist I didn't want to have any dealings with those who threw stones. (Don't all black hats and beards live in Mea Shearim and throw stones?)

But he didn't engage in debate with me. Instead, to my everlasting consternation, he looked out of the window at the setting sun, mumbled a "beg your pardon", quickly rose from his seat, tied some kind of cord around his waist, and started to pray. Quietly, but deliberately. Quickly, but with articulation. At the very least I must be given credit for recognising that it was prayer.

I did not quite know what to do. If memory serves, this was the first time I had ever seen anyone *davening Mincha*; certainly the first time anyone *davening Mincha* outside a synagogue, without a prayer book, and without someone to call the pages. Without doubt, the first time anyone had ever *davened* in my laboratory. And, above all, the first time anyone *davened* anything without an obligation to say *Kaddish*.

I don't think I will ever forget the flood of thoughts that swept through me during the few minutes of that winter twilight. On the one hand, I was completely nonplussed. What should I do? Can I smoke? Should I stand up? Could I return to my writing? How long is this going to last? (My major previous experiences with prayer, it must be stated, involved lengthy sermons and/or *Barmitzvah* speeches.) My secretary poked her head in to say good night and has never really recovered. The telephone rang and I didn't know whether I was permitted to answer. What would the guard do with his gun when he came to close the vault?

On the other hand, I was annoyed and righteously indignant. After all, I had given this man a fixed appointment. Now he was using most of it for some type of mediaeval ritual. That's the trouble with religious Jews, I thought. They come to ask a favour and then ignore you. What *Chutzpah*!

But through the emotions of consternation and indignation, I remember being impressed. This young Rabbi, new in town, in need of favours from

people like me, desperately trying to get something started in a community which didn't know him and wanted him less—this young Rabbi felt a higher obligation. Regardless of what he needed from me, his hierarchy of values was such that temporal needs like my name or my cheque or even my approval came second to the prime need: to pray at the time fixed by law.

I liked that. Though I didn't lend my name as a sponsor to his banquet, I liked that. That night I told my wife that a different type of person visited my office: someone who was sincere, someone whose religion meant more than the external trappings. Thus we invited the Rabbi and his wife (a Phi Beta Kappa in mathematics) to our home to meet some of our friends. I wanted to show off someone who was real. Someone who *davened Mincha* in a microbiology laboratory. Someone who could write computer programmes and wear a *shaytl*.

The evening was the first of many. Many days and weeks and months, indeed years, were spent in debate and dialogue. The four of us became friends, even good friends, but it was a friendship of dialogue. I debated and he taught. I quoted history and philosophy. He quoted *Torah*. We tried to point out the error of their ways, but they were more tolerant than we. Ultimately, their tolerance and patience, their humanity and sincerity, their knowledge and concern convinced us that we had something to learn. Nearly a year after our first meeting I visited New York and discovered that our friends were not exceptions but prototypes. Fifteen months after that first meeting, our friend brought me my first set of *Tefillin* and showed me how to put them on. And a year after that his wife helped my wife start a kosher kitchen. And similarly, in a slow and gradual fashion, we were helped with all of the other features of our current life: *Shabbos*, *Taharas Hamishpocho*, keeping my head covered at work, etc. It was all done gradually. Each step was taken hesitatingly.

There are those who say that we were psychologically or spiritually prepared for these transformations long before we ever met our friends from Lubavitch. There are those who say that our original encounter merely was coincidental. That our path to *Torah* Judaism was paved by too many complex influences to isolate a single moment in time and place. This is probably true. But I will never forget a winter afternoon, six years ago, when a young *Chassid* asked for a ten-minute appointment and spent five minutes of the time *davening Mincha*.

encounters with Lubavitch
by Dr J. J. Ross

Lubavitch and I have been crossing paths for almost as long as I can remember. It must have been shortly after my *Barmitzvah* in Johannesburg when I met my first Lubavitch *Chassid*—the genuine article, I mean.

Rabbi Weinberg, an emissary of the Lubavitcher Rebbe, has, I believe, since visited South Africa on several occasions. But I remember the impression he made on me on that first visit of his shortly after the war.

He was a new phenomenon, *Yiddish*-speaking but young and dynamic. We had him at our home for some sort of youth gathering, and I can remember him addressing a meeting where there were several Rabbis who spoke. Rabbi Weinberg seemed to me the most authentic and genuine representative of the Jewish spirit present. His rich repertoire of Jewish sources, especially of stories and *mesholim*, left an exciting and pleasurable after-taste.

I did not meet with Lubavitch again until I visited the Ponevez Yeshivah in Bne Braq. There I established a very close relationship with several young men who had spent a short time at the Lubavitch Yeshivah in Tel Aviv before moving to Ponevez.

Some of these students had kept strong connections with Lubavitch, and all of them retained a nostalgia and warmth for *Chabad Chassidism*. I absorbed from them some of their respect for Lubavitch and I have retained these feelings till the present day.

I encountered Lubavitch once more during my student years in Cambridge. If I recall correctly, I met Rabbi Benzion Szemtov in a train travelling from Letchworth to London. I saw him quite often after that in London, and even spent a *Seder* night at his home.

Through him I got to know some of the Lubavitch *Chassidim* in Stamford Hill and was befriended in particular by a young man whose hospitality I enjoyed on several occasions. It is with genuine regret that I now realise that I have not had the occasion to meet him or his charming Irish-born wife since I have been back in London. During this period I regularly had lessons in *Tanya* with one of the older *Chassidim* and moved closer to identification with *Chabad* than I have ever been, before or subsequently. I have often wondered whether it could be said that an attempt was made to "convert" me to *Chabad*, at this or at any other period.

It would be flattering to my pride to imagine that they thought this worth while, but I do not think that in fact any such effort was ever made. At any rate, by the time I had returned for my second period at the Ponevez Yeshivah, I had more or less allowed any association with Lubavitch to lapse, and felt myself completely at home in the undiluted Lithuanian *yeshivah* spirit.

In the years that have elapsed since then I have moved away only a little from the complete identification with the *yeshivah* spirit which I then uncritically assumed. But I should like to fancy that I can nonetheless appraise what seemed and still seems important, congenial and characteristic of Lubavitch.

Lubavitch has for me always stood for the following three things:

1. While to some extent, especially in the older generation, it continues to give the impression of a distinct tribe or race consisting of a number of closely knit families spread in many countries who have in common their Russian origin and a heritage of *Chabad* teaching, Lubavitch, especially since the Second World War, has become a revivalist movement in Judaism.

In pursuing this aim it has come to grips with the basic circumstance of contemporary Jewish existence, the fact that the Jewish masses have largely become estranged from Jewish tradition. Its revivalist bent has therefore had to direct itself first to a conversion of the masses to Jewish observance and only then to the recruiting of these souls to Lubavitch.

2. One of the primary instruments, however, by means of which the task of converting Jews to Jewish observance has been pursued, is connected with the second aim rather than the first. The feeling has been created of a

world-wide movement, cutting across geographical or institutional barriers. An element of revolutionary excitement is fostered in which people are encouraged to feel that there is a jettisoning of established patterns of communal life which, since the age of emancipation, is undoubtedly based on a certain amount of compromise in favour of an older and more authentic Judaism of the heart and the mind.

This is not to suggest, of course, that Lubavitch in any way necessarily wishes to undermine existing institutions of education and religious life in this or in any other country. On the contrary, it often pursues the policy of taking over such institutions and seeing that they are run by *anshei shlomeinu* in accordance with the right spirit. However, the primary loyalty which is developed is loyalty to the movement, rather than loyalty to institutions or to office-holders.

In this respect Lubavitch seems to me a genuine *Chassidic* movement pursuing a social philosophy that was characteristic of the rise and spread of *Chassidus* in the eighteenth century. My sympathy for Lubavitch at this point stems, however, not so much from any support of *Chassidus*, but rather from a feeling that certain institutions have become so out of touch with communal needs that they have to be supplemented by an additional form of spiritual impetus. I see the *yeshivah* movement, for example, as another revolutionary movement, not as well-organised or monolithic as Lubavitch, but unconsciously changing existing institutionalised patterns and transferring spiritual leadership to *roshei yeshivah*. Of course, the respective ideologies of these two movements do not contain this as a declared aim; but at the level of social life this seems to me to be one of the most important implications of their doctrines.

3. Lubavitch representatives are sincere, dynamic and constructive. There is a feeling of youthfulness, which is supported by the fact that field workers are young and of a decidedly non-clerical character. They inspire confidence by their sincerity, even where audiences are not ready to accept what they have to say. They are outward-looking and refuse to restrict their activities to the religiously observant inner circles of the community.

Unlike many young men associated with the *yeshivah* movement, they are not hampered by an ideology which encourages them to concentrate their efforts on their own self-improvement or on the aggrandisement of the status of limited groups of *bnei Torah*.

Of course, this plank in the *yeshivah* ideology is counterbalanced by the insistence of *hafotzas Torah* as one of the primary aims of the *ben Torah*;

but in practice, the extent to which the pupils of different *yeshivos* allow the pursuit of *hafotzas Torah* to overcome their inward-looking insistence on self-improvement varies from *yeshivah* to *yeshivah* and seems to depend upon the personality and influence of different *roshei yeshivos*.

But in *Chabad*, the outward-looking ideology which attributes Messianic significance to the conversion of souls to *shmiras mitzvos* and ultimately to *Chassidus*, provides representatives of the Lubavitch movement with a certain buoyancy and lack of self-consciousness which is wholly admirable.

I cannot guarantee that my interpretation of these aspects of Lubavitch will meet with the approval of *Chabad* circles. But I think they represent a certain angle on the popular image of Lubavitch. In fact I am a little surprised that my personal interpretation of the characteristics of Lubavitch conforms so closely to the popular image. Does this mean, perhaps, that its popular image reflects its true character? Or is it rather a sign that I do not know Lubavitch at any more than a superficial level?

Apart from an episode during my years of service in Bar-Ilan University, when I rendered some small assistance in establishing a regular group which studied the *Tanya*, I have come in contact with Lubavitch once more only recently, in connection with my efforts to help to place Jewish education in this country on a more organised basis, and to raise the level of teacher-training as part of a general heightening of standards in Jewish studies in the schools.

I am delighted to find that in the fifteen years which have elapsed since I first met the few Lubavitch *Chassidim* in London whom I have previously mentioned, Lubavitch has grown into a powerful force on the educational scene. Its highly successful kindergarten, primary schools and girls' senior school in Stamford Hill, now supplemented by its boys' grammar school in Hampstead Garden Suburb, as well as the various educational activities such as afternoon schools, *shiurim*, summer-camps and field work among students at the universities, provide an example which other sections of the local community might do well to emulate.

Above all, the outward-looking policy of the Lubavitch movement makes it one of the most flexible and successful partners in waging what is after all the most important battle to be fought in this as in other Jewish communities—the battle for Jewish education, for *hafotzas Torah*.

At a farbrengen *with the Rebbe* שליט"א *in Brooklyn, N.Y.*

with the Rebbe

My encounters with *Chabad* have been at many levels, each stimulating and rewarding in its own way—but I wish it was possible for everyone to attend a *farbrengen* of the Rebbe.

The Rebbe speaks. His words, flowing as from a fountain of youth, are literally absorbed by thousands of ears, devoured by thousands of eyes burning with hope, and inspire thousands of souls with a love of their faith and their fellow.

Anyone witnessing this scene in the midst of twentieth-century New York must be convinced that here beats a generous heart radiating faith, knowledge and hope to us all.

Jacques Lipchitz

an extra dimension

By now the reader will have discovered that there is a particular Chassidic *insight to all aspects of life.* Chabad *philosophy permeates both social and cultural activity. The Holy Days which are such an important part of Jewish tradition assume an additional meaning when viewed with this* Chabad *insight. There follows a few examples of* Chabad Thought *on the major Jewish Festivals which we hope will open up for the reader an extra dimension to their significance.*

שבת

Shabbos—its meaning and lesson

In the book of Exodus, Sabbath observance is mentioned twice in conjunction with a passage regarding the construction of the Sanctuary. There is, however, an important difference between the two passages. In Chapter 32, we find G–d's command to Moses to exhort the people regarding the *Shabbos*, a command which terminates the detailed plans for building the Sanctuary. Later, in Chapter 35, however, Moses adjures the people to observe the *Shabbos*, and then imparts to them the details of the Sanctuary's structure. In Moses' command, the order of the passages is reversed and *Shabbos* observance is placed before the plans for the Sanctuary. Indeed, this juxtaposition is so important that from it our Sages deduce the various categories of work which are prohibited on *Shabbos*.

In order to understand this intentional reversal of the Divine command, let us first consider the saying of our Sages, that on *Shabbos* every Jew possesses an additional soul. Who can truly say that on *Shabbos* he feels totally different from the rest of the week; that he is aware of some extra vitalising force pulsating within him?

Our mystics have explained that, of all the soul powers and abilities that a human being possesses, the power and ability to exercise will, supersedes all others. The perceptive properties of the senses are all confined to certain organs. Even the sense of touch (which has no special limb or organ) is limited, in that different parts of the hand are sensitive to different feelings. Will, on the other hand is universal. It may be exercised uniformly over any part of the body.

There are, however, two distinct levels at which will is experienced.

"There is will and there is will", say our Sages. There is will which is derived from the intellect and is subordinate to it. The intellect decides that a certain will must be brought to bear, and the result is that that will is exercised accordingly.

On a higher plane, however, a form of will may be manifested which lies beyond the scope of the mind. It is an intrinsic desire which the intellect cannot explain, derived from some inner bond with the object of the desire. It is with this will that martyrs have given up their lives for that which they hold dear. It lies outside the grasp of the intellect, for the mind would never decide through logic and reason to sacrifice life for an ideal.

This higher manifestation of will stems from a bond so deep-rooted that it remains incomprehensible to the mind and imperceptible to the senses, becoming manifest only at certain times.

One of these occasions, we are told, is on *Shabbos*. The meaning of *Shabbos* is so bound up with the plan and purpose of our lives, that the very foundations of faith are built upon it. Indeed, the meaning of *Shabbos* expresses all that a Jew must live and strive for. It is an everlasting sign between man and G–d that He is our Creator, and as such brought us into being in order to fulfil some Divinely ordained function.

The Jew who recognises the implications of *Shabbos* and orients his life accordingly, declares his belief in his own Divine calling. The Jew who fails to appreciate the meaning of *Shabbos* has yet to realise the true purpose in his life.

For this reason, every Jew is endowed on *Shabbos* with an additional soul —the manifestation of a higher will, which stems from the intrinsic and immutable bond between him and his Creator. On *Shabbos* he undergoes a change. The limitations of his weekday self fall away, and an overwhelming awareness of his Divine origin permeates his entire being, revitalising him with a force he will carry with him throughout the coming week—a Divinely inspired foundation for the lofty edifice of fulfilling a Divine purpose.

And yet this is not felt. This additional soul, this wondrous manifestation remains but a potentiality, never finding positive expression. It is bestowed once a week upon every Jew, and he is oblivious to its presence.

What vitiates his awareness and prevents him from undergoing a sublime experience is his own gross nature. A foot which is placed inside a darkened room, and then into a room which is brilliantly lit, will not distinguish between light and darkness, for it is not the correct instrument for this. The Jew who knows only mundane and materialistic values is like this—his sensitivity to the Divine becomes dulled and he is not a proper instrument for distinguishing between the presence or non-presence of a lofty spiritual revelation.

The soul of a Jew may be compared to a diamond. Nobody would imagine that the stone, when it is brought up out of the ground, could shine and glitter. The dirt must first be washed off; the stone must be separated from its bed of rock; it must be pounded, cut and polished, and only then does it appear as a sparkling gem, reflecting light in all directions in a thousand delicate shades of the colours of the spectrum.

This is the function of the lower level of will, that which is born of intellect. The Jew must weigh up his spiritual standing and decide for himself which path brings him to his purpose. Only then does he become attuned to receive and be aware of the higher manifestation of will, the additional soul he is invested with every week, and the potentialities it gives him.

When G–d commanded Moses regarding *Shabbos*, He did so after describing to him the plans for the Sanctuary. The building of the Sanctuary was no simple task. The *Talmud* describes at length the fine detail and immense complexity of the work involved. Thus, in the order of His command regarding a physical task, G–d intimated the order of man's spiritual task. The awareness of the meaning of *Shabbos* and all it implies can only be realised after hard toil.

Moses, however, when he imparted the Divine message to the people, reversed the order, for the work does not end here. The experiencing of a sublime manifestation is not the fulfilment of man's purpose in this world, but only the means to achieve it. On *Shabbos*, the Jew must become elevated to a higher plane and be imbued with a revivifying force which will uphold him during the coming week.

As the *Zohar* says: "All the (following) days are blessed from *Shabbos*." It is upon *Shabbos* that one's week is built, and it is by utilising *Shabbos* throughout the week that one comes a little closer each successive day to fulfilling his Divinely ordained purpose.

Rosh Hashonoh

Before *Rosh Hashonoh* we have the month of *Elul*, a preparatory season for the Ten Days of *Teshuvah*. *Elul*, as noted frequently, is an acrostic for "*Ani ledodi vedodi li*", the passage in *Shir Hashirim* describing Israel's devotion to G-d. "I am my beloved's (G-d), and my beloved is mine." Note the order; Israel's devotion comes first, while G-d's love is His response. Israel takes the initiative.

At the other end of the calendar, we find *Pesach* described in a companion verse, "*Dodi li ve'ani lo*". "My beloved is mine and I am my beloved's." Here the order is reversed—G-d's love for Israel precedes Israel's response to G-d. G-d took the initiative.

Of course, these verses, and the Holy Days they represent, indicate two different approaches inherent in *Yiddishkeit*. Approaches that are complementary, not contradictory. *Chassidus* explains that both orders are equally valid, for each has its proper mood, season and purpose. Sometimes we call; at other times we answer.

Egypt was a land of consummate degeneracy and evil. Our enslaved ancestors were so lost, and so agonising was their slavery, that they could not even listen to Moses announcing the redemption. Their merit was in the past (Abraham, Isaac and Jacob) or in the future (the promise of *Torah*). But G-d "appeared" spontaneously as it were, by His initiative, to redeem us, and only then did Israel respond by "fleeing" the defilements of Egypt.

Torah, the Rebbe has frequently emphasised, is not simply a story, even in its narrative portions. *Torah* is "teaching". What can we learn from this aspect of Egypt?

There are qualities with which we are endowed, not because of our virtues or efforts, but as an inheritance. Generally, there are three ways of acquiring an object from another person; by purchasing, by gift or by inheritance. In purchasing there is an exchange, value for value. A gift is not paid for; it is not given as an obligation discharged, but neither is it generally given to a "stranger". Something on the recipient's part inspired the gift. Inheritance, though, does not involve the recipient's merits at all; he is simply his parents' child. *Morosho kehillas Yaakov* describes *Torah* as Israel's heritage. What did we receive in the form of inheritance?

Neshomah, the G–dly soul within each of us, is part of our endowment at birth. In the recesses of the soul there is a "concealed love" for G–d that needs only to be aroused. The most estranged of Israel possesses an inextinguishable spark. These are not earned by our labours; they are instances of "*Dodi li*", G–d's call to Israel in every generation. He granted us these of His own accord, by His initiative, and we are now expected to make use of them. Our response is the next step. The G–dly soul must rule and master the desire of the flesh. The "concealed love" must be brought forth, awakened, given life, to impel the Jew to live *Yiddishkeit* with enthusiasm. These are our efforts, but they come only after the gift was freely given to us.

But suppose the Jew foolishly squanders his inheritance? Suppose his deeds and life create a barrier between him and his Father in Heaven? Here we come to *Elul*, to the *Rosh Hashonoh* season. "*Ani ledodi*", I am G–d's, the first step, and only then "*Dodi li*", does G–d respond to man.

Man makes the overture. He takes the initiative by reconsidering his actions of the past year and measuring them according to the standards of *Torah*. He must determine to correct whatever was deficient. This is the theme of *teshuvah*, return, that dominates these fateful weeks. Man comes back, man worships, man makes the start of the fresh year what it should be. We are then assured of "*Dodi li*", that G–d will make the year one of blessing and good in answer to Israel's prayers.

Rosh Hashonoh is Coronation Day for G–d as our King and for Israel as His people. The word *melech* is a constant refrain throughout the prayers of the Ten Days of *Teshuvah*, and G–d's *malchus* is the first of the three sections of the *Rosh Hashonoh Musaf*. What do we mean by *melech*? In fact, is not G–d King regardless of what we do? What, then, is meant by "coronation"?

Loshon hakodesh, the sacred language of *Torah*, is precise, with often untranslatable, yet vital shades of meaning that convey profound ideas.

Melech is translated as "king". But there are related words in *loshon hakodesh*, for example *moshel*, or "ruler". How is *melech* different from *moshel*? The definition will enhance our understanding of *Torah*'s attitude to the relationship between man and G–d, and will add to our appreciation of *Rosh Hashonoh* as well.

A *moshel* rules. The consent of the governed is not required. His rule might extend over men—as in the case of a dictator. He might be a shepherd of animals without intelligence, or even the manager of inanimate possessions. The *moshel* does as he pleases, and his subjects, whatever they may be, are his pawns. G–d is sometimes called *Moshel*, for He has established laws of nature, for example, that are dictates of His wish. Trees grow, planets move, not because they wish to, or because they recognise the wisdom of doing so. There is no "consent" here. The absolute Ruler decrees, and there is no violating His law.

But just as G–d is *moshel*, He is *melech*. The *melech*, unlike the *moshel*, does not impose his rule on unwilling subjects. They must desire his rule, even in the face of the potential *melech's* reluctance, a reluctance overcome by the people's importuning and submission. But the key to *malchus* is consent. The subjects face alternatives of requesting or rejecting the ruler. Not by compulsion, but purely of their own volition, they choose to accept His dominion. In *Maariv* we say: "*Umalchuso berotzon kiblu*", Israel accepted G–d's kinghood willingly, exactly as we have explained *malchus*.

This power of election, the ability to make decisions, is the unique quality of man, unshared by any other creature. "Choose life", Moses pleads with his people, because the choice is open to man. This is the teaching of *Torah*, instructing and inspiring man to make the decisions G–d wishes.

What is the particular connection of this with *Rosh Hashonoh*? The term "*Rosh*" is used here deliberately. *Rosh* means both "head" and "first". The "head" is the "first", the highest, of the body's organs, possessing the higher faculties like sight, hearing, speech and thought. The head commands the other organs of the body to act according to its instructions. If the head is in good condition, then the rest of the body may function well, but the least defect in the brain may have an immeasurable effect on the body.

On *Rosh Hashonoh* the higher soul-faculties are revealed. Quite simply, this means that the Jewish heart is more sensitive on this day; that every Jew feels more deeply his kinship with his Creator than during the rest of the year. *Rosh Hashonoh* sets the pace; as *Rosh Hashonoh* goes, so goes the rest of the year. A wasted *Rosh Hashonoh* will result in a Jewishly indifferent year, and a *Rosh Hashonoh* spent in the proper manner gives life and spirit to the whole year.

Throughout the year, the Jew must live the life of *Yiddishkeit*, observing *mitzvos* and studying *Torah*. To a large degree this is determined by *Rosh Hashonoh*, just as the well-being of the head determines the state of the body. Before the specific decrees of the king are accepted and observed, the king's general authority must be established. The people's submission to his rule at the coronation affects their later observance of his wishes.

The *Mishna* explains that *Shema* precedes *vehoyo*, so that man will "first accept the Kingdom of Heaven and then accept the *mitzvos*." In this sense *Shema* and *Rosh Hashonoh* play similar rôles, for both initiate the *Torah* life; both are general foundations followed by specific observance of individual *mitzvos* throughout the year and throughout the life of the Jew.

In this light we can understand *Rosh Hashonoh* as the Day of Judgement. "Today the world was conceived", we say in the *Musaf* prayer. "Today, all the creatures of the universe stand in judgement."

The establishment of a king does not depend solely upon the desire of the subjects; the king, too, has to want to rule. It is when he sees that the subjects are preparing themselves to accept his sovereignty that he will deign to rule.

So it is with G–d. "Today, all the creatures of the universe stand in judgement", for G–d to examine, weigh up and decide whether He will continue to rule over them for another year. Only by submitting ourselves to His rule and resolving to observe His wishes do we demonstrate to G–d that we want Him to continue being our King—"*Ani ledodi*." Then He, in His mercy will accept the kingship and continue to want us as His people— "*Dodi li*."

Yom Kippur

The period commencing on *Rosh Hashonoh* and ending on *Yom Kippur* is referred to as the Ten Days of *Teshuvah*. This implies that both *Rosh Hashonoh* and *Yom Kippur* are included in these penitential days, and that they are all part of a significant period which culminates on the day of *Yom Kippur*. From this it can be inferred that from the very moment *Rosh Hashonoh* begins we are in fact preparing for *Yom Kippur*.

In the days of the Temple, the essence of *Yom Kippur* was that the service could only be performed by the *Kohen Godol*. During the rest of the year the service in the Temple could be performed by any of the *Kohanim*.

There were two distinct groups of services performed by the *Kohen Godol* on *Yom Kippur*. One group was performed while he wore all the eight garments referred to as the "golden garments", and the second group was carried out while he wore only his pure white linen garments.

The Temple contained three specific areas. The *Azoroh*, the *Hechal*, and the Holy of Holies.

The services in the first two areas were performed by the *Kohen Godol* wearing his golden garments. For the services in the Holy of Holies, the *Kohen Godol* wore the white garments.

The Temple is now destroyed and these services are no longer performed. There remains, however, the spiritual Temple which is extant in each and every Jew. A Temple unscathed, always complete, and beyond destruction even by the Jew himself, let alone by our enemies.

Each Jew is the *Kohen Godol* of his own spiritual Temple and when *Yom Kippur* arrives he, like the *Kohen Godol* of old, must perform all the services there himself. There are still two types of "service" to be performed. The service of the Holy of Holies in the white garments, and the other services in the golden garments.

Maimonides writes that the reason for the *Kohanim* performing their duties in special garments, and for the *Kohen Godol* performing his duties on *Yom Kippur* in the golden garments, was that for matters of holiness one must use the most beautiful and best materials available. Therefore, as gold is held in high esteem and makes a deep impression upon a person, the service in the Temple, particularly on *Yom Kippur*, had to be performed in golden clothes.

This being so, it is difficult to understand why the service in the Holy of Holies, which was of even greater spiritual standing, was performed in white garments.

The matter may be explained as follows. Each Jew must serve the Al–ty to the limit of his personal ability. When a Jew is approached to give charity, he cannot claim that he has discharged his religious responsibilities by studying *Torah* or by praying. This is a sphere in which he must use his "golden garments" in the service of G–d.

On the other hand, a Jew must remember that he cannot discharge his other responsibilities in spiritual and worldly matters merely by supporting places of learning or charitable endeavours. Here each Jew must wear white garments, pure garments, symbolising spiritual perfection un-tarnished by material and physical matter.

While it is incumbent on a Jew to use his "golden garments" for service outside the Holy of Holies, once inside, in each individual's soul, gold must not enter. There, rich man and poor man alike must don white, pure garments. And just as the *Kohen Godol* of old did not first wear one set of garments and then later the other, but constantly changed from one to the other during the course of the day's services, so must we, today, do the same. For in the concept of a Jew, spiritual and material matters cannot be divorced from each other.

This, then, is the significance of the Ten Days of *Teshuvah* which begin with the blowing of the *shofar* on *Rosh Hashonoh* and culminate in the services on *Yom Kippur*.

In the days of the Temple, the Holy of Holies contained only the Ark housing the tablets engraved with the *Torah*. The bond of the Jew with *Torah*, the Law of Life, is similarly indelibly engraved. On *Yom Kippur* each Jew must enter the Holy of Holies which is within himself. He must not think: "How can I enter when I am not dressed up?" He must realise that to enter the Holy of Holies does not require "dressing up", but rather simple, pure, heartfelt thoughts. And when he emerges he must have resolved to serve the Al–ty at all times with both his golden and his pure, white garments.

Finally, after the whole service on *Yom Kippur*, the *Kohen Godol* used to say a short prayer invoking a good year for himself and for all Jews.

Today, each Jew, while doing service in his Holy of Holies, can do the same. A few chosen words in a chosen moment, expressed by an individual in pure thought, can bring not only for his immediate family, but for all his brethren, a good and sweet year in all matters, spiritual and material.

the Succah

"You shall dwell in booths for seven days . . . so that your generations shall know that I have caused the children of Israel to dwell in booths when I brought them out of the land of Egypt. . . ."

(Lev. 23:42–43)

Although the festival of *Succos* is also associated with other *mitzvos* (such as the *lulav* and *esrog*), it takes its name from the *succah*, the temporary booth in which the *Torah* instructs us to live during this festival.

One reason advanced for this is that the *mitzvah* of dwelling in a *succah* has an additional merit in that it takes effect from the beginning of the festival and not, as in the case of the *lulav* and *esrog*, from the first morning of *Succos*. Furthermore, the *mitzvah* of building a *succah* requires preparation before the commencement of the festival, and this adds further to the merit of this *mitzvah*. After fulfilling the *mitzvah* of *lulav*, one is exempt for the remainder of the day. The *mitzvah* of dwelling in the *succah*, however, applies to the whole of the festival—from the moment it begins until it ends.

To delve more deeply into this theme: Most *mitzvos* involve only one part of the body, while the *mitzvah* of dwelling in the *succah* involves the whole of the body which is encompassed by it. Thus, any personal action which would not normally be a *mitzvah* is hallowed and becomes a *mitzvah* by being performed within the *succah*.

The *Gemorrah* states: "He who has no home is not a man", meaning that he who has no home is incomplete, for a place of domicile is essential to a whole man. The possession of a dwelling-place completes a man's status, and he does not forfeit this status even when he is not in his dwelling-place. The *succah* is the symbol of the Jew's spiritual status and, as in the case of a physical domicile, this status is independent of whether or not a person is physically within the walls of this dwelling, as long as he knows where his home is and expects to return to it.

It is expected of every Jew that, "in all your ways, you shall know Him". Not only during the time we are learning *Torah* or are occupied in prayer should we be serving G–d, but even when we are occupied with worldly matters, these too should be bound up with the Al–ty.

The essential lesson of *Succos* is that by dwelling in a *succah* we do connect our personal, mundane affairs with the Al–ty and raise them to the level of sanctity. We should gain strength from this to be subservient to G–d in all our daily affairs throughout the year.

The *Gemorrah* refers to the *mitzvah* of *succah* as an "easy *mitzvah*". Indeed, when a Jew really resolves that, come what may, he will be a servant of the King of Kings, then it is truly a "simple matter" to conduct his worldly affairs in such a manner as to make this world a hallowed place— a true sanctuary—for the Al–ty to dwell therein.

the Lulav—symbol of Torah study

During the festival of *Succos*, we Jews observe a most interesting and basic commandment—the *mitzvah* of "*bentsching esrog*"—of reciting the proper blessing over the "Four Kinds" of plants specified in the *Torah*: the *esrog*—a species of citrus fruit; the *lulav*—a branch of the palm tree; *hadassim*—myrtle branches, and the *arovos*—branches of willow.

The correct way of observing this *mitzvah* is by binding the myrtle and willow branches to the *lulav*, then holding the *lulav* in the right hand. The *esrog* is held separately in the left hand. We recite the blessing: "Who commanded us about holding the *lulav*", and place both hands together so that the *esrog* in the left hand touches the other kinds in the right hand.

There is an explicit reason for every one of the details of "*bentsching esrog*".

Our Sages teach us that the "Four Kinds" of plants we use represent four kinds of Jews. The *esrog*, which has a distinctive taste as well as aroma, symbolises those Jews who are *Torah* scholars, as well as devout observers of the *mitzvos*. The *lulav*, the branch of the palm tree which has a good taste but no aroma, represents the Jews who concentrate on the study of *Torah*. *Hadassim*, myrtle branches, which have a lovely smell but no taste, symbolise the Jews who exert their major efforts on the observance of *mitzvos*. While *arovos*, willow branches, which have neither taste nor smell, represent those Jews who are lacking in both *Torah* study and observance of *mitzvos*.

Since the aim and purpose of life is *Torah* study and the observance of G-d's will as expressed in the *mitzvos*, it would seem that the *esrog*, symbolising as it does both facets of a Jew's ideal, enjoys pre-eminence among the "Four Kinds". And so we bring the *esrog*, alone in the left hand, to touch the other kinds in the right hand.

This teaches us that whilst every Jew has the duty of helping other Jews, one who realises in his person the ideal goal that is demanded of us has the greater responsibility of approaching his fellow-Jews to try and help them, especially in those basic aspects of *Yiddishkeit* which they lack, and with which he is so fortunately blessed. With love, insight and ceaseless effort, he should try to influence his fellow-Jew till he, too, achieves the qualities of *esrog*.

Although we bring the *esrog* so close to the other kinds that they touch, we do not bind the *esrog* to the others in the same way that they are bound to each other. Our ideal is a Jew who is not only a *Torah* scholar, and as such can be quite indifferent to the rest of the world, but who is also a devoted observer of *mitzvos*. This necessitates his active participation in worldly matters, and association with, and concern for, his fellows. This participation can result in many a test of his *Torah* loyalty. He must, there-fore, continually rededicate himself to an appreciation of the *Torah* way of life, so as not to be lured by the superficial splendour of material things at the expense of compromising his own values, which help him to achieve the true purpose of life.

The *lulav* symbolises those Jews who concentrate on *Torah* study, with the extraordinary devotion previously described, which in turn earns them the Divine gifts of special power and ability to learn and understand *Torah* under all conditions, without being occupied or concerned with anything else.

Such a person, whose special quality is his unconcern about any and all worldly matters, cannot be harmed by being bound to the Jews repre-sented by the myrtle and willow, far removed as they are from the ideal. His superiority and strength may influence them for the better, but his very removal from material things makes it almost impossible for them to affect him.

It is not necessary to bind the *lulav* and *esrog* to each other, for each represents a different period in a Jew's ideal development—each perfect in its own time.

It is significant, however, that the *mitzvah* of "*bentsching esrog*" cannot be performed if any one of the four species is lacking. Whilst the *esrog* em-bodies all qualities and the *lulav* and *hadassim* represent specific virtues, the *mitzvah* is not perfect and the *berocho* may not be recited over them unless the humble *arovo* is there as well.

The meaning is obvious. Israel has a totality in its fullness and completeness and must of course have men of wisdom and deeds. But if the *arovo*, a Jew devoid of learning and deficient in deeds, does not participate and is not reckoned among Israel, then Israel is incomplete.

In his last address to the people, Moses speaks of all of Israel standing before G–d, from the highest to the most humble. This ideal of the wholeness, the inclusive nature, of the Jewish people is paramount.

In each Jew there is room for improvement but each Jew has his part to play and each is indispensable to the Jewish way of life.

Simchas Torah

Throughout the ages *Simchas Torah* has been observed, not with the cold, spiritless, dutiful "marching" with the *Torah* which takes place in so many congregations today, but with a warmth, enthusiasm and fervour which are an inspiration to those who witness and participate in the celebration.

One still witnesses true *simcha*, sees joy pouring forth from the innermost crevices of the soul. Not a joy characterised by levity and frivolity, but rather by deep soul-searching and all-encompassing exaltation at one and the same time. It is not the kind of joy which drags one down to the trivialities of life, but rather a joy which elevates one above the narrow and petty, to achieve a new perspective of life, and to gain a deeper purpose for it.

A lesson of *Simchas Torah* can be learned from the custom that all Jews dance together on this Festival of Rejoicing.

ALL Jews. Aged and dignified Rabbis and *Chassidim*—men who are steeped in the most profound and intricate phases of *Torah* learning, persons whose very countenances radiate thoughtfulness and wisdom—dance joyously before the *Torah*, with the vigour and the apparent enthusiasm of children. These intellectual and spiritual giants who measure their every word, whose every gesture bespeaks dignity and deliberation, rejoice before the *Torah* with the sprightliness, the agility, the utter abandon and enthusiasm one often sees in youngsters—behaviour, it would seem, entirely inconsistent with the dignity and gravity associated with intellectual status.

ALL Jews. At these same gatherings one sees equally fervent Jews of lesser intellectual ability—students, those with little learning, and children, all dancing together with the same abandon.

Dancing together, truly rejoicing with the *Torah*, imbued with the conviction of its absolute relevance, its utter indispensability to life. To them, life without *Torah* is unthinkable. Only a life of *Torah* has purpose and meaning. Thus, when they look at the *Sefer Torah*, rolled up and covered, they realise, each within the bounds of his own intellect, that in this scroll and what it represents, is their raison d'être, their tree of life.

The less learned are moved by the flood of joy emanating from the more intellectual, who are in turn moved by the simple exuberance emanating from the faith of the less learned; resulting in a unified display of joy in the *Torah*.

This then is the message of *Simchas Torah*. When all Jews rejoice together with the *Torah* because they know that the *Torah* is the precious possession of all Jews, then they become one unit bound up with the Al–ty Himself.

the miracle of Chanukah

Our *Talmud* Sages describe the miracle of *Chanukah* as follows:

During the occupation of the Holy Land by the Greeks, they entered the *Hechal* and defiled all the oil there. However, when the Hasmoneans defeated them, one cruse of oil was found which had evidently not been touched by the Greeks. It contained oil sufficient for one day only. The *Menorah* was rekindled and the oil miraculously lasted for eight days (until new oil could be prepared for the *Menorah*).

From the text of the *Talmud* it is clear that the defilement of the oil was not accidental, but intentional and systematic. This poses the question: If the purpose of the Greeks was to put out the *Menorah* and prevent it being rekindled, why did they merely defile the oil? They could more effectively have used it up or destroyed it completely.

Furthermore, we must assume that the Greeks had defiled all the oil within reach of the Jews throughout Jerusalem and its environs, for if any (ritually clean) oil had been available in the vicinity there would have been no need for a miracle. Consequently, the situation would have been more accurately described merely by the words, "defiled all the oil", without the additional qualification, "in the *Hechal*". This qualification seems even more conspicuously superfluous, when one takes into account that the storage place for the oil was not in the *Hechal*, but in the adjoining *Azoroh*.

The answer is this: By emphasising that the Greeks defiled all the oil in the *Hechal*, our Sages indicated to us that the true objective of the Greeks was not to prevent the rekindling of the *Menorah*, but to ensure that it could be rekindled only with defiled oil. This was why they purposely left a supply of defiled oil in the Sanctuary.

Herein lies the essential aspect, as well as the message of *Chanukah*, the Festival of Lights, as our Sages indicated in their succinct description of the miracle of *Chanukah*.

Chanukah recalls the collision of two worlds. The Jewish world of faith, *Torah* and a particular way of life based on pure monotheism, with its concept of holiness down to the minutest detail in one's daily life, and the Hellenistic culture, with its polytheistic and largely materialistic concept of life.

By force of arms, the Greeks attempted to impose their culture on conquered people and lands. However, their aim was not to eradicate indigenous cultures, but rather to Hellenise and assimilate them. This was also the policy of Antiochus when the Holy Land came under his domination. Thus, we say in the special *Chanukah* prayer, *Ve'al hanissim:* "The Greek Empire (was determined) to make (the Jews) forget Thy *Torah*, and to make them transgress the statutes of Thy Will."

The Greeks were willing to recognise the *Torah*, or even accept it as a perfect and beautiful literary creation, a work of poetry, wisdom and profound philosophy, provided it was considered as a human creation, something like their own mythology (which was a human invention, and where the deities were represented in human shapes and forms, with human characteristics, passions, etc.).

As such, the *Torah* could be, in fact ought to be, changed and modified from time to time, in order to harmonise with the character of the ruling class and the novel ideas and mores of the period. This, of course, would do away with the permanence and immutability of religious institutions, such as *Shabbos*, circumcision, and so on.

In other words, it was not the suppression of the *Torah* that they aimed at, but the denial of it as the G–d-given word. Similarly, they were not averse to the moral and ethical values contained therein, but they prohibited the Divine Statutes, the so-called "supra-rational" precepts which, more than any other, distinguish the Jewish way of life and make it specifically Jewish, holy and pure.

Moreover—and this was the greatest danger posed by the Greek penetration of the *Hechal*—they favoured, and actually endeavoured to bring about, the rekindling of the *Menorah*, specifically in its hallowed place in the *Hechal*. From there it would spread its radiance everywhere as before, but the light would come from oil that had the Greek "touch"—the touch of the heathen that defiles the oil.

The *Menorah*, which was kindled with pure and consecrated oil, was the visible symbol of the purity of the Jewish way of life, and its perpetual light flashed this message from the *Beis Hamikdosh* to every Jew, wherever he might be. The Greeks were resolved to change this.

Indeed, there were Jews, too—Jewish Hellenists—who felt that a "touch" of the more "modernistic" and "sophisticated" Greek culture ought to be applied to the Jewish faith, religion and *Torah*. But a handful of Hasmoneans, whose vision had not been blurred, recognised that this "touch" would be a fatal blow striking at the inner sanctum of Jewish life.

Divine providence saw to it that a cruse of oil, pure and uncontaminated, should be left with which to rekindle the *Menorah*, and that it should not only hold its own, but should grow, spread and keep the perpetual light burning.

What was true "in those days" is just as true "in this season", in our day and age. What is true of the Jewish people as a whole is, of course, true also of each individual Jew.

Under the assault of environmental influences, a Jew may find his "Sanctuary"—his attachment to, and identification with, G–d through the observance of the *Torah* and *mitzvos*—invaded and contaminated by ideas and mores which are alien to the Jewish way of life, incompatible with it and inimical to it.

But in the inner sanctum of his soul there is always a "cruse of oil"—that spark of G–dliness which is his Divine soul, indestructible and beyond the reach of defilement that remains pure and holy. The Jew has but to kindle it and he will find that although it may at first give only a tiny light of brief duration, it will, in time, light up one's whole being until it becomes a perpetual light.

However, the Jew must not think only of himself. The commandment: "Love thy fellow as thyself", demands the same attitude towards one's fellow-Jew. No Jew should ever be given up. It is necessary to kindle in him that pure and holy light, even if it appears to be good only for no more than one day. For even that in itself is worth-while, and more, it will steadily grow from day to day, gradually illuminating his whole life.

Chanukah reminds us that the greatest danger to the Jewish way of life lies not in the threat of shutting out or extinguishing its light completely, but rather in the tendency to defile it by supplying unholy oil to its *Menorah*. This tendency expresses itself in many ways. In the worship of materialism and material successes; in the presentation of certain man-made ideologies and "isms" as panaceas for all human ills; in the idolatry of science and technology and the tendency to measure everything by the yardstick of human reason, none of which necessarily rules out "religious experience", but either confines it to a narrow domain or, worse still, produces a pseudo-religiosity where consecration and commitment are sacrificed to convenience and compromise and where crass pragmatism and rationalism, instead of unadulterated truth and holiness, are the guiding principles.

Chanukah teaches us that the sanctity and purity of Jewish life must be preserved at all costs. Not only should the external and material aspects of daily life be precluded from contaminating the purity and holiness of the *Torah* and *mitzvos*, but the *Torah* and *mitzvos* should bring sanctity into the material aspects of daily life, in accordance with the principle: "Know Him in all thy ways." The message of the *Chanukah* lights contains three basic points, which are applicable—in an immediate and practical way—to the crucial problems of our day:

(*a*) The *Chanukah* lights (symbolising the light of the *Torah* and *mitzvos*) have to be kindled after dark. This indicates that one should not be discouraged by the prevailing "darkness" outside; for even a little light of *Torah* and *mitzvos* can dispel a great deal of darkness, and how much more so a great deal of light.

(*b*) The *Chanukah* lights are required to be kindled in such a way that their light should be seen outside. This indicates that it is not enough to illuminate one's own home with the light and warmth of *Torah*-true *Yiddishkeit*, but one must also spread it outside, in the neighbourhood and in the community at large.

(*c*) The *Chanukah* lights are kindled in a growing number each night of *Chanukah*, teaching us to make a steadily growing effort to spread the light of *Torah* and *mitzvos*, and that these efforts are in themselves an assurance of ever-growing success.

Purim

The story of *Purim*, as related in the Book of Esther, gives us a clear analysis of the "Jewish problem".

Dispersed over 127 provinces and lands, their own still in ruins, the Jews undoubtedly differed from one another in custom, dress and language according to the place of their dispersal, in very much the same way as Jews in different countries differ nowadays.

Yet, though there were Jews who would conceal this Jewishness, Haman, the enemy of the Jews, recognised the essential qualities and characteristics of the Jews, which made all of them, with or without their consent, into "one people", namely: "Their laws are different from those of any other people."

In his desire to annihilate the Jews, Haman sought to destroy "all the Jews, young and old, children and women". Undoubtedly, there were in those days, too, Jews who adhered strictly to the *Torah* and *mitzvos*, as well as Jews whose religious ties with their people were weak, or who sought to assimilate themselves, yet none could escape being classified as belonging to that "one people", and every single one was included in Haman's cruel decree.

In all ages there have been Hamans, yet we have outlived them. Wherein lies our secret of survival?

The answer will be evident from the following illustration. When a scientist seeks to ascertain the laws governing a certain phenomenon, or to discover the essential properties of a certain element in nature, he must undertake a series of experiments under the most varied conditions, in order to discover those properties or laws which obtain alike under all conditions.

No true scientific law can be deduced from a minimum number of experiments, or from experiments under similar or only slightly varied conditions, for the findings as to what is essential and what is secondary or quite unimportant would then not be conclusive.

The same principle should be applied to our people. It is one of the oldest in the world, beginning its national history from the Revelation on Mount Sinai, some 3,300 years ago. In the course of these long centuries our people has lived under extremely varied conditions, in most diverse times and in different places all over the world.

If we wish to discover the essential elements that are the cause and very basis of the existence of our people and its unique strength, we must conclude that it is not its peculiar physical or intrinsic mental characteristics, not its language, manners and customs, or even its racial purity (for there were times in the early history of our people, as well as during the Middle Ages and even recent times, when whole ethnic groups and tribes became proselytes and part of our people).

The essential element which unites our "dispersed and scattered people" and makes it "one people" throughout its dispersion and regardless of time, is the *Torah* and *mitzvos*, the Jewish way of life which has remained basically the same throughout the ages and in all places.

The conclusion is clear and beyond doubt: It is the *Torah* and *mitzvos* which have made our people indestructible on the world scene in the face of massacres and pogroms aiming at our total physical destruction, and in the face of ideological onslaughts of foreign cultures aiming at our total spiritual destruction.

Purim teaches us the age-old lesson, verified time and time again, that no manner of assimilationism, not even if extended over several generations, provides an escape from the Hamans and Hitlers; nor can any Jew sever his ties with his people by attempting such an escape.

On the contrary, our salvation and our existence depend precisely upon the fact that, "Their laws are different from those of any other people."

Purim reminds us that the strength of our people as a whole, and of each individual Jew and Jewess, lies in a closer adherence to our ancient spiritual heritage, which contains the secret of a harmonious, healthy and happy life.

All other things in our spiritual and temporal life must be free from any contradiction of the basis and essence of our existence, and must be attuned accordingly, in order to make for the utmost harmony, and add to our physical and spiritual strength, both of which go hand in hand in Jewish life.

excerpt from a Passover message

The festival of *Pesach* is inaugurated by the central theme: "When thy son will ask thee", and the *Haggadah* is based on the commandment of the *Torah*: "Then shalt thou tell thy son. . . ."

There are various ways of asking questions and formulating the answers, depending upon whether the son belongs to the category of the "Wise", the "Wicked", the "Simple", or the "One who knows not how to ask".

While the "Four Sons" differ from one another in their reaction to the *Seder* service, they have one thing in common: they are all present at the *Seder* service. Even the so-called "wicked" son is there, taking an active, though rebellious, interest in what is going on in the Jewish life around him. This, at least, justifies the hope that some day the "wicked" one also will become wise, and all Jewish children attending the *Seder* will become conscientious Jews, observing the *Torah* and *mitzvos*.

Unfortunately, there is in our time another kind of Jewish child: the child who is conspicuous by his absence from the *Seder* service; the one who has no interest whatsoever in *Torah* and *mitzvos*, laws and customs; who is not even aware of the *Seder shel Pesach*, of the Exodus from Egypt and the subsequent Revelation at Sinai.

This presents a grave challenge, which requires attention long before Passover and the *Seder* night. No Jewish child should be forgotten and given up as lost. No effort should be spared to save that "lost" child, and bring him or her to the *Seder* table. With determination and a true sense of compassion and responsibility, we need have no fear of failure.

In order to remedy an undesirable situation of any kind, it is necessary to attack the roots of the evil. The same is true in this case. The regrettable truth is that much of the blame for this "lost generation" lies squarely on the shoulders of the previous generations.

It is largely the result of an erroneous psychology and misguided policy on the part of some immigrants arriving in a new and strange environment. Finding themselves a small minority and encountering certain difficulties, which are unavoidable in all cases of resettlement, some parents had the mistaken notion, which they injected also into their children, that the way to overcome these difficulties is quickly to become assimilated with the new environment, by discarding the heritage of their forefathers and abandoning the Jewish way of life. Finding the ensuing process somewhat distasteful, as such a course is bound to be full of spiritual conflict, some parents were resolved that their children would be spared the conflict altogether.

In order to justify their desertion and appease their injured conscience, it was necessary for them to devise some rationale and they deluded themselves and their children by the claim that the Jewish way of life and observance of the *Torah* and *mitzvos* did not fit with their new surroundings. They looked for, and therefore "found", faults with the true Jewish way of life, while everything in their non-Jewish environment seemed to them only good and attractive.

By this attitude these parents hoped to ensure their children's existence and survival in the new environment. But what kind of existence is it, if everything spiritual and holy is traded for the material? What kind of survival is it, if it means the sacrifice of the soul for the amenities of the body?

Moreover, in their retreat from *Yiddishkeit*, they turned what they thought was an "escape to freedom" into an escape to servitude, pathetically trying to imitate their non-Jewish environment and failing to see that such imitation, by its caricature and inferiority complex, could only call forth mockery and derision and offend the sensibilities of those whose respect and acceptance they were so desperately trying to win.

The same false approach, whereby the misguided minority seeks to ensure its existence by self-dissolution, which essentially means suicide or is at any rate, self-crippling, has not only dominated individuals, but has unfortunately been made the creed of certain groups thrown together by a set of circumstances.

This has given rise to certain dissident movements on the Jewish scene, which either openly or clandestinely seek to undermine the *Torah* which Moses received from the one G–d and transmitted to our people; the Divine *Torah* which gives our people its unique and distinctive character among the nations of the world. These movements, while differing from each other, have one underlying ideology in common, that of "Let us be as the nations, as the families of the countries, to serve wood and stone."

The dire consequences of this utterly false approach have been that thousands upon thousands of Jews have been severed from their fountain of life, from their fellow-Jews and from their true faith. Deprived of spiritual life and content, children have grown up who no longer belong to the "Four Sons" of the *Haggadah*, not even in the category of the "wicked" one. They are almost a total loss to themselves, to their fellow-Jews and to true *Yiddishkeit*, which are inseparable.

The event of the Exodus from Egypt and the festival of Passover are timely reminders, among other things, that the hope for survival, deliverance and freedom does not lie in an attempt to imitate our environment, but rather in unswerving loyalty to our traditions and true Jewish way of life.

Our ancestors in Egypt were a small minority, and lived in the most difficult circumstances. Yet, as our Sages relate, they preserved their identity and, with pride and dignity, clung tenaciously to their way of life, traditions and uniqueness. Precisely in this way was their existence assured, as was also their true deliverance from physical and spiritual slavery.

It is one of the vital tasks of our time to exert all possible effort to awaken in the young generation, as also in those who are advanced in years but still immature in deeper understanding, a fuller appreciation of true Jewish values, of *Torah*-true *Yiddishkeit*. Not one which goes under a false label of misrepresented, compromised, or watered-down "Judaism", but a full and genuine *Yiddishkeit*. With this new appreciation will come the realisation that only true *Yiddishkeit* can guarantee the existence of the individual, of each and every Jew, at any time, in any place and in any circumstances.

There is no room for hopelessness in Jewish life, and no Jew should ever be given up as a lost cause. Through the proper, compassionate approach of *ahavas Yisroel*, even those of the "lost" generation can be brought back to the love of G–d, *ahavas Hashem*, and love of the *Torah, ahavas haTorah*, and not only be included in the community of the "Four Sons", but in due course be elevated to the rank of the "wise" son.

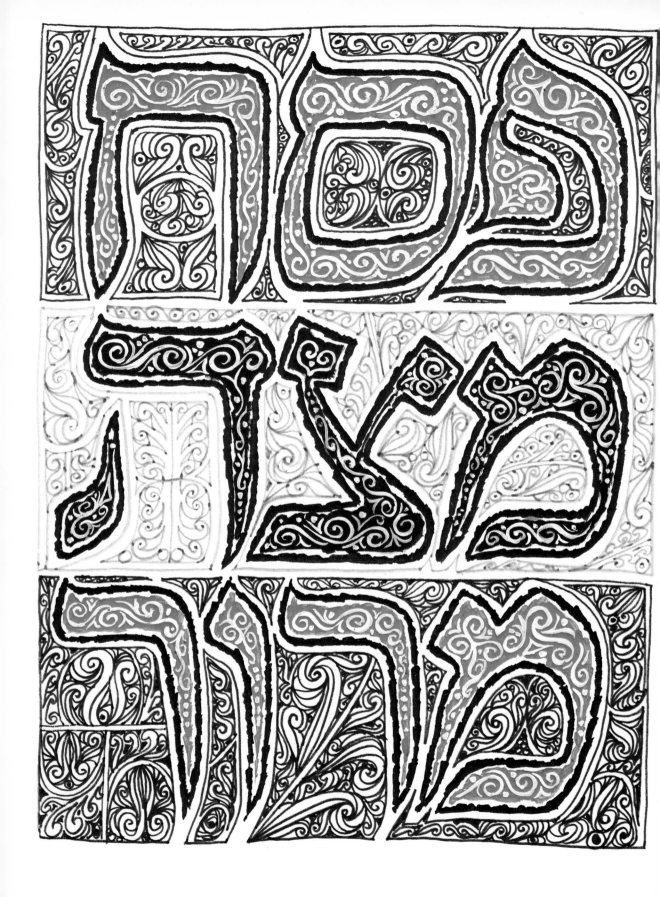

Pesach, Matzoh, Morror

There is a special *mitzvah* of "*Vehigadato*" on Pesach, a law that you should relate and explain the essence of the festival to your child.

Rabbi Gamliel, the *Nassi*, stated that the essence of the festival is contained in the following three words: "*Pesach*", "*Matzoh*", "*Morror*". The *Haggadah* quotes him as saying that one who does not recite these three at *Pesach* has not fulfilled his obligation to celebrate the festival.

The significance of Rabbi Gamliel's dictum can also be interpreted in the light of modern life. We live, thank G–d, in an enlightened and advanced country, where we enjoy peace, abundance and even luxury. Yet, amid this plenty, these technological and cultural achievements, our generation thirsts for Jewish knowledge. In the words of the prophet Amos: "Behold the days come . . . that I will send a famine in the land, not a famine of bread, nor a thirst for water, but of hearing the words of the L–rd."

The degree of ignorance of Judaism and Jewish values among so many groups staggers the imagination. Worse, it leads to too many poor misguided "sheep" straying from our fold. Perhaps the basic motivation of this "exodus" stems from the fact that the assimilationists never learned the significance of the word *Pesach*, a word which refers essentially to self-sacrifice, and preparedness for suffering, exile and insecurity.

For is it not a fact that *Pesach*, and everything involved in the liberation from bondage, was based on these qualities? Therefore, anyone who seeks the easy way in life; who wishes to swim with the current and not against it; who is not prepared to be part of a creative minority, bound by its historical past and destiny, and serve as a light to the nations; who prefers the easy and socially acceptable life rather than the eternal *Torah* way, has learned nothing from the eternal message of the word "*Pesach*".

Matzoh is the symbol of freedom. On each of the first two nights of *Pesach*, at the *Seder*, when we demonstrate our sense of complete freedom, it is mandatory for each man, woman and child to eat *matzoh*, even the sick, for whom this may be difficult.

This sense of freedom is intertwined with a recognition that true freedom can be achieved only in the service of the L–rd. The *matzoh* remained a flat unleavened bread because, when the Jewish people were being freed from slavery, it was the sun which baked this bread; a symbol of the eternal presence of G–d and His guiding hand in the destiny of His people.

Therefore, while we enjoy our freedom from physical enslavement, we must secure our moral and religious freedom. This is the concept of *matzoh*. Anyone who is a slave to his uncontrolled desires, is not truly free, but enslaved. He cannot unshackle himself unless he accepts the word of the *Torah*, and fastens his faith in the Al–ty.

The idea conveyed by the word "*morror*", which reminds us of the bitterness of our days in Egypt, is that no matter how bitter our lot, how helpless our situation, how awesome the odds against us and frightening the forces seeking to destroy us, how insecure and unstable our present and terrifying our future, we must never despair.

In the midst of the indescribable persecutions and sufferings, the terrible tragedies and emergencies that fill the pages of our national history, there have always arisen leaders who have shown the way, and breathed new spirit into the shattered lives of their people. Events totally unexpected, miracles hardly imagined possible, have occurred to save the Jewish community.

How often it has happened that an individual has given up all hope because of varying personal problems, frustration and disappointment. In the midst of this despair and disillusionment, a remarkable thing happens. He is healed from his illness; he makes a financial recovery; he is reinstated in the good graces of society. He begins to breathe new self-confidence and becomes ambitious again. An act of G–d indeed. Fortunate is the man who recognises the hand of G–d in this hour.

The festival of *Pesach* demands a re-appraisal of oneself and one's degree of confidence and faith in G–d, learning from the history of our forefathers in Egypt. Their bitter lot and subsequent redemption should inspire everyone to a renewal of faith, and endow him with the mettle for courageous and confident living.

These thoughts are conveyed through the three meaningful words: *"Pesach"*—dedication and sacrifice; *"Matzoh"*—true spiritual and moral freedom through *Torah* living; *"Morror"*—complete faith under even the bitterest conditions. If one has absorbed this message, one has indeed fulfilled the obligations of the festival.

on the significance of Sefirah

The period of *Sefirah* connects the festival of Passover with the festival of *Shovuos*. We begin counting the days of the *Omer* immediately after the day of the Exodus from Egypt, the day of liberation from slavery, and continue to count for forty-nine days, at the end of which we celebrate the festival of receiving the *Torah*, marking the culminating point of the liberation.

The purpose of counting or measuring any quantity is to ascertain the exact number or measure of a certain thing, the quantity of which is variable. A census of the population, for example, is taken from time to time, since the population can either increase or decrease, and we want to ascertain its progress. Similarly, statistics are kept of various factors, conditions, etc. Were such factors stationary and unchangeable, or were they uncontrollable, there would be no real purpose served in going over such statistics periodically.

Now, time is something over which man has no control or influence. Time just marches on, and we can neither slow its march nor speed it, nor can we make an hour last more or less than sixty minutes. From this point of view, the idea of *Sefirah* would seem incomprehensible.

Moreover, even where things of variable quantity are concerned, the idea of counting or measuring signifies importance. We are not satisfied merely with an estimate or general appraisal, but wish to establish the exact number of units.

We have said that, unlike most other things which are changeable in quantity, time is unchangeable and beyond our control. But this is true only superficially. Actually, time holds out for us possibilities which do not exist in other things. For, while man's influence over things under his control is limited, his influence over time is, in a sense, unlimited.

Time is like a "vessel" which is highly elastic, and, with an infinite absorptive capacity. It has the power of expanding or contracting, depending upon how much or little we put into it. We can fill our time with unlimited content, or waste it away, and the very same unit of time may mean an infinity to one, or shrink to nothingness for another. Its true measure varies in direct proportion to what is achieved in it.

Herein lies the special significance of *Sefirah*—of counting the days to the time of receiving the *Torah* on Sinai.

For the *Torah*, "whose measure is longer than the earth and broader than the ocean", containing the infinite wisdom of G–d, was given to finite beings, men limited to a life-span of short duration, of "three-score years and ten, or, if in strength, four-score years". At most, "his days shall be one hundred and twenty years". Can a being so limited in time do justice to such an unlimited gift? Can a finite being like man have any grasp of the infinite *Torah*?

That is why, in preparation for receiving the *Torah*, we were commanded to count the days in order that we should be impressed with the significance of time.

It is thereby emphasised that although we cannot alter the flow of time, either by stretching it or by retracting it, this is so only superficially. In reality, each particle of time, even a day, gives us almost infinite possibilities. Therefore, although human life is limited on this earth to a certain number of years, one is not limited in one's possibilities of using them to accomplish as much as would take others thousands of years.

Although, formally, time is fixed and can only be measured but not influenced, nevertheless, if it be measured in terms of its content and our accomplishment in the sphere of our infinite and eternal *Torah* and *mitzvos*, we are able not only to "stretch" time, but even to turn it into infinity and eternity. In other words, we can transfer and elevate our own time beyond and above time.

This, in essence, is the significance of *Sefirah*, the counting of the days to *Shovuos*, as a preparation for receiving the *Torah*.

Shovuos

The *Torah* was given in an unclaimed wilderness, to symbolise everyone's freedom to "take" *Torah*. It is the property of no one but him who learns it. But why was it given in a desert, with no vegetation for food, no water, no shelter or clothing?

Israel followed *Moshe Rabbenu* into that forbidding waste-land of Sinai with no assurance of even the basic necessities of life. All that the people possessed was *emunah*. Food would be provided—and the *manna* came because of *Moshe*'s merit; there would be water—and the spring appeared because of Miriam's merit; the clouds sheltering them were because of Aharon's merit. Because Israel took this bold step out of its familiar Egyptian background into an "unsown land", it was privileged to receive the *Torah*.

Men are prone to set pre-conditions for *Torah* study. One might need sufficient leisure time. Another might require a degree of financial security. Another might feel he is not "prepared" or fit for the exalted act of *Torah* study—his is a more humble station; some day, perhaps. . . .

For all these the Sinai desert tells us that we are to immerse ourselves in *Torah* learning without prior conditions. Our needs, spiritual and physical, will be provided for. We need not make all the arrangements in advance.

The giving of the *Torah* is bound up with the third month, *Sivan*, in *Chumash* and in the *Gemorrah*. ("A three-fold instruction to the three-fold people in the third month.") Since the ultimate is unity, oneness as in *Shema*, why the emphasis on three?

Chassidus frequently cites the parable of the king's son who was taken far from king and palace, to a coarse and grubby people, in order to test his devotion to his father, and to see whether he could conduct himself as the king's son should, though in a strange environment. The parallel would be a descent of the soul from its abode with G–d into this physical world of spiritual darkness and concealment of G–dliness.

Unity untested is uncertain unity. Contact with this world and coping with it while still retaining adherence to G–d, brings about true unity with G–d. Maintaining adherence to G–d in a hostile worldly environment can take two forms: One when man totally ignores his environment and repudiates it out of hand; the other, making the environment itself an instrument of G–dliness.

In the first case, the hostile environment remains a contradiction to G–dliness, but one personally ignores it. In the second, a more profound and truer one, unity is expressed through the once-hostile environment.

Nissan, Iyar and *Sivan* are three months that exemplify different expressions of unity with G–d. *Nissan* is called the "first month", when G–d revealed Himself spontaneously, and Israel "fled" from the abominations of Egypt. Contact and exposure to evil are abhorred.

Iyar, the second month, is the month of *sefiras ha'omer,* counting the days, purifying and refining the character traits. They become subservient to G–d's wish as expressed in *Torah.* Man does not act contrary to *Torah,* his impulses are as demanding as ever though they are controlled.

Sivan is the third month, the month of *Torah.* In performing a *mitzvah,* man and *mitzvah* are distinct. In learning *Torah,* man's intelligence is "united" with G–d's intelligence. Here, the lowly and the exalted unite (the Divine is not out of reach, nor is the lowly rejected) and create a new state *kula chad,* all are One, G–d, *Torah,* and Israel.

Years ago, the Rebbe demanded that every individual set aside regular periods for in-depth *Gemorrah* study, not simple skimming or scanning; *be'iyun* not *lemigras.* This is based on a *Mishna:* "A wealthy person who brings a poor man's offering has not fulfilled his duty." Wealth means intellectual riches, and poverty, intellectual penury. Whoever is intellectually wealthy, capable of serious study, but remains content with superficial learning, does not discharge his obligation to study *Torah.*

Indeed, he might, in a refined way, involve himself with *bitul Torah.* He uses his external faculties in superficial learning, the external aspect of thought and mind, his power of speech. His power of elaboration, of profound immersion, of creativity—his *Chabad* powers, in short—lie dormant, unexercised. Only half a man has learned, and the external half, at that. All his powers must labour at *Torah*, and then will be fulfilled the promise: "Exert yourself, and you will find (succeed)." Without exertion, man cannot "find".

Conclusion of the ceremony held in New York on 9th Shevat 5730—16th January 1970—to mark the completion of the writing of the Sefer Torah initiated by the previous Lubavitcher Rebbe, Rabbi Joseph Issac Schneersohn in 5702—1942.

glossary

Acharonim. lit. Later ones. Jewish codifiers and commentators from about the sixteenth century to the present day.

Adar sheni. *Adar* 2. Additional month occurring after *Adar* (1) in the Hebrew calendar in a leap year. There are seven leap years in every nineteen years in the Hebrew calendar.

Ahavas Hashem. Love of G–d.

Ahavas haTorah. Love of the *Torah.*

Ahavas Yisroel. Love of fellow Jew.

Akeres habayis. Foundation of the household. A term used in relation to the Jewish housewife.

Aliyah. lit. Going up. Term used in connection with being called up to the reading of the *Torah* in the synagogue. Also used in connection with immigration to Israel.

Alma deiscasyiah. Hidden (unrevealed) world.

Alma deisgalyah. Open (revealed) world.

Alter Rebbe. lit. Old Rabbi. Among *Chabad-Chassidim,* the term *Alter Rebbe* refers to Rabbi Shneur Zalman of Ladi. Was first used during the time of Rabbi Menachem Mendel of Lubavitch (third generation), to differentiate between the incumbent Rebbe (always known as "the Rebbe"), the previous Rebbe ("the Mittler Rebbe") and the first Rebbe ("the Alter Rebbe").

Amidah. lit. Standing. The prayer of the Eighteen Benedictions, recited standing.

Ani ledodi vedodi li. "I (Israel) am my Beloved's (G–d's) and my Beloved is mine." (Cant. 6:3.)

Anshei shlomeinu. lit. Men of our peace. Fraternity. A term used to denote particular groups in general, and especially in frequent use among *Chassidim* when referring to their own group(s). The term is of Biblical origin. (Jer. 38:22; Obadiah 1:7; Gen. 34:21.)

Arba minim. lit. Four kinds. Specific four species: palm, myrtle, willow (these three comprise the *lulav*), and *esrog.*

Arovo (pl. **Arovos**). Branch(es) of willow. One of the "Four Kinds" of plants used at *Succos.*

Ashkenazi (pl. **Ashkenazim**). Term originally applied to Jews of Germany and northern France, as distinct from Jews living in the Spanish and Mediterranean countries, called *Sephardim.* Later, the Jews of Poland, Russia and the Scandinavian countries were also called *Ashkenazim.*

Asiya le'ela. Deed above all else.

Avodah. Service. Refers to the service and worship of G–d.

Azoroh. The special area of the *Beis Hamikdosh* in which the people assembled.

Baal haTanya. The author of the *Tanya.*

Baal Shem Tov. Master of the good name. Applied to Rabbi Israel Baal Shem Tov.

Baal teshuvah. A penitent.

Barmitzvah. lit. Son of the command. The ceremony marking a boy's thirteenth birthday, when he attains adulthood in Jewish life and becomes religiously responsible for his own conduct.

Battim. lit. Houses. The square boxes of the *Tefillin* housing the scrolls on which the portions from the *Torah* are inscribed.

Beis Hamedrash. lit. House of study. Synagogue and house of study.

Beis Hamikdosh. lit. House of holiness. The ancient Temple in Jerusalem.

Be'iyun. With concentration. In depth.

Ben Torah (pl. **Bnei Torah**). lit. Son(s) of the *Torah.* Men who study the *Torah.*

Bentsch; bentsching (Yiddish). To say Grace after a meal. To bless. To pronounce a blessing (e.g. over an *esrog*).

Berg Yidden. Mountain Jews.

Berocho (pl. **Berochos**). Blessing(s). Benediction(s).

BeShT. Popular name by which Rabbi Israel Baal Shem Tov is known. An acrostic of Baal Shem Tov.

Betzibur. With the congregation.

Bimah. Elevated platform in the synagogue on which the desk stands for reading the *Sefer Torah* and *Prophets*.

Binoh. Understanding; comprehension; intellectual grasp. One of the three primary intellect powers. (See also *Chabad*.)

Bitul (*Torah*). Wrongful abstention from *Torah* study.

Bnei Torah. See *Ben Torah*.

Boruch sheomar. "Blessed be He Who spoke (and the world came into existence)." The first two words of one of the morning prayers.

Chabad. Acrostic of *Chochmoh* (wisdom), *Binoh* (understanding), *Daas* (knowledge). Branch of *Chassidic* movement, founded by Rabbi Shneur Zalman, based on intellectual approach to the service of G–d.

Chadorim. See *cheder*.

Chag. Festival.

Chagat. Acrostic of *Chesed, Gevurah, Tiferes*. The primary emotional powers.

Challoh. Traditional Sabbath bread.

Chanukah. Feast of Dedication; begins *Kislev* 25 and lasts for eight days.

Chassid (pl. **Chassidim**). Adherent(s) of the *Chassidic* movement; follower(s) of a *Chassidic* Rabbi.

Chassidei Chabad. Collective term for *Chabad Chassidim*.

Chassidic. Appertaining to *Chassidism* and *Chassidus*.

Chassidism. Movement founded by Rabbi Israel Baal Shem Tov.

Chassidus. Philosophy of *Chassidism*.

Chazir. Pig; prohibited under Jewish law.

Cheder (pl. **chadorim**) lit. Room(s). Now used to denote elementary religious school where the curriculum is exclusively religious, i.e. Bible, *Talmud*, etc. Formerly also used to denote any school of religious instruction. For example, the Maggid of Meseritch's *cheder* was for pupils who already knew the whole *Talmud* by heart.

Chesed. Kindness; one of the emotion attributes. (See also *Chagat*.)

Chinuch. Education.

Chochmoh. Wisdom; concept. One of the three primary intellect powers. (See also *Chabad*.)

Chometz. Leaven. Any fermented food or beverage which one is prohibited to consume, or possess, during Passover.

Chukim. Statutes. One of the three categories of commandments. Divine commandments for which no explanation is given.

Chumash. (pl. **Chumashim**). Pentateuch; Five books of Moses.

Chutzpah. Cheek!

Daas. Knowledge; concentration; depth. One of the three primary intellect powers. (See also *Chabad*.)

Daven, davening To pray.

Derech Hashem. Way to G–d.

Derech mitzvosecha. *Way of Your Commandments*; one of the religious-philosophical works of Rabbi Menachem Mendel of Lubavitch (known as the *Tzemach Tzedek*).

Dodi li ve'ani lo. "My Beloved is mine and I am His." (Referring to the relationship between G–d and Israel.) (Cant. 2:16.)

Echod. One.

Edos. Testimonies, one of the categories of commandments; i.e. testimonial and memorial observances.

Elokim. G–d.

Elul. Last month of the Hebrew calendar. Period of repentance in preparation for *Rosh Hashonoh*.

Emunah. Faith.

Eretz Yisroel. Land of Israel.

Erev. Evening. Used to mean "day before", as, for example, *erev Shabbos*.

Esrog. The citron fruit used at *Succos*. One of the "Four Kinds".

Etz Chaim. Book written by Rabbi Chayim Vital, renowned mystic and disciple of Rabbi Yitzhak Luria. It contains 600 chapters of Rabbi Luria's explanations of the *Zohar*.

Farbrengen(s) (Yiddish). Gathering of *Chassidim* to discuss *Chassidus*, recount tales of the *Rebbes* and *Chassidim*, and to give each other moral exhortation. In addition to its immediate purpose, a *farbrengen* serves to strengthen the bonds among *Chassidim*.

Fedayeen. An Arab terrorist organisation.

Gam zu letovah. "This too is for the good."

Gaon (pl. **Gaonim**). Excellency; title of honour for distinguished *Talmudists*.

Gartel (Yiddish). A cord worn by Orthodox men, particularly *Chassidim*, to separate the upper and lower parts of the body, during prayer.

Gemorrah (pl. **Gemorros**). The work based on, and directly interpreting the *Mishna*. Together they constitute the *Talmud*.

Gevald (Yiddish). An exclamation of anguish.

Gevurah. Mighty; severity; restraint; one of the emotion attributes. (See also *Chagat*.)

Gomur. Complete.

Hadassim. Branches of myrtle. One of the "Four Kinds" of plants used at *Succos*.

Hafotzas Torah. The spreading of *Torah*.

Haggadah. lit. The telling. Traditional text read on the first two nights of Passover. (*Seder* nights.)

Hakofos. Circuits around the *Bimah* in the centre of the synagogue, especially on *Simchas Torah*, while carrying the *Torah* scrolls.

Hakriah Vehakdusha. A monthly publication by the Agudas Chassidei Chabad during the Second World War.

Halachah. Jewish law.

Halachic. Appertaining to *Halachah*.

Hashem. lit. The Name; alternative name for G–d.

Hashem Elokainu. The L–rd our G–d.

Havdalah. Prayer marking the end of the Sabbath and/or Festival.

Hechal. Inner sanctum of the *Beis Hamikdosh*.

Hislahavus. Fervour.

Hisvaadus. *Chassidic* gathering. (See also *Farbrengen*.)

Hodu. "Give thanks." One of the morning prayers.

Ish. Man.

Ish Elokim. Man of G–d.

Ivrit. The Hebrew language.

Iyar. A month of the Hebrew calendar (following the month of *Nissan*).

Judenrein (German). Cleansed of Jews.

Kabbalah. lit. Received tradition. Esoteric Jewish lore; mysticism; inner interpretation of the *Torah*.

Kabbalistic. Appertaining to *Kabbalah*.

Kaddish. Mourner's prayer for a deceased close relative, usually said by the son; it is also used to refer to the son who recites the prayer.

Kashrus. *Torah* dietary observances.

Kavannah. lit. Intent. Purpose and devotion.

Kesuvim. Holy Writings. Part of the *Tenach*.

Kiddush. Prayer of sanctification recited on the Sabbath and on Festivals, usually over a cup of wine.

Kiddush Hashem. Sanctification of the Name. To sanctify the name of G–d by noble deeds or martyrdom.

Kisei Hakovod. The Throne of Glory.

Kislev. A month of the Hebrew calendar (third from *Tishrei*).

Kodosh. Holy.

Koheles. Ecclesiastes. The book "*Koheles*" is contained in the "Writings" (*Kesuvim*), the last section of the Bible. It is universally quoted because it contains numerous sayings of wisdom in reference to man's conduct, his relationship with other people and his manifold experiences in life.

Kohen (pl. **Kohanim**). Priest(s); descendants of Aaron.

Kohen Godol. lit. The Great Priest. The high Priest in the *Beis Hamikdosh* of old.

Kosher. lit. Fit. Food permitted by the Dietary Laws.

Kula chad. All one.

Lag b'Omer. Thirty-third day of the Omer. Occurs on *Iyar* 18. Traditionally observed as a reminder of the cessation of a plague which threatened to destroy the students of Rabbi Akiva. *Lag b'Omer* is also observed as the anniversary of the death of Rabbi Shimon ben Yochai.

Lechoo nerannenno. "Come let us give song." Opening prayer of the Friday night service.

Lehavdil. To distinguish or to separate.

Lemigras. To study superficially (as distinct from studying in depth).

Likutei Amarim. lit. "Collected Essays", otherwise the *Tanya*.

Limud Torah. *Torah* study.

Loshon. lit. Language, tongue.

Loshon hakodesh. Holy language, holy tongue, i.e. Hebrew.

Lubavitch. "Town of love" in the county of Mohilev, White Russia. It became the residence of the heads of the Lubavitch-*Chabad* movement in 1814, when Rabbi Dovber, son and successor of Rabbi Shneur Zalman settled there. For over a century (until 1916) and four generations of *Chabad* leaders it remained the centre of the movement. Hence, the leaders of *Chabad* became known as the "Lubavitcher Rebbes" and their *Chassidim* as "Lubavitcher *Chassidim*".

Lulav. Palm branch. One of the four species of plants used on *Succos*.

Maariv. Evening prayer.

Maasei hamenorah. The making of the *menorah*.

Maggid. Preacher.

MaHaRaL. Famous Chief Rabbi of Prague, Rabbi Judah Ben Bezalel Lowe (1520–1609), popularly known as the *MaHaRaL*. Great *Talmudic* authority, philosopher, mystic and writer.

Malach (pl. **malochim**). Angel(s).

Malchus. Kingdom.

Manna. The miraculously supplied food eaten by the Israelites in the desert.

Mashke. Drink; usually refers to alcoholic beverage.

Mashpiah. Instructor of *Chassidus*; especially responsible for the spiritual development of young *Chassidim*.

Maskil (pl. **maskilim**). Intellectual(s). Adherent of the Haskala movement. A movement in Eastern Europe in the eighteenth and nineteenth centuries which sought to secularise Jewish life.

Masmid. A very ardent student. Diligent.

Matzoh (pl. **matzos**). Unleavened bread, eaten on Passover, in place of leavened bread.

Mazel. lit. Fortune. Auspiciousness.

Mechitza. Partition.

Megillah. Scroll or roll. The Book of Esther is popularly referred to by this term.

Melava malka (pl. **melavei malka**). lit. Escorting the Queen. Applied to the meal and the special festivities after the termination of the Sabbath. Jewish tradition compares the Sabbath to a "Queen".

Melech. King.

Memaleh. Permeating (light).

Menorah. Hebrew name of the golden seven-branched candlestick in the sanctuary of the Tabernacle, and in the *Beis Hamikdosh* of old.

Me'od. Very.

Mesholim. See *Moshol*.

Meshulach. Emissary.

Mesibos Shabbos. Sabbath meeting.

Mesiras nefesh. Self-sacrifice.

Mezuzah (pl. **mezuzos**). The sacred scroll, containing portions of the *Shema*, affixed on the door-posts of a Jewish home.

Midrash. Rabbinical homiletical literature, exegesis.

Midrashic. Appertaining to *Midrash*.

Mikvah (pl. **mikvaos**). lit. A gathering of waters; for ritual immersion.

Mincha. Afternoon prayer.

Minhag. Custom.

Minyan (pl. **minyonim**). Quorum of ten males for congregational worship.

Mishna. The codification, by Rabbi Judah Hanassi, of the Oral Law.

Mishpatim. lit. Judgements. One of the categories of commandments; moral and ethical precepts.

Misnagid (pl. **misnagdim**). lit. Opponent(s). Generally used to denote opponents to *Chassidus*.

Mittler (Yiddish). The middle one.

Mittler Rebbe. The *Mittler Rebbe*—Rabbi Dovber, son of Rabbi Shneur Zalman, founder of *Chabad*.

Mitzvah (pl. **mitzvos**). Commandment(s); religious obligation, good deed.

Mochol. Circle-dance.

Modeh ani. lit. "I give thanks." First prayer on awakening in the morning.

Modzitzer. A member of the Modzitz *Chassidic* group.

Mohel. A person who performs ritual circumcision.

Morosho kehillas Yaakov. An inheritance of the congregation of Jacob. (Deut. 33:4.)

Morror. Bitter herbs. Used at the *Seder*, in memory of the bitter enslavement of the Israelites in Egypt.

Moshe Rabbenu. Moses our teacher.

Moshel. Ruler.

Moshiach. Messiah.

Moshol (pl. **mesholim**). Parable(s).

Motzei Shabbos. After the termination of the Sabbath.

Musaf. lit. Additional. Term originally used to describe the additional offering. Now used to describe additional service of prayer on *Shabbos*, *Rosh Chodesh* and the main Festivals.

Mussar. Reproof, ethics, morals. Literature stressing piety and refinement of character.

Nassi. Prince.

Ne'ilah. "Closing" prayer on *Yom Kippur*.

Neshomah. Soul.

Nigun (pl. **nigunim**). Melody (melodies).

Nissan. Spring month in the Hebrew calendar.

Nistarim. lit. Hidden ones. Mystics.

Ohev Yisroel. The lover of the Jewish people.

Omer. A Hebrew dry measure, probably between three and four quarts. An *omer* of barley was brought to the Temple as an offering on the second day of Passover, at the start of the barley harvest. (see *Sefirah*.)

Omud. Reader's desk.

Oneg Shabbat (pl. **onegei Shabbat**). Sabbath delight.

Ooforatzto. "And you shall spread out." (Gen. 28:14.) Lubavitch motto for disseminating *Torah* and *mitzvos* with *Chassidic* enthusiasm.

Or ein sof. Infinite light. This is the usual *Kabbalistic* metaphor for Divine influence.

Pegisha. Meeting; encounter.

Pesach. Passover; begins on the eve of *Nissan* 15.

Pesukei dezimro. lit. Verses of song. Introductory psalms and prayers to the morning service.

Pirkei Ovos. *Ethics of the Fathers*. A popular tractate of the *Mishna*.

Pnei Yehoshua. Famous commentary on the *Talmud*, by Rabbi Yaakov Yehoshua.

Ponim. Face.

Pora adumoh. The red heifer used in purifying the ritually impure.

Purim. Feast of Lots or Feast of Esther. *Adar* 14.

Rabbi. lit. Teacher.

Rachmonoh liboh boey. G–d wants the heart.

Rambam. *RaMBaM*, the popular name by which Rabbi Moshe ben Maimon (Moses Maimonides) (1135–1204) is known. Greatest Jewish philosopher and Codifier of the Middle Ages and distinguished physician. Among his numerous writings his two greatest literary works are his Code *Mishneh Torah* (*Repetition of the Law*) and his philosophical work *Moreh Nevuchim* (*Guide for the Perplexed*). These two works have left an indelible mark on Jewish life and scholarship. As a tribute to his greatness it was said of him that: "From Moses unto Moses there arose none like Moses."

Ramban. *RaMBaN*, the popular name by which Rabbi Moses ben Nachman (1194–1270) is known. Born in Spain, he became the authoritative *Talmudist* of his time. In 1263 he participated in a public religious disputation which took place at Barcelona in the presence of King James I. Although the *Ramban* defended Judaism so brilliantly that he was rewarded by the king, the Dominicans would not concede defeat and accused Rabbi Moses ben Nachman of blasphemy. Forced to leave Spain in 1267, he set out for Palestine. Here he spent his remaining years reorganising the Jewish communities and writing his commentaries on the Bible.

Rashi. Abbreviated name of Rabbi Solomon Yitzchaki (1040–1105). French rabbinical scholar. At the age of twenty-five he became Rabbi at Troyes, France, where he spent most of his life. The major commentator on the Bible and *Talmud*.

Rav. Teacher. Rabbi Shneur Zalman, founder of *Chabad*, was popularly known as the *Rav*.

Rebbe. Rabbi and teacher. Leader of a *Chassidic* group.

Rikkud. Dance.

Rosh. Head, first.

Rosh Chodesh. First day of a Hebrew month.

Rosh Hashonoh. Beginning of the Jewish year. First and second days of *Tishrei*. *Rosh Hashonoh* is the two-day festival at the beginning of the Jewish New Year.

Rosh Yeshivah (pl. **roshei yeshivos**). Head(s) of advanced school(s) of religious studies.

Sabra (pl. **sabras**). Hebrew term applied to the native-born of Israel. It is in fact the name of a prickly cactus plant of Israel. The fruit is prickly on the outside but sweet and good-tasting.

Sedei Chemed. *Halachic* encyclopaedia.

Seder. lit. Order. The Passover banquet is called "*Seder*" because it follows a traditional order of ceremonies, symbols and prayers found in the *Haggadah*.

Seder shel Pesach. Order of *Pesach*.

Sefer Torah (pl. **Sifrei Torah**). Scroll(s) of the Law.

Sefirah. Counting. The period of seven weeks counted day by day from the second day of *Pesach* to *Shovuos*. Also called the Counting of the *omer*, because it commenced with the bringing of the measure of barley to the Temple. In our times a period of semi-mourning.

Sefiras ha'omer. Counting of the *omer*.

Semicha. Rabbinical diploma.

Sephardi (pl. **Sephardim**). Pertaining to Jews of Spanish or Portuguese origin. Even after the expulsion of Jews from Spain and Portugal at the end of the fifteenth century, the *Sephardi* Jews, in whichever countries they settled, preserved their own ritual traditions and customs, and their own dialect called Ladino. They use the *Sephardi* pronunciation of Hebrew, which is basically that which is used in Israel.

Shabbaton. A name given by Lubavitch in English-speaking countries to a Sabbath "get-together".

Shabbos (pl. **Shabbosos**). Sabbath(s); Saturday(s).

Shacharis. The morning prayers.

Shalach monos. The sending of gifts to friends on *Purim*.

Shalosh seudos. Third meal on *Shabbos*.

Shatnez. The prohibition of wearing linen and wool in one garment.

Shaytl. Wig worn by Orthodox married women as a covering for the hair. Jewish law requires married women to cover their hair.

Shechinah. Divine Presence.

Sheliach (pl. **shelichim**). Emissary (emissaries); ambassador(s).

Shema. Hear. Passage of the *Chumash* recited daily, in the morning and evening. (Deut. 6. 4–9.)

Shemini Atzeres. Eighth day of assembly. The concluding day of *Succos* regarded as a separate festival. The *mitzvah* of *lulav* and *esrog* is not observed on this day.

Shemura Matzos. Guarded *matzos*; hand-baked *matzos*.

Shevat. Month of the Hebrew calendar.

Shir Hashirim. lit. Song of Songs. Book in *Torah*; one of the five *Megillas*. *Shir Hashirim* was written by King Solomon and refers to the relationship between G–d and Israel.

Shiur (pl. **shiurim**). Lesson(s).

Shlito. May he live for many good days.

Shmeussen. lit. Talks.

Shmiras mitzvos. lit. Keeping of the commandments.

Shmona esrei. lit. Eighteen. Prayer recited three times daily, four times on Sabbaths, five times on *Yom Kippur*. Also referred to as the *Amidah* or Standing Prayer, because one recites it standing.

Shochet (pl. **shochetim**). Ritual slaughterer(s).

Shofar. Ram's horn sounded during the month of *Elul*, on *Rosh Hashonoh* and at the close of *Yom Kippur*.

Shovuos. Festival of Weeks, commemorating the Giving of the *Torah*, on *Sivan* 6 and 7.

Shtetl (Yiddish). Small town; village.

Shul (Yiddish). Synagogue.

Shulchan Aruch. lit. "Set table". Code of *Torah* Law, compiled by Rabbi Joseph Caro (1488–1575). *Talmud* presents the broad discussion of the law, the background, while the *Shulchan Aruch* is a "set table", an orderly presentation of practical law and usage, regulating every aspect of the Jew's daily life and conduct.

Siddur (pl. **siddurim**). Prayer book(s).

Sifrei Torah. See *Sefer Torah*.

Simcha. Joy.

Simcha shel mitzvah. Joy in the performance of a commandment.

Simchas Torah. Festival of Rejoicing with the *Torah*, celebrated on *Tishrei* 23 in the diaspora and on *Tishrei* 22 in Israel.

Sivan. A month in the Hebrew calendar; (third from *Nissan*).

Sofer (pl. **sofrim**). Scribe(s).

Sovev. Encompassing (light).

Succah. A hut or booth in which the Autumn Feast of Tabernacles is observed.

Succos. Festival of Tabernacles, begins *Tishrei* 15.

Taharas Hamishpocho. Family purity.

Tallis (pl. **taleisim**). Prayer shawl(s) worn by men during morning worship and during *Yom Kippur*.

Talmud. Post-Biblical Rabbinical literature, including *Mishna* and later teachings, concluded around sixth century of the common era.

Talmud Torah (pl. **Talmud Torahs**). Hebrew school(s) provided by the community, as distinct from the private *cheder*.

Talmudic. Talmudical. Relating to the *Talmud*.

Talmudist. One who studies the *Talmud*.

Tammuz. Month of the Hebrew calendar. Falls in the summer.

Tanya. Famous philosophical work, by Rabbi Shneur Zalman of Ladi, in which the principles of *Chabad* are expounded. The name is derived from the initial word of this work. Also called *Likutei Amarim*.

Techias Hameisim. Resurrection of the dead.

Tefillah. Prayer.

Tefillin. Phylacteries worn by men during weekday morning worship; they contain verses from the Bible including *Shema*.

Tehillim. Psalms.

Tenach. Popular name for the Bible. From the three initial letters of *Torah* (Pentateuch), *Neviim* (Prophets) and *Kesuvim* (Holy Writings).

Teshuvah. Return; repentance.

Teva. Nature.

Teves. Month in the Hebrew calendar. Falls in the winter.

Tiferes. lit. Beauty. Composition of first two emotion powers with kindness predominating. (See also *Chagat*.)

Tishrei. A month in the Hebrew calendar; following Elul.

Torah. Used variously for *Chumash*, especially in scroll form, or for the entire body of Jewish religious Law (Bible, *Talmud*, *Midrash*, etc.).

Tosephos. Additions. Applies to the commentaries to especially difficult passages in the *Talmud*, written by a number of teachers from the twelfth to fourteenth century.

Tov. Good.

Tov me'od. Very good.

Tu b'Shevat. The fifteenth day of the month of *Shevat*. In the *Mishnah* it is called the "New Year of the Trees". In Israel the day is reserved for the planting of trees, especially by schoolchildren. In the diaspora, Jewish children celebrate this day by holding special parties; they partake of many kinds of fruits.

Tzaddik. Righteous man.

Tzaddik gomur. Completely righteous man.

Tzaddik v'tov lo. Righteous man who prospers.

Tzedoko. Charity.

Tzemach Tzedek. lit. Seed of righteous. Famed *Halachic* and Responsa work by Rabbi Menachem Mendel, third generation of *Chabad* leaders. The author is usually called the "*Tzemach Tzedek*" after the name of his great work. Sages of Israel are often better known by their works than by their personal names.

Tzitzis. Fringes.

Umalchuso berotzon kiblu. "They accepted His Kingdom willingly." From the liturgy.

Ve'al hanissim. "And for the miracles." Special prayer recited on *Chanukah* and on *Purim*.

Vehigadato. "And you shall relate." Reference to the *mitzvah* of relating the story of Passover to the children, hence the *Haggadah*.

Vehoyo. "And it will come to pass. . . ." Opening words of the second paragraph of the three paragraphs of the *Shema*.

Yahrzeit (Yiddish). "Year time." Anniversary of a death.

Yashar. Upright.

Yeshivah (pl. **Yeshivos**). Advanced school(s) of *Talmudic* studies. In the U.S.A. it is used in reference to Jewish Day School(s).

Yeshivah Gedoloh. Advanced *Yeshivah*.

Yetzer hara. Evil inclination.

Yevsektzia (abbr. from Russian: "Jewish branch"). Jewish branch of the Russian Communist Party 1918–1930. It sought to destroy the Jewish religion. Was responsible for the destruction of Jewish institutions, closing of synagogues and the liquidation of Jewish communal organisations.

Yid (pl. **Yidden**). Jew(s).

Yiddish. Jewish language.

Yiddishkeit. Jewishness. A term covering the traditional culture of Jewry.

Yishuv. lit. Settlement. Popularly applied to the Jewish community in the Holy Land.

Yisroel. lit. Israel. Used in reference to the Jewish people.

Yom echod. One day.

Yom Kippur. Day of Atonement; *Tishrei* 10.

Yom Tov (pl. **Yomim Tovim**). Feast(s); festival(s).

Yud tes Kislev. *Kislev* 19. The festival of *Yud tes Kislev* commemorates the release from prison of Rabbi Shneur Zalman of Ladi, founder of *Chabad*.

Zemiros. Songs.

Zohar. Classic *Kabbalistic* work by Rabbi Shimon ben Yochai.

list of contributors and biographical notes

ALTEIN, MORDECAI
Rabbi, Congregation of Lubavitch, Bronx, New York. Studied in various *yeshivos* in U.S.A. and in Lubavitch *yeshivos*, Otvock, Poland, and New York. One-time Principal, Lubavitch Yeshivah, Pittsburgh, U.S.A.

BLOCK, IRVING L.
Born U.S.A., 1930. B.A. (Philosophy), Vanderbilt University, 1952. A.M., Ph.D. (Philosophy), Harvard University, 1958. Associate Professor of Philosophy, University of Western Ontario. Studied at Lubavitch Yeshivah, Brooklyn, New York. Noted writer and contributor to philosophical journals.

DAREN, KENY (Mrs)
Educated in the Beth Jacob Teachers' Seminary of Brooklyn, New York. Assistant Principal of Yeshivah Achei Tmimim of Pittsburgh, U.S.A. Noted lecturer on the rôle of the Jewish woman and the relevance of *Chassidus* in a modern society.

FORTE, ARYE
Educated at *yeshivos* in Israel and England where he was ordained as Rabbi. Member of teaching staff of Lubavitch House Schools.

GREENE, VELVL WILLIAM
Born Canada. Graduated from the University of Manitoba with a degree in Agriculture. M.S., Ph.D. in Bacteriology and Biochemistry, University of Minnesota, where he holds a joint appointment in the College of Medical Sciences as an Associate Professor of Public Health and Microbiology. Research worker in the fields of Environmental Microbiology and Contamination Control and has lectured on these subjects in thirty-three States, Canada and Europe. Consultant to the Aerospace Industry, to hospitals and to N.A.S.A.'s Planetary Quarantine Programme. President of the Herzl Camp Association. Active member of the Board of the Minneapolis Torah Academy, the Minneapolis Talmud Torah, the Merkos L'Inyonei Chinuch and of the College and University Council of the Lubavitch Youth Organisation.

HECHT, ABRAHAM B.
Rabbi, Shaare Zion Congregation, Brooklyn. Studied in *yeshivos* in U.S.A. and in Lubavitch Yeshivah, Otvock, Poland. Ordained as Rabbi at the Lubavitch Yeshivah, Brooklyn, New York. B.A. and M.A. (Yeshivah University), D.D. (Philathea College, Ontario). President, Rabbinical Alliance of America. Noted author, lecturer and educator.

JAFFE, ZALMON
Chairman of the Manchester and District Branch of the Lubavitch Foundation. Former President of the Manchester Shechita Board.

KRANZLER, GERSHON
Ph.D. (Colombia University). Professor of Sociology, Towson State College and Johns Hopkins University, Baltimore. One-time Principal of Yeshivah High School for boys and girls. Author of numerous books and articles including *Williamsburg—a Jewish Community in Transition*, which won prize in 1967 as best study of Jewish life in the U.S.A. and Canada.

LIEBB, JULIUS
Attended Lubavitch Yeshivah. Graduated B.A., Magna Cum Laude (Yeshivah University), M.A. in English Literature (Columbia University). Educator and editor of books for schools. Presently engaged in producing an Anthology titled *Understanding People —Representative Types*.

LIPCHITZ, JACQUES
World-famous sculptor.

MILLER, W. G.
Features editor of a monthly magazine. Previously with the industrial and scientific staff of the *Financial Times*. Broadcaster on B.B.C. European Service and a contributor to a number of newspapers and magazines in England and abroad.

MINDEL, NISSAN
Studied in European *yeshivos* where he received his Rabbinic ordination. Studied law and political science at the University of Manchester, graduating with B.A. and M.A. Received Ph.D. degree in Semitic languages from Columbia University. Has been associated with the Lubavitch-*Chabad* movement since 1940 as an executive of the Merkos L'Inyonei Chinuch. Also serves the editorial board of the Lubavitch publications division and the Chabad Research Centre. A noted author and translator.

POSNER, ZALMAN I.
Rabbi of Nashville, Tennessee, U.S.A., Orthodox Community. Educated and ordained as Rabbi at Lubavitch Yeshivah, New York. Founder of Nashville Hebrew Day School. Translator of a number of *Chassidic* classics. Noted writer and lecturer on Jewish subjects, particularly *Chassidus*.

ROSEN, BELLA (Mrs)
Educated Cardiff and Switzerland. Assisted her late husband, Rabbi Dr Kopul Rosen, in founding and establishing Carmel College. Degree in Hebrew and Arabic, Oxford (1966), and Diploma of Education, Oxford (1967). Vice-President and Cultural Chairman Mizachi Women's Organisation. Member of Education Committee of the London Board of Jewish Religious Education, Governor of the J.F.S. Interests: Jewish education in any of its ramifications.

ROSS, J. J.
Rabbi. M.A. (Capetown), Ph.D. (Cantab.). Formerly Deputy Principal and Tutor. Lecturer in Talmud and Philosophy, Jews' College; Chairman, Department of Philosophy, Bar-Ilan University, and Visiting Assistant Professor, Brown University, Providence, R.I.

SHOCHET, I.
Ph.D., educated at Lubavitch Yeshivah, New York, where he was ordained as Rabbi. Lecturer at Toronto University.

SUDAK, NACHMAN
Educated in *yeshivos* in Russia, Israel and U.S.A. Received *Semicha* at Lubavitch Yeshivah, Brooklyn, New York. Principal of Lubavitch Foundation of Great Britain since 1959.

SUFRIN, ARON DOV
Educated at Manchester and Gateshead *yeshivos*. Director of Education of the Lubavitch Foundation of Great Britain since 1959.

VOGEL, SHRAGE FAIVISH
Educated in *yeshivos* in England and New York. Ordained as Rabbi at Lubavitch Yeshivah, Brooklyn, New York. Executive Director of Lubavitch Foundation since 1960.

WOUK, HERMAN
Author. Visiting Professor of English, Yeshivah University. Novels: *Aurora Dawn*; *The City Boy*; *The Caine Mutiny*; *Marjorie Morningstar*; *Youngblood Hawke*. Plays: *The Traitor*; *The Caine Mutiny Court Martial*; *Nature's Way*. Non-fiction: *This is my G–d*.

acknowledgements

All copyright materials in this volume have been reprinted with the permission of the following publishers and holders of copyright.

Di Yiddishe Heim

"Kehot" Publication Society

Especial thanks are due to Rabbi M. A. Hodakov, Rabbi Dr N. Mindel and Rabbi N. Sudak for their assistance and guidance during the compilation of this volume, and to Rabbi I. H. Sufrin for his painstaking care in reading the proofs and for his many valuable suggestions.

note

The traditional way of writing G–d's name (with a dash) has been used throughout this publication. The sources of this tradition are to be found in the *Shulchan Aruch, Yoreh Deah*, Chapters 179 and 276 and commentaries. *Rav's Shulchan Aruch, Orach Chaim*, Chapter 85, par. 3.

Suggested Reading on Chabad-Chassidus in English

RABBI SHNEUR ZALMAN OF LADI, Vol. I Biography, by Nissan Mindel. 1969.

LIKUTEI AMARIM (TANYA), by Rabbi Shneur Zalman, Part I. Translated with Introduction by Nissan Mindel. 1962.

—PART II—SHAAR HAYICHUD VEHAEMUNAH. Translated with Introduction by Nisen Mangel. 1965.

—PART III—IGERES HATESHUVA. Translated with Introduction by Zalman I. Posner. 1965.

—PART IV—IGERES HAKODESH. Translated with Introduction by Jacob I. Schochet. 1968.

—PART V—KUNTRES ACHRON. Translated by Zalman I. Posner. 1968.

MEMOIRS, by Rabbi Joseph I. Schneersohn. Translated by Nissan Mindel. Volumes I–II. 1956; 1960.

SOME ASPECTS OF CHABAD CHASSIDISM, by Rabbi Joseph I. Schneersohn. Translated with Biographical Sketch by Nissan Mindel. 1961.

ON THE TEACHINGS OF CHASSIDUS, by Rabbi Joseph I. Schneersohn. Translated with Supplements by Zalman I. Posner. 1959.

ON LEARNING CHASSIDUS, by Rabbi Joseph I. Schneersohn. Translated with Supplements by Zalman I. Posner. 1961.

THE "TZEMACH TZEDEK" AND THE HASKALAH MOVEMENT, by Rabbi Joseph I. Schneersohn. Translated with Supplements by Zalman I. Posner. 1962.

THE COMMANDMENTS, by Nissan Mindel. 1961.

RABBI SHNEUR ZALMAN OF LADI, by Gershon Kranzler. 1959.

ARREST AND LIBERATION OF RABBI SHNEUR ZALMAN OF LADI (The History of Yud-Tes Kislev), by A. C. Glitzenstein. Translated by Jacob I. Schochet. 1964.

Published by "Kehot" Publication Society